Brown v. Board of Education
Its Impact on Public Education
1954-2004

D0145020

THURGOOD
MARSHALL
SCHOLARSHIP FUND

A Publication of the
Thurgood Marshall Scholarship Fund

Brown v. Board of Education
Its Impact on Public Education
1954-2004

Introduction by Juan Williams

Edited by Dara N. Byrne, Ph.D.

Thurgood Marshall Scholarship Fund

Brown v. Board of Education: Its Impact on Public Education 1954-2004
A Publication of the Thurgood Marshall Scholarship Fund
Funded by the Andrew W. Mellon Foundation

Cover Photograph
The Trouble We All Live With by Norman Rockwell
Used by permission of Norman Rockwell Museum, Stockbridge, MA

Cover Design: George Byfield

Brown v. Board of Education:
Its Impact on Public Education 1954-2004
Copyright © 2005 by Thurgood Marshall Scholarship Fund

Includes bibliographical references

Word For Word Publishing Co., Inc.
Brooklyn, New York
800-601-WORD (9673)

Library of Congress Cataloging-in-Publication Data: 2005935611
ISBN: 1-889732-43-5

Printed in the United States of America.

ACKNOWLEDGMENTS

To Thurgood Marshall, who helped to open the door for our children to pursue their greatest potential for academic success. Mrs. Cecilia Marshall, John Marshall and Goody Marshall, and the extended Marshall family, thank you for sharing your legacy with public HBCU students, faculty and staff. John, special thanks for your leadership and for sharing your lessons learned with our students.

To Dr. Lydia English and Program Officers at the Andrew W. Mellon Foundation, who believed in this project and endorsed it with interest and understanding. History salutes the foundation's board and staff for the great work that you do to make our country strong.

To the incredible team of people who work at the Thurgood Marshall Scholarship Fund who unselfishly give of their time and energy each day to achieve the mission and goals of the organization. Maria, Lisa, Beverly, LaQuanda, Roger, Glen, Habeeb, Paul, Lamar, Ola, Renau, Shannon, Charles, Shineaca, Eve and Candice; you all make it seem so easy with your zeal for empowering our young men and women to achieve their personal best. Eve and Candice, the two of you are shaping the future for young men and women through the Small Schools Initiative, for many years to come.

A special thank you to the entire board of directors, presidents, alumni and donors who keep the organization strong and vibrant. Jim Clifton, Brent Clinkscale, James Mitchell, Michael Rhodes and Noel Hankin, your leadership continues to drive opportunities for public HBCUs to realize greater potential.

Dr. Payne, you are an inspiration—thank you for dreaming the impossible and planting the seeds for the Thurgood Marshall Scholarship Fund.

Adrienne Ingrum, you always make it happen—your partnership makes it a pleasure to work with you on projects. Dr. Dara Byrne, through your natural talent for writing, editing and managing creative projects, the world will continue to hear your voice. The life you breathed into this project sustains itself in every page that is turned.

To the distinguished members of the Scholarly Review Committee who, along with Dr. Payne, helped to shape the direction of this publication—Dr. Molefi Kete Asante, founding editor of the *Journal of Black Studies*; D. Kamili Anderson, director of the Howard University Press; Dr. V.P. Franklin, editor of the *Journal of African-American History*; Dr. Faustine Jones-Wilson, editor-in-chief emerita of *The Journal of Negro Education*.

To the awesome team of scholars and experts who lent their voices to the historical document, you are carrying on Thurgood Marshall's legacy.

Thank you Carolyn M. Davis and the wonderful team at Word For Word Publishing Co., for all your hard work.

To my good friend, Juan Williams. Thank you for commemorating the memory of Thurgood Marshall and HBCUs—our children and institutions of learning are indeed fortunate to have you as an advocate.

—Dwayne Ashley
Thurgood Marshall Scholarship Fund

CONTENTS

FOREWORD

UPHOLDING THE PROMISE
OF *BROWN V. BOARD OF EDUCATION*

Dwayne Ashley

When one considers the significance and impact of the U.S. Supreme Court decision in *Brown v. Board of Education of Topeka* in 1954, it was and still is considered to be one of the most prolific events in the history of America and with ample reason. It was the beginning of a time when the doors of opportunity that had long been closed to black Americans were cracked open.

In 1952, the *Journal of Negro Education* published an article by Thurgood Marshall that provided a comprehensive survey of the NAACP's efforts to eliminate segregation in education. In the article entitled, "An Evaluation of Recent Efforts to Achieve Racial Integration Through Resort to the Courts," Marshall wrote of his belief that the segregated schools were in effect, serving up more than an inadequate education; segregated schools were instilling feelings of inferiority, self-hatred, low self-esteem and an overall "warped" outlook on life.

Marshall wrote regarding segregated schools, 'What he (the black child) learns, feels and how he is affected there is apt to determine the type of adult he will become.'

While it is apparent that Thurgood Marshall's belief about the negative impact that segregated education had on the immediate and long-term egos of blacks, he wrote with equal conviction in the 1952 article that an inadequate education was also directly linked to black adults' inability to thrive in higher education.

While Negroes had the right to attend state graduate and professional schools, most Negroes who had been educated in segregated schools were handicapped because their early training was both inadequate and inferior. This, he stated, made it apparent that segregation in public elementary and high schools would have to be challenged and that the "separate but equal" doctrine was not providing equal education opportunities to all Americans. Indeed those opportunities would not be achieved in a segregated system.

A quality education, he would say then and after *Brown,* was a right that all Americans must have access to for human dignity and to advance as successful individuals and contributing members of American society and the world.

Black Americans and white Americans have always known that education is the pathway to positions of leadership, the ability to earn a living and the road to advancement of one's self and society. For black Americans, education meant something more than the ticket to success; education meant freedom, independence and dignity of self beyond measure. To be black and uneducated meant that even if the physical chains of bondage were removed, one would still have many of the vast limitations that he or she experienced as a slave.

So great was the belief among former slaves that an education was the key to the kind of freedom that blacks did and would not know even after the Emancipation, a penniless Harriet Tubman began a fund-raising campaign to support schools for newly freed blacks in the South. For example, in the late 1860s, Tubman was provided with the proceeds from a book published on her life. Tubman, a woman who possessed unspeakable courage, unselfishness and a visionary outlook, used a portion of the $1200 to support southern schools for black children—even though she desperately needed money for her own living expenses and those of her ailing parents.

The thirst for knowledge and education has been in the souls of black men, women and children since slave masters held them chained to the very plantations and houses that they dreamed of fleeing from to freedom. Many took great chances with their very lives just to learn the alphabet. Frederick Douglass, the internationally famous abolitionist and former slave, wrote of the many risks he took to learn how to read and write.

In his book, *Narrative of the Life of Frederick Douglass, An American Slave*, he tells of learning the alphabet from Mrs. Auld, the wife of his master. These daily lessons continued until the slave master learned of them and forbade his wife to teach young Douglass any further. Quoting Mr. Auld, Douglass recounted him saying: "If you give a nigger an inch, he will take an ell…Now if you teach that nigger to read, there will be no keeping him."

His master's declaration unlocked a great mystery that had gripped Douglass all of his life. In his book he spoke of the revelation by stating that, "I now understood what had been to me a most perplexing difficulty–to wit, the white man's power to enslave the black man. It was grand achievement and I prized it highly. From that moment, I understood the pathway from slavery to freedom." The pathway to which he referred of course, was education.

Years later, while serving another family, the mistress of the house followed him from room to room and watched him intently to make sure he had no time or access to reading materials. Douglass, however, declared that her efforts were expended in vain because his former mistress' teachings had given him "the *inch* and no precaution could prevent him from taking the *ell.*" The mystery was unlocked and Douglass' quest for education would not be dampened even by the threat of the loss of his own life.

After slavery was abolished and blacks eventually no longer had to risk their lives to become educated, a small but growing new class of blacks emerged; first came the great preachers and teachers who were leaders in establishing schools along with other free blacks. In those early decades, blacks were more focused on establishing the schools and on educating children than on the fact that the schools were grossly inferior to those of whites.

When Booker T. Washington arrived in June 1881 to head Tuskegee, the school for black children that is today Tuskegee University, he found a leaky, dilapidated structure that often required a student to hold an umbrella over him while he taught. Notwithstanding, in his book, *Up from Slavery,* Washington said that he had never seen a group of children so earnest and willing to endure the grave inadequacies of the facility to learn.

From those early days through the 1950s, these were often the conditions under which black teachers taught and black children strived to learn with little hope of change. Unbeknownst to those teachers, students, their parents and the majority of Americans, the NAACP, as early as 1930, had started an attack on the inequalities in public education.

Following the filing of five lawsuits by blacks seeking better facilities, conditions and education for their children, Thurgood Marshall filed a lawsuit asking for an end to the "separate but equal" doctrine in 1949. On May 17, 1954, the U.S. Supreme Court made its landmark ruling ending segregation in public education.

Reflecting on the aftermath of the ruling in May 2004, Jack Greenberg (who was part of Marshall's NAACP team which argued the case before the Supreme Court) was quoted in *The*

Atlanta Journal-Constitution regarding "unimaginable" opposition to the ruling–opposition that included black families being terrorized when they tried to send their children to white schools.

In many parts of the South it took as long as 10 years before full compliance with the law took place and even then, only 2 percent of black students in the South attended schools with whites. In some areas of the country, it took courage beyond measure and a desire to better one's self beyond what should be required for those children to walk through the doors of opportunity where they were not welcomed or wanted and in some cases, were terrorized.

A case in point is the children who came to be known as "The Little Rock Nine." If one wonders what motivated those children to endure death threats by the throngs of angry mobs who greeted them daily for three weeks to attend Central, that question was perhaps best answered by Melba Pattillo Beals, one of the Little Rock Nine. In the book *Voices of Freedom* by Henry Hampton and Steve Fayer, Beals said: "I wanted to go to Central High School because they had more privileges. They had more equipment; they had five floors of opportunities."

Beals, in effect, provided the summation of the significance of *Brown v. Board of Education.* The doors of opportunity, once closed to black Americans for centuries, were opened by *Brown* and Thurgood Marshall, through his commitment to equality and civil rights and his passionate conviction that education and opportunity were keys to survival, prosperity and the dignity of black folks.

Brown did not make America a perfect place for blacks to live, work and educate their children. In some cases, its legacy may not be tangibly traceable to a sudden groundswell of black children who were welcomed into the new world of opportunity that white schools provided to white children. What then, are the significant legacies of *Brown?* There are many.

First, *Brown* forced America to confront something that they had long denied: Separate was *not* equal. Second, the highest court in the land confirmed to black men, women and children that as Americans, they had a right to a quality education. Those same black men, women and children found their voices, dignity and courage during the years that the case was being fought and in the years after the ruling. Today, many blacks who were part of the first generation of children to be educated in white schools describe the dignity that they felt in not having to attend inferior schools; this was the "dignity of self" that Marshall wrote about in 1952.

Brown gave black Americans their first inroad to the creation of the black middle class—an educational and economic class that continues to grow and expand 50 years later. Finally, and perhaps most enduring, is that millions of blacks can now set high standards for educational, professional and personal achievement and actually have the opportunity to accomplish their goals.

Through the opportunity to receive a quality education, others still have achieved positions at the top of the private and public sectors. Black Americans who have reached such pinnacles of success include Kenneth Chenault, chairman & CEO of American Express; Richard Parsons, CEO of media giant Time Warner; Ann Fudge, chairman & CEO of Young & Rubicam; Arthur Harper, president & CEO of GE Equipment Services; Stanley O'Neal, chairman of the board, president & CEO of Merrill Lynch; and Alwyn Lewis, chairman & CEO of K-Mart. Individuals such as Colin Powell, the first black Secretary of State and Condoleezza Rice, the first black female Secretary of State and Franklin Raines, chairman & CEO of Fannie Mae and many others have also reached great positions of leadership in the public sector.

While there is still much to be done to truly bring equality in education to blacks, what has been accomplished in the 50 years since *Brown* is nothing short of remarkable and historically black colleges and universities (HBCUs) have and continue to play a prominent role in the education of blacks. During their more than 160 years of existence, they have educated millions of scholars, physicians, lawyers, scientists, educators, writers and entrepreneurs. HBCUs have made a tremendous contribution to *Brown*'s and Marshall's legacies by educating generations of young black men and women; that education provided generations of blacks with a gateway into the middle class and even into the ranks of the wealthy.

When and if HBCUs are adequately supported, they actually do fulfill the purpose of the decision in the landmark case because they serve a role in the integrated American society. HBCUs have always welcomed all students, despite race, creed or color. In past years and today, many of these institutions are educating white students (some such as Bluefield State College and Lincoln University in Missouri are even predominantly white) and the schools are currently attracting a growing number of Hispanic students. Societal support of HBCUs will ensure that they are competitive and are of the level of quality that will appeal to a wide range of people who, by virtue of attending the schools, are assuring society that those colleges and universities will remain integrated institutions.

Thurgood Marshall, one of the greatest lawyers in history and of course, the first black to sit on the U. S. Supreme Court, is a product of an education at HBCUs. A graduate of Lincoln University (Pennsylvania) and Howard University School of Law, much of Marshall's work during his 60-year career demonstrated a lifelong commitment to ensuring that the black race has access to a quality education. Like the many who had come before him, Justice Marshall knew that education was the key to blacks' survival, independence, dignity and the assurance that future generations will be prepared to lead.

To that end, he only granted permission to one organization to bear his name and that was the Thurgood Marshall Scholarship Fund (TMSF), which was established in 1987. Based in New York, it is the only national organization of its type providing merit-based scholarships and programmatic support to students attending the nation's 47 public HBCUs. TMSF also provides capacity-building support to the 47 institutions. Both of Marshall's alma maters are member schools of TMSF's federation.

To date, TMSF has provided more than $50 million in scholarships and programmatic support to thousands of students and capacity-building support to the schools. TMSF prepares leaders for the future by providing students with leadership skills, career-development opportunities and scholarships and by building the capacity of its member schools.

Whereas TMSF's support provides Thurgood Marshall scholars with scholarships, the organization's support also impacts the more than 215,000 students being educated on the campuses of its member public HBCUs. Through its mission to provide capacity-building support to its members, TMSF impacts areas such as the schools' technology upgrades, executive staff training and enhancement of various academic programs.

TMSF's mission serves as a living legacy of Thurgood Marshall's life, work and commitment to ensuring that all Americans would have the opportunity to fulfill the basic right to attain a quality education. It is also TMSF's mission to uphold the promise of *Brown v. Board of Education* and to carry out Justice Marshall's vision for creating an organization such as TMSF that would be dedicated to preparing new generations of leaders through higher education.

This book is a perfect complement to TMSF's mission, to Thurgood Marshall and to the purpose and legacy of *Brown v. Board of Education*. While it gives some of the top scholars an opportunity to inject thought-provoking examinations of *Brown*'s impact on law, HBCUs and on public policy, curriculum and resources, it also helps focus attention on *Brown*'s impact on the education in America as a whole and the intent to eradicate centuries of under educating generations of black Americans.

Was *Brown* a success? Perhaps not completely because there is still a great divide between the quality of education for blacks and whites in this country.

However, the decision in *Brown v. Board of Education* helped America to face the fact that undereducated Americans depletes the nation, lessens all Americans as human beings and prevents America from making real change and there is profound value in that. *Brown* at 50 provides a multifaceted view of its impact and legacy and *Brown* at 100 will give an even more enduring story of how the case changed America's future.

One thing that will not change in the next 50, 100 or 150 years is that for black Americans and indeed for all Americans, education is the key to dignity, freedom and the opportunity to achieve self-actualization. *Brown*'s gift to present and future generations is to ensure that those opportunities are available to all who seek them. However, it is up to America to make sure that *Brown* is all that it was designed to be and that the work of all who made it possible live on through well-educated children.

Thurgood Marshall Scholarship Fund
Preparing a New Generation of Leaders

Since 1987, Thurgood Marshall Scholarship Fund has been the strongest voice for students attending the nation's public historically black colleges and universities. Founded under the leadership of Dr. N. Joyce Payne, Director of the Office for the Advancement of Public Black Colleges (a division of the National Association of State Universities and Land-Grant Colleges), in cooperation with Miller Brewing Company, the NBA, Sony Music Corporation and the American Association for State Colleges and Universities, TMSF was created to prepare a new generation of leaders through scholarships, programmatic and capacity-building support in partnership with its 47 member colleges and universities.

Public Historically Black Colleges and Universities have been educating young men and women for over 170 years. TMSF is the only national organization to provide merit scholarships, programmatic and capacity-building support to 47 public HBCUs. Since its inception, TMSF has provided more than $50 million in scholarships and programmatic support to students attending our 47-member public HBCUs and five historically black law schools. More than 5,000 young men and women have earned their degrees because of the generous scholarship support provided by the Fund.

TMSF member schools are a critical source of higher education for African-Americans. More than seventy-seven percent of all students enrolled in historically black institutions attend TMSF member schools. Public HBCU alumni have become leaders in the business, government and entertainment industries. However, few of these achievements would be possible without the support of the Thurgood Marshall Scholarship Fund.

Today, the Fund is stronger than ever and continues to keep Justice Thurgood Marshall's legacy alive through its work to empower young men and women to reach their full potential.

PREFACE

READING *BROWN V. BOARD OF EDUCATION: ITS IMPACT ON PUBLIC EDUCATION 1954-2004*

Dara N. Byrne

Brown v. Board of Education: Its Impact on Public Education 1954-2004 presents a range of research from scholars at Historically Black Colleges and Universities as well as notable research by those at other leading institutions. The perspectives in this book are diverse and multi disciplinary, and many of the chapters examine the often overlooked local and regional implications of the decision. In so doing, *Brown v. Board of Education: Its Impact on Public Education 1954-2004* aims to broaden your understanding of *Brown* by making widely available a rich cross-section of research that is rarely assembled under one cover.

The scope of this book was a cumulative effort. We were fortunate to enlist the assistance of some of the most noted editors and publishers of African-American research who selected the chapters based on a blind proposal review. The Scholarly Review Committee was comprised of Molefi Kete Asante, professor of African-American Studies at Temple University and founding editor of the *Journal of Black Studies*; D. Kamili Anderson, director of the Howard University Press and former associate editor of the *Journal of Negro Education*; Dr. V.P. Franklin, professor of history and education at Teachers College of Columbia University and editor of the *Journal of African-American History*; Faustine Jones-Wilson, professor emerita of education at Howard University, former Associate Editor of the *Journal of Education for Students Placed at Risk (JESPAR)*, and editor in chief emerita of *The Journal of Negro Education*; and Dr. N. Joyce Payne, founder of the Thurgood Marshall Scholarship Fund and director of the Human Resources and Minority Programs for the National Association of State Universities and Land-Grant Colleges.

This book is divided into three parts. The chapters in Part I examine a variety of legal issues, from jurisprudence to the *Ayers v. Fordice* case to gender considerations. Part II addresses the impact of the *Brown* decision on Historically Black Colleges and Universities. The six chapters in this section provides a comprehensive picture of the successes, challenges and current initiatives at HBCUs. Part III looks at the intersection between *Brown* and public policy; in fact, many of these authors concurrently discuss pedagogy, praxis and access to resources.

Brown v. Board of Education: Its Impact on Public Education 1954-2004 maintains its commitment to the mission of the Thurgood Marshall Scholarship Fund and the vision of its namesake. In addition to providing a comprehensive focus on HBCUs, each of the chapters in this volume provokes critical questioning and honest reasoning about fulfilling the promise of equal access to public education.

INTRODUCTION

THE RULING THAT CHANGED AMERICA1

Juan Williams

Fifty years later, the *Brown* decision looks different. At a distance from the volcanic heat of May 17, 1954, the real impact of the legal, political and cultural eruption that changed America is not exactly what it first appeared to be. On that Monday in May, the high court's ruling outlawing school segregation in the United States generated urgent news flashes on the radio and frenzied black headlines in special editions of afternoon newspapers. One swift and unanimous decision by the top judges in the land was going to end segregation in public schools. Southern politicians reacted with such fury and fear that they immediately called the day "Black Monday."

South Carolina Gov. James Byrnes, who rose to political power with passionate advocacy of segregation, said the decision was "the end of civilization in the South as we have known it." Georgia Gov. Herman Talmadge struck an angry tone. He said Georgia had no intention of allowing "mixed race" schools as long as he was governor. And he touched on Confederate pride from the days when the South went to war with the federal government over slavery by telling supporters that the Supreme Court's ruling was not law in his state; he said it was "the first step toward national suicide." The *Brown* decision should be regarded, he said, as nothing but a "mere scrap of paper."

Meanwhile, newspapers for black readers reacted with exultation. "The Supreme Court decision is the greatest victory for the Negro people since the Emancipation Proclamation," said Harlem's *Amsterdam News*. A writer in the *Chicago Defender* explained, "neither the atomic bomb nor the hydrogen bomb will ever be as meaningful to our democracy." And Thurgood Marshall, the NAACP lawyer who directed the legal fight that led to *Brown,* predicted the end of segregation in all American public schools by the fall of 1955.

Slow progress, backward steps

Ten years later, however, very little school integration had taken place. True to the defiant words of segregationist governors, the Southern states had hunkered down in a massive resistance campaign against school integration. Some Southern counties closed their schools instead of allowing blacks and whites into the same classrooms. In other towns, segregationist academies opened, and most if not all of the white children left the public schools for the racially exclusive alternatives. And in most places, the governors, mayors and school boards found it easy enough to just ask for more time before integrating schools.

That slow-as-molasses approach worked. In 1957, President Eisenhower had to send troops from the 101st Airborne into Little Rock just to get nine black children safely into Central High School. Only in the late '60s, under the threat of losing federal funding, did large-scale school integration begin in Southern public schools. And in many places, in both the North and the South, black and white students did not go to school together until a federal court ordered schoolchildren to ride buses across town to bring the races together.

Today, 50 years later, a study by the Civil Rights Project at Harvard University finds that the percentage of white students attending public schools with Hispanic or black students has steadily declined since 1988. In fact, the report concludes that school integration in the United States is "lower in 2000 than in 1970, before busing for racial balance began." In the South, home to the majority of America's black population, there is now less school integration than there was in 1970. The Harvard report concluded, "At the beginning of the 21st century, American schools are now 12 years into the process of continuous resegregation."

Today, America's schools are so heavily segregated that more than two-thirds of black and Hispanic students are in schools where a majority of the students are not white. And today, most of the nation's white children attend a school that is almost 80 percent white. Hispanics are now the most segregated group of students in the nation because they live in highly concentrated clusters.

At the start of the new century, 50 years after *Brown* shook the nation, segregated housing patterns and an increase in the number of black and brown immigrants have concentrated minorities in impoverished big cities and created a new reality of public schools segregated by race and class.

The Real Impact of *Brown*

So, if *Brown* didn't break apart school segregation, was it really the earthquake that it first appeared to be?

Yes. Today, it is hard to even remember America before *Brown* because the ruling completely changed the nation. It still stands as the laser beam that first signaled that the federal government no longer gave its support to racial segregation among Americans.

Before *Brown*, the federal government lent its power to enforcing the laws of segregation under an 1896 Supreme Court ruling that permitted "separate but equal" treatment of blacks and whites. Blacks and whites who tried to integrate factories, unions, public buses and trains, parks, the military, restaurants, department stores and more found that the power of the federal government was with the segregationists.

Before *Brown,* the federal government had struggled even to pass a law banning lynching.

But after the Supreme Court ruled that segregation in public schools was a violation of the Constitution, the federal attitude toward enforcing second-class citizenship for blacks shifted on the scale of a change in the ocean's tide or a movement in the plates of the continents. Once the highest court in the land said equal treatment for all did not allow for segregation, then the lower courts, the Justice Department and federal prosecutors, as well as the FBI, all switched sides. They didn't always act to promote integration, but they no longer used their power to stop it.

An irreversible shift had begun, and it was the direct result of the *Brown* decision. The change in the attitude of federal officials created a wave of anticipation among black people, who became alert to the possibility of achieving the long-desired goal of racial equality.

There is no way to offer a hard measure of a change in attitude. But the year after *Brown,* Rosa Parks refused to give up her seat to a white man on a racially segregated bus in Montgomery, Ala. That led to a year-long bus boycott and the emergence of massive, nonviolent protests for equal rights. That same year, Martin Luther King, Jr. emerged as the nation's prophet of civil rights for all Americans.

Even when a black 14-year-old, Emmit Till, was killed in Mississippi for supposedly whistling at a white woman, there was a new reaction to old racial brutality. One of Till's elderly relatives broke with small-town Southern tradition and dared to take the witness stand and testify against the white men he saw abduct the boy. Until *Brown,* the simple act of a black man standing up to speak against a white man in Mississippi was viewed as futile and likely to result in more white-on-black violence.

The sense among black people—and many whites as well—that a new era had opened created a new boldness. Most black parents in Little Rock did not want to risk harm to their children by allowing them to join in efforts to integrate Central High. But working with local NAACP officials, the parents of nine children decided it was a new day and time to make history. That same spirit of new horizons was at work in 1962 when James Meredith became the first black student to enroll at the University of Mississippi. And in another lurch away from the traditional support of segregation, the federal government sent troops as well as Justice Department officials to the university to protect Meredith's rights.

The next year, when Alabama Gov. George Wallace felt the political necessity of making a public stand against integration at the University of Alabama, he stood only briefly in the door to block black students and then stepped aside in the face of federal authority. That was another shift toward a world of high hopes for racial equality; again, from the perspective of the 21st century it looks like another aftershock of the *Brown* decision.

The same psychology of hope infected young people, black and white, nationwide in the early '60s. The Freedom Rides, lunch-counter sit-ins and protest marches for voting rights all find their roots in *Brown.* So, too, did the racially integrated 1963 March on Washington at which Martin Luther King, Jr. famously said he had a vision of a promised land where the sons of slaves and the sons of slave owners could finally join together in peace. The desire for change became a demand for change in the impatient voice of Malcolm X, the militant Black Muslim who called for immediate change by violent means if necessary.

In 1964, a decade after *Brown,* the Civil Rights Act was passed by a Congress beginning to respond to the changing politics brought about by the landmark decision. The next year, 1965, the wave of change had swelled to the point that Congress passed the Voting Rights Act.

Closer to the Mountaintop

This sea change in black and white attitudes toward race also had an impact on culture. Churches began to grapple with the Christian and Jewish principles of loving thy neighbor, even if thy neighbor had a different color skin. Major league baseball teams no longer feared a fan revolt if they allowed more than one black player on a team. Black writers, actors, athletes and musicians– ranging from James Baldwin to the Supremes and Muhammad Ali–began to cross over into the mainstream of American culture.

The other side of the change in racial attitudes was white support for equal rights. College-educated young white people in the '60s often defined themselves by their willingness to embrace racial equality. Bob Dylan sang about the changing times as answers "blowing in the wind." Movies like *Guess Who's Coming to Dinner* found major audiences among all races. And previously all-white private colleges and universities began opening their doors to black students. The resulting arguments over affirmative action in college admissions led to the Supreme Court's 1978 decision in the *Bakke* case, which outlawed the use of quotas and its recent ruling that the University of Michigan can take race into account as one factor in admitting students to its law school. The court has also had to deal with affirmative action in the business world, in both hiring and contracts–again as a result of questions of equality under the Constitution raised by *Brown*.

But the most important legacy of the *Brown* decision, by far, is the growth of an educated black middle class. The number of black people graduating from high school and college has soared since *Brown*, and the incomes of blacks have climbed steadily as a result. Home ownership and investment in the stock market among black Americans have skyrocketed since the 1980s. The political and economic clout of that black middle class continues to bring America closer to the mountaintop vision of racial equality that Dr. King might have dreamed of 50 years ago.

The Supreme Court's May 17, 1954 ruling in *Brown* remains a landmark legal decision. But it is much more than that. It is the "Big Bang" of all American history in the 20th century.

THE FIVE CASES THAT LED TO *BROWN*

Belton (Bulah) v. Gebhart: Two separate cases with the same issues–families frustrated by inequitable conditions in African-American schools–were filed in Delaware in 1951. At the state's request, the cases were heard at the Delaware Court of Chancery, a move that backfired when the chancellor ruled that the plaintiffs were being denied equal protection under the law and ordered that the 11 children involved be immediately admitted to the white school. The school board appealed the decision to the Supreme Court. Even though the state's segregation law was not struck down, this was the only case of the five to bring relief to the plaintiffs at the state level.

Bolling v. Sharpe: In 1950, a parent group sued to get 11 young African-American students admitted to John Philip Sousa Junior High School in Washington, D.C. The students were turned away, although the school had several empty classrooms. After the U.S. District Court ruled that segregated schools were constitutional in the District of Columbia, NAACP attorneys appealed. In 1954, the U.S. Supreme Court removed *Bolling v. Sharpe* from its *Brown* decision and rendered a separate opinion on the case because the 14th Amendment was not applicable in the District of Columbia.

Briggs v. Elliott: Named for Harry Briggs, one of 20 parents who sued the Clarendon County, S.C. school board, the lawsuit was filed in November 1949 by the NAACP's Thurgood Marshall. Initially, black parents asked the county to provide school buses for their children, but Judge J. Waties Waring urged the plaintiffs to file a lawsuit to challenge segregation itself. Waring's 28-page dissent in an unsuccessful district court battle is considered a blueprint for much of the Supreme Court's decision in *Brown.*

Brown v. Board of Education: Thirteen parents, working with local lawyers and representatives from the NAACP Legal Defense and Educational Fund, filed a lawsuit in February 1951 to force children to be admitted to their neighborhood schools. At the time, black children were required to attend schools that were designated for African-Americans. While the request was denied in the U.S. District Court, the panel of judges agreed with psychological evidence that African-American children were adversely affected by segregation. The U.S. Supreme Court later quoted the findings in its 1954 opinion.

Davis v. Prince Edward County: After 450 students participated in a two-week student strike to protest deplorable conditions at Robert R. Moton High School in Farmville, Va., the NAACP filed a lawsuit in May 1951 seeking the end to segregation in the state's schools. A three-judge panel at the U.S. District Court unanimously rejected the students' request, which was appealed to the Supreme Court. After *Brown* and *Brown II*, which required districts to desegregate with "all deliberate speed," were announced in 1954 and 1955, white Virginians launched a massive resistance campaign. In 1959, the Prince Edward County Board of Supervisors refused to appropriate funds to the school board; the public schools remained closed for five years.

Source: Brown v. Board of Education National Historic Site

Part I

ITS IMPACT ON LAW

Chapter 1

CRUMBS FROM THE TABLE OF PLENTY: *BROWN* AND THE ONGOING STRUGGLE FOR EDUCATIONAL EQUITY IN AMERICAN SCHOOLS

Gloria J. Browne-Marshall

Upon the 50th Anniversary of the *Brown* decision, one is compelled to examine whether time has produced progress in educational equity.[1] Did America fail to take positive advantage of the opportunity *Brown* presented? The Honorable Constance Baker Motley states the "Supreme Court's decision in *Brown* is not only a statement of what the Equal Protection clause requires but, more broadly speaking, a statement of what justice requires."[2] Or, is it as legal scholar Derek Bell has noted:

> From the cold perspective of history, the *Brown* decision in 1954 is the 20th century equivalent of the Emancipation Proclamation. Both had symbolic value for black people, promising racial justice, and neither provided substantive government enforcement to eliminate the oppression blacks suffered.[3]

This chapter examines *Brown* in a sociolegal and historical context[4] as the issue of racial oppression under law has been at the foundation of American society since its very inception.

An Historical Overview

The Jamestown colony was formed as a British business venture in 1607. A mere ten years later, male and female Africans were brought to Jamestown, Virginia.[5] These Africans were not considered chattel slaves.[6] Prior to the arrival of Africans, most distinctions between peoples were based on class and intra-European ethnic divisions.[7] White immigrants were brought to the English colonies to meet the inordinate need for labor.[8] Although the Africans in the colonies were not slaves, they did not have legal protections equal to that of the white nonservant colonists from Europe.[9] As the benefits of slavery increased the profits of the

European colonists, legal protections for blacks within the colony became the exception to the rule.[10] By 1659, Africans in Virginia were relegated by statute to the lowest human status.[11] Indians were also enslaved in several of the colonies.[12] White indentured servants also served as uncompensated laborers to the colony.[13] However, unlike the Irish or Scottish indentured servant, the African's time of servitude continued as a laborer in perpetuity.[14]

The restrictions on Africans grew in direct correlation to the desire on the part of colonists for labor.[15] England had a profitable market in the crops grown in Virginia. By 1705, statutes and custom had all but rendered the African laborer outside of "the family of man."[16] The African was deemed chattel or moveable property rendering education nonsensical; they were believed to be "uneducable."[17] It was believed that if a slave were to be taught how to read, "there would be no keeping him. It would forever unfit him to be a slave. He would at once become unmanageable, and of no value to his master."[18] Thus, learning to read and write, on the part of Africans, was discouraged by whites and later criminalized.[19]

At the time the colonists were depriving Africans of their humanity, the Declaration of Independence renounced King George as a tyrant.[20] The document speaks of "suffering" and "the history of the [then-] present King of Great Britain" who has caused the colonists "repeated injuries."[21] The colonist, with the aid of Africans, defeated the English in the Revolutionary War. The United States of America ratified its Constitution in 1789.[22] The preamble of the U.S. Constitution provides that "securing liberty to ourselves and our posterity" as one of the many reasons for establishing this Constitution.[23] It notably refers to Africans in America, slave and free, as three-fifths of a person for the purpose of determining the number of representatives to the United States Congress.[24] By 1836, Africans have provided two hundred years of free labor to these United States, the majority of whom were captives of slave-labor camps known as plantations.[25] However, a relative handful of Africans in America, such as Fannie M. Jackson Coppin, received a college education.[26]

Although certain states allowed varying degrees of liberty, Africans in America were subject to the whim of whites.[27] They were forbidden to defend themselves or their loved ones, perse- cuted by law enforcement, deprived of humanity, and treated as an inferior class.[28] In the U.S. Supreme Court decision *Dred Scott v. Sandford*, Mr. Scott brought suit for assault after Sandford beat Scott's wife and daughter.[29] The 7-2 decision delivered by Justice Taney is deserving of intense examination for its instigating thoroughness. Justice Taney determines that the Court does not have jurisdiction over the *Scott* case only after declaring that the U.S. Constitution never contemplated citizenship for Africans.[30]

> What the construction was at that time, we think can hardly admit or doubt. We have the language of the Declaration of Independence and of the Articles of Confederation, in addition to the plain words of the Constitution itself; we have the legislation of the different states, before, about the time, and since, the Constitution was adopted; we have the legislation of Congress, from the time of its adoption to a recent period; and we have the constant and uniform action of the Executive Department, all concurring together, and leading to the same result. And if anything in relation to the construction of the Constitution can be regarded as settled, it is that which we now give to the word 'citizen' and the word 'people.'[31]

Mr. Scott's suit was dismissed for lack of jurisdiction because he is neither person nor citizen.[32] Justice Roger Taney made clear that in addition to being enslaved "a black man had no rights a white man need respect."[33]

The Struggle for Recognition Under Law

The Civil War brought the issue of black personhood to the fore. The war had at its core the conflict between political and economic philosophies represented by powers in the North and South. The North, experiencing the throes of the Industrial Revolution, sought factory laborers, whereas the South, an agrarian economy, depended heavily on the free labor of enslaved Africans.[34] Africans fought for their freedom in the war. Their participation was a great influence in the North's victory in the Civil War. Southerners, once Republicans, renounced their party allegiance and registered as Democrats. The Emancipation Proclamation freed the enslaved Africans residing in states that had seceded from the Union. In

1865, the 13th Amendment to the U.S. Constitution ended slavery.[35] In 1868, Africans in America were granted due process rights, equal protection and the privileges and immunities of United States citizenship.[36] African-American men were then granted the right to vote in 1870.[37]

Hundreds of organizations were created in the 1800s by blacks to fund educational initiatives, improve moral conditions, enlighten the black community about temperance, defeat segregation, promote cultural pride, lobby political forces, protect black children, highlight achievements and remove obstacles to progress.[38] Elementary and high schools, trade schools and colleges were created by blacks and a few white philanthropists to teach the millions of newly released black people who had been prohibited formal education.[39] However, blacks remained vulnerable to oppression and white malevolence.[40] There was relatively little money or motivation for the education of blacks because it represented a change in social status for them and whites wanted none of that.[41]

The participation of blacks in elections was met by the creation of terrorist organizations such as the Ku Klux Klan.[42] For example, where 130, 344 African-Americans had been registered voters in Louisiana in 1896, by 1900 only 5,320 remained.[43] Constitutional protections were meaningless as whites forced free blacks into shareholding, political disfranchisement and legal vulnerability reminiscent of slavery. The black community was helpless to defend itself from murderous lynch mobs.[44] Lynching was a tool of intimidation and terrorism utilized by some whites against blacks.[45] It was considered most effective when whites, male and female, stood back in silence or cheered in approval.[46] Lynching took place in the North as well as the South.[47] Blacks escaped to the North only to find tensions arose over the competition for employment. Blacks were met with oppression in both the North and South. During the period 1890 to 1920, race riots occurred in several different cities as whites opposed the inclusion of the black worker.[48] About 185, 000 blacks had come to cities such as Chicago, Cleveland, Philadelphia, Pittsburgh and New York since 1890.[49] They were as ill-prepared for anomie and brutal competition within urban culture as the Italians, Poles and Hungarian immigrants were arriving at the same time.[50] However, racism would mark blacks for special abuse.[51]

Laws restricting the actions of blacks and segregating them from whites were created in both the North and South.[52] These laws effectively relegated blacks to that of second-class citizens. It was the challenge to a Louisiana statute segregating blacks to the soot-filled front cars of the local railroad that was at issue in *Plessy v. Ferguson*.[53] Justice Brown delivered the now-infamous opinion in which Plessy's claims of discrimination were soundly defeated.[54] The opinion which institutes "separate but equal," the American version of apartheid, sets forth public education specifically as an area in which the races should be separated.

> The most common instance of this is connected with **establishment of separate schools for white and colored children** which has been a valid exercise of the legislative power even by courts of states where the political rights of the colored race have been longest and most earnestly enforced.[55] *[emphasis added]*

Justice Brown dismisses any assumed criticism of this constitutional overreaching by allowing the states to determine the breadth of their segregation laws; he states:

> Laws permitting, and even requiring, their separation in places where they are liable to be brought into contact do not necessarily imply the inferiority of either race to the other, and have been generally, if not universally, recognized as within the competency of the state legislatures in the exercise of their police power.[56]

There have always been a relative handful of whites who have withstood social ostracism, threats and assault to support the rights of black people.[57] The opinion in *Dred Scott* denying personhood to blacks was not unanimous.[58] Nor was the *Plessy* opinion.[59] Justice Harlan's dissent in *Plessy* provides early insight into the path America could have taken had she the fortitude. Justice Harlan states that:

> The white race deems itself to be the dominant race in this country. And so it, in prestige, in achievements, in *education,* in wealth, and in power. So, I doubt not it will continue to be for all time if it remains true to its great heritage

and holds fast to the principles of constitutional liberty. But in view of the Constitution, in the eye of the law, there is in this country no superior, dominant, ruling class of citizens. There is no caste here. Our Constitution is color-blind, and neither knows nor tolerates classes among citizens.[60] *[emphasis added]*

He continues with this prescient statement: "In my opinion, the judgment this day rendered will, in time, prove to be quite as pernicious as the decision made by this tribunal in the *Dred Scott* case."[61]

The oppression of blacks was widespread as evidenced by the number of lynchings during the relevant period 1882 to 1920. The numbers are based on self-reported government statistics gathered from county law-enforcement agencies which may be under-estimated.

TABLE 1 Persons Lynched, by Race: 1882 to 1920[62] Source: United States Series H 1168-1170.			
Year	Total	White	Black
1882	113	64	49
1883	130	77	53
1884	211	160	51
1885	184	110	74
1886	138	64	74
1887	120	50	70
1888	137	68	69
1889	170	76	94
1890	96	11	85
1891	184	71	113
1892	230	69	161
1893	152	34	118
1894	192	58	134
1895	179	66	113
1896	123	45	78
1897	158	35	123
1898	120	19	101
1899	106	21	85
1900	115	9	106
1901	130	25	105

TABLE 1 (Continued) Persons Lynched, by Race: 1882 to 1920[62] Source: United States Series H 1168-1170.			
Year	Total	White	Black
1902	92	7	85
1903	99	15	84
1904	83	7	76
1905	62	5	57
1906	65	3	62
1907	60	2	58
1908	97	8	89
1909	82	13	69
1910	76	9	67
1911	67	7	60
1912	63	2	61
1913	52	1	51
1914	55	4	51
1915	69	13	56
1916	54	4	50
1917	38	2	36
1918	64	4	60
1919	83	7	76
1920	61	8	53

TABLE 2 Lynching of Blacks in 1882-1930 by State.[63]	
Source: *Ida B. Wells-Barnett: An Exploratory Study of an American Black Woman, 1893-1930*	
Certain discrepancies in the numbers are recognized in that the United States census indicates 230 persons, including whites, lynched in 1892.	
Alabama	22
Arkansas	25
California	3
Florida	11
Georgia	17
Idaho	8
Illinois	1
Kentucky	9
Louisiana	29

Maryland	1
Mississippi	16
Missouri	6
Montana	4
New York	1
North Carolina	5
North Dakota	1
Ohio	3
South Carolina	5
Tennessee	28
Texas	15
Virginia	7
West Virginia	5
Wyoming	9
Arizona Terr.	3
Oklahoma	2

During the latter part of the 19th century, America was in the throes of moral reform. However, for the most part, white reformers of the period ignored the murder by lynching of blacks.[64] Black leaders, male and female, toured the United States and Great Britain lecturing on lynching, Jim Crow and mounting oppression suffered by black men, women and children.[65]

In 1909, the NAACP was formed to construct a strategy to address the conditions under which blacks endured in America.[66] "The NAACP began as the Conference on the Status of the Negro [with] two divergent conceptions of itself: the first, as primarily a white organization dedicated to African-American uplift through well-financed suasion; the second, as an interracial phalanx challenging the mainstream public to accept ever-greater civil and social rights for the nation's historic minority."[67] The Niagara Movement, comprised of black intellectuals, demanded constitutional rights and freedoms, merged with the politically powerful organization of whites.[68] W.E.B. DuBois, the prominent intellectual and most vocal member of the NAACP, set his sights on combating racial oppression fostered by *Plessy*.[69]

The Legal Strategy

Under the leadership of Charles Hamilton Houston, a legal strategy was implemented that consisted of laying an incremental foundation of Supreme Court jurisprudence which would lead unequivocally to an end to racial segregation.[70] Houston described the work of lawyers as that of "social engineers."[71] Most states practicing segregation in higher education lacked a separate black graduate school, medical school or law school; this failure became the impetus for court challenges on behalf of those black applicants.[72] By 1947, cases challenging segregation were pending in Oklahoma, Texas, Louisiana and South Carolina.[73]

The *Brown* opinion was, by most accounts, a political compromise.[74] The country was in the midst of the Cold War with the Soviet Union and international criticism surrounding the treatment of blacks in America was of growing concern to the State Department.[75] President Harry Truman signed an Executive Order desegregating the military in 1948.[76] Chief Justice Warren, former governor of California, ascended to the Court in 1953 as a nominee of President Eisenhower.[77] Although Justice Warren was resolutely against the practice of segregation, the Constitution, as interpreted by the Court in prior decisions, supported *de jure* segregation.[78] Justice Warren needed to draft the legal argument in a manner that would result in unanimity on the Court due to the social and political obstacles awaiting the decision.[79]

The Court wrestled with the breadth of the 14th Amendment and the legislature's intent at the time of its ratification.[80] The NAACP used Justice Harlan's dissent in *Plessy* to form the basis of legal arguments in *Brown*.[81] Social scientists led by psychologist Kenneth Clark presented studies which demonstrated the invidious emotional scars, "badge of inferiority," which was left on black children attending segregated schools.[82] One could juxtapose this theory and argue that white children suffered from an invidious badge of illusionary superiority as well. *Plessy* was overturned on the basis that there was ignorance on the part of the *Plessy* Court regarding the psychological effects of segregation.[83] As if Justice

Brown and the *Plessy* majority would have held differently after reviewing the science.

The social, political, legal and spiritual value of the *Brown* decision began a national move for equal rights under law. Unfortunately, Linda Brown and the other plaintiffs in this class action failed to receive the requested injunctive relief that would have allowed them to attend the requested white schools.[84] The remedy would be argued at a later date. In 1955, after hearing arguments by the NAACP for immediate integration of public schools, the Court ruled that the school districts would develop their own plans for desegregation monitored by the local United States District Courts.[85] The Court, in *Brown II*, requested that the school districts desegregate their schools "with all deliberate speed."[86] The *Brown II* decision was viewed as a disappointment by civil rights attorneys of the time.[87] It was yet another compromise decision.[88] The *Brown II* opinion set forth a list of criteria the United States District Courts were to follow in making a determination that school districts were complying in "good faith" with the Court's Order.[89] Without a specific time frame for implementation, Marshall and other advocates feared the states would resist integration.[90] Those fears were well-founded.

Massive Resistance

Desegregation was met with vigorous resistance by local school districts and white parents. Segregationists argued in a "Southern Manifesto" that *Brown* was a unconstitutional violation of states' rights and all "lawful means" should be used to reverse it.[91] Several deviously creative school plans would permit students to voluntarily attend the school of their choice. The Court held that such a voluntary plan to integrate is tantamount to maintaining a segregated system.[92] Due to intimidation, few white students enrolled in the majority black schools; black students who attempted to enroll in white public schools were assaulted and threatened with death.[93] For example, civil rights leader Fred Shuttlesworth was brutally beaten by a white mob when he attempted to enroll his child in an all-white school.[94] In 1957, Governor Faubus of Arkansas called forth the state's National Guard to prevent black children from enrolling in white public schools.[95] When the children secretly enrolled, Faubus allowed white mobs to surround the school.[96] Notwithstanding America's racial history, President Eisenhower reluctantly sent in the 101st Airborne paratroopers to restore order and escort the black children to Central High School in Little Rock.[97] President Eisenhower stated that the enforcement of *Brown* "should not be allowed to create hardship or injustice [for whites]."[98] There is little evidence that the black children and adults injured while attempting to attend an integrated school were ever financially compensated by state or local governments.

School districts attempted to use Justice Harlan's dissent in *Plessy* against the plaintiffs by producing an alleged "color-blind" school assignment plan; it was also struck down by the Court.[99] The color-blind plan was defeated because the Court began to appreciate that "the background of segregation" such a "limit on remedies would render illusory the promise of *Brown*."[100] Unfortunately, the school districts litigated issues that forced the Court to once again establish that the state's affirmative duty to desegregate their schools.[101] After several years fending off protests and legal challenges to busing, the Court upheld Charlotte, North Carolina's policy of busing students as a legitimate method for integrating public schools.[102] The Court, in one of the few apparent fits of frustration, reversed the Fourth Circuit and upheld the District Court's busing plan which "promises realistically to work, and promises realistically to work now."[103] However, the tactics of evasion practiced by the school districts continued for decades as lawyers for black children found themselves enmeshed in time-consuming and resource-draining litigation.[104]

Busing for integration purposes was a short-lived success. Black children bore the greatest weight of busing, awaking early and returning home late, in order to attend formerly all-white schools across town.[105] White flight proliferated within cities falling under desegregation orders as white parents removed their children from public schools or relocated to the suburbs.[106] The Court in *Jenkins* held that suburban school-district policies did not violate the rights of black schoolchildren.[107] Therefore, any attempts by city school districts to fashion an inter-district school assignment plan reaching into the suburbs is unconstitutional.[108] One may argue that whites did not leave the public schools to avoid racial integration; it was merely coincidental timing.[109] However, their departure might have been motivated, the end result is the same.

Between 1968 and 1980, white-student enrollment declined in all major city schools.[110]

TABLE 3	
City	% Decline in White Students
New York City	45.7
Los Angeles	63.4
Chicago	62.1
Philadelphia	41.2
Detroit	77.8
Houston	62.8
Baltimore	58
Memphis	54.6
San Diego	37.9
Washington, DC	59.9
Milwaukee	58.2
New Orleans	71
Cleveland	66.3
Atlanta	85.7
Boston	63.3
Denver	58.7

Presently, the majority of the population of urban public schools is students of color.[111] A study by the Civil Rights Project at Harvard University finds that "since 1986, in almost every district examined, black and Latino students have become more racially segregated from whites in their schools.[112]

The literature suggests that minority schools are highly correlated with high-poverty schools and these schools are also associated with low parental involvement, lack of resources, less experienced and [less] credentialed teachers and higher teacher turnover—all of which combine to exacerbate educational inequality for minority students."[113] On January 8, 2002, President George W. Bush signed legislation intended to raise the academic standards of all children in public education,

especially those children in "failing" schools.[114] Unfortunately, the federal funding necessary for state implementation of No Child Left Behind Act of 2001 is in question.

The *Brown* Decision and Higher Education

Affirmative action in higher education may be viewed as the next epoch of *Brown* in that it would provide the opportunity that would have otherwise been available *but* for racial discrimination. However, by 1978, the country's majority population, if reflected through the opinions of the U.S. Supreme Court, refused to acknowledge the connection between the history of American racism and affirmative action. Only the remnants of past racial discrimination are at issue before the Court. By focusing on the "remnants" of past discrimination one may argue that the American majority society, as represented by the courts, assume that race-based discrimination and racial segregation no longer exists. During the 1970s, whites rioted in northern cities such as Boston as well as in the South as black parents attempted to integrate public schools with "all deliberate speed." Yet, the Court found that the University of California could not provide a remedy in the absence of judicial, legislative or administrative findings of constitutional or statutory violations.[115]

In *Bakke*, the Court addressed whether voluntary measures at the University of California Medical School, intended to remedy the present effects of their past discrimination, were constitutional.[116] The University of California at Davis Medical School was reserving sixteen of the 100 spaces in its class for minority group members when Allan Bakke, a rejected white applicant, brought suit alleging discrimination because of his race in that was prevented from competing for those 16 reserved seats and that the special two-track admissions system violated the Equal Protection Clause.[117]

His claim is labeled "reverse discrimination" in that the plaintiff, a white male applicant, alleges he was the object of discrimination due to his race; the school's admissions policy denied him admission to medical school and allegedly admitted less qualified black applicants.[118]

Supreme Court Justices Stevens, Burger, Stewart and Rehnquist held in *Regents v. Univ. of California v. Bakke* that the admissions program violated Title VI of the Civil Rights Act of 1964 while U.S. Supreme Court Justice Brennan, White, Marshall and Blackman held that the program could be constitutionally upheld under an intermediate scrutiny test in that both Title VI and the Fourteenth Amendment would permit the University to take voluntary, race-conscious steps, even granting numerically-based racial preferences when the program is designed to remedy the effects of past discrimination.[119]

Justice Powell held that a strict scrutiny test would be utilized in all cases using racial classifications and so found that the two-track admissions program at the Medical School violated the Fourteenth Amendment.

> "The guarantee of equal protection cannot mean one thing when applied to one individual and something else when applied to one a person of another color."[120]

In interpreting the Fourteenth Amendment, Justice Powell states that:

> "Nothing in the Constitution supports the notion that individuals may be asked to suffer otherwise impermissible burdens in order to enhance the societal standing of their ethnic group. Second, preferential programs may only reinforce common stereotypes holding that certain groups are unable to achieve success without special protection based on a factor having no relationship to individual worth."[121]

The country was still unclear as to when race would meet the strict scrutiny test. Civil rights organizations could only wait until the next test case. It would arise as a challenge by a white applicant denied admission to the University of Texas School of Law.[122] In *Hopwood v. Texas,* another "reverse discrimination" case, the Fifth Circuit Court of Appeals held that the law school's consideration of race as a factor in admissions violated the Equal Protection Clause.[123] The *Hopwood* court "agreed with the white plaintiffs that any consideration of race or ethnicity by the law school for the purpose of achieving a diverse student body is not a compelling interest under the Fourteenth Amendment."[124]

The majority of judges comprising the *Hopwood* panel proffered three reasons for concluding that the use of race to achieve a diverse student body is not a compelling interest under the Fourteenth Amendment:[125] First, the majority of the panel rejected U.S. Supreme Court Justice Powell's view in *Bakke* as non-binding because it was a dissenting or "lonely opinion;" second, the panel suggests that *Bakke* "appears to have decided that there is essentially only one compelling state interest to justify racial classifications and that is remedying past wrongs;" third, the panel opined that the use of race to achieve diversity undermines the primary objective of the Fourteenth Amendment–ending racially-motivated state action.[126] The State of Texas did not appeal the decision of the Fifth Circuit to the U.S. Supreme Court.

Meanwhile, in the public school arena, another "reverse discrimination" claim was filed in North Carolina against the Charlotte-Mecklenburg School District. In 1998, a white elementary school student claimed the school district violated her constitutional rights in assigning her to a school based on her race in order to achieve racial balance.[127] The school district was still under a decades-old desegregation order at the time.[128] Although the Charlotte-Mecklenburg School District admitted to failing to fulfill its *Green* obligations, the District Court judge found the district unitary and ruled in favor of the white plaintiff.[129] On appeal to the Fourth Circuit, that court held that the school district had not achieved unitary status based on the factors set forth in *Green* and therefore the school district could utilize a white student's race in achieving racial balance within its schools.[130]

Post-*Bakke*, the Supreme Court has had relatively few modern opportunities to determine racial equity issues in higher education.[131] It last "addressed the use of race in public higher education over 25 years ago" in the *Bakke* case.[132] Then, in 2003, the Court was presented with "two reverse discrimination" cases against the University of Michigan. Both cases were brought by white applicants challenging their denial of admission and alleged race discrimination because black applicants were admitted using an admission policy which takes race into account.[133] The United States Supreme Court upheld racial diversity as a compelling state interest in admissions at the University of Michigan Law School in *Grutter v. Bollinger.*[134] The Court, in *Grutter,* allowed the use of race as one element of a complex list of criteria.[135] In the companion case *Gratz, et al., v. Bollinger, et al.*, the United States Supreme Court held that the University of Michigan's admission process for its College of Literature, Science and the Arts violated the rights of white applicants.[136] The college admissions process at issue awarded twenty points to applicants from under-represented minority groups.[137]

The University of Michigan is a state school.[138] The Equal Protection Clause provides that no state shall "deny to any person within its jurisdiction the equal protection of the laws."[139] The

Bakke strict scrutiny test is the legal standard of judicial review utilized by the U.S. Supreme Court in determining whether the consideration of race in the admissions process was unconstitutional.[140] In 1995, the Supreme Court determined that: "All racial classifications imposed by whatever federal, state or local government actor, must be analyzed by a reviewing court under strict scrutiny.[141] The Court relied on a test set forth in *Richmond v. J.A. Croson Co.*[142] Therefore, the admissions policy must substantially advance a compelling state interest and the means chosen to do so must be narrowly tailored to accomplish this goal."[143] The policy must be narrowly tailored in scope and application. "To be narrowly tailored, a race-conscious admissions program cannot use a quota system" or insulate a particular group from competition.[144]

In applying strict scrutiny, the Court, in a divided opinion delivered by Justice O'Connor, held that the use of race in *Grutter* met the constitutional standard.[145] The Court, in *Grutter*, determined that the University of Michigan Law School had a compelling interest in having a diverse student body.[146] Law schools such as that at the University of Michigan, "represent the training ground for a large number of our nation's leaders."[147] Thus, the state seeks to expose the law students "to widely diverse people, cultures, ideas and viewpoints" in order to equip them for leadership in an increasingly global business world as well as a diverse American society.[148] The admissions policy at the University of Michigan Law School was also deemed narrowly tailored because it was applied in a "flexible, nonmechanical way."[149]

Whereas the Court in *Gratz* deemed the policy as well as the manner in which it was applied to be a quota which shielded black applicants from competing with their white peers.[150] The comparison of the Court's decisions in *Grutter* and *Gratz* demonstrates the complexities involved in any governmental attempts to address racial disparities in public education. Justice Powell found the "principle evil" of the University of California's medical school admissions policy given to African-American applicants based solely on race.[151] The Court finds unconstitutional any policy which provides an "automatic acceptance or rejection" of applicants based on race.[152]

Upholding diversity as a compelling state interest in *Grutter* was heralded as a hard-won celebrated step forward in civil rights jurisprudence. However, one could also argue that the splintered

Grutter majority and contentious dissent evidence the failure of American society to make substantive progress in the fifty years following *Brown*. It may appear mere ingratitude. But America has chosen to ignore the nearly 400 years of economic, political, social and spiritual oppression based on race. In light of America's history, one could well argue that allowing a handful of black students to attend a state law school in order to better prepare future white leaders of the free world to deal with a diverse populace or to simply provide these leaders with an appearance of "legitimacy in the eyes of the citizenry" is but crumbs from a table of plenty.[153] *Brown* presented the government with an opportunity for positive change in education and constructive change on every level of America society. Those governmental failures continue to undermine the victory that was *Brown*.

> When the government, therefore, has secured to each of its citizens equal rights before the law and equal opportunities for improvement and progress, it has accomplished the end for which it was organized and performed all of the functions respecting social advantages with which it is endowed.[154]

Certainly, Justice Brown failed to envision his statement as an impassioned plea for racial justice in American public education. However, his prescient words offer ironic encouragement to advocates living in a new millennium and fighting this centuries' long struggle to gain educational equity for black children.

Chapter 2

THE IMPACT OF THE 1993 *BROWN III* DECISION ON TOPEKA PUBLIC SCHOOLS

Judith Lynne McConnell, Blythe F. Hinitz & Gloria A. Dye

Introduction: Forty-five Years of *Brown* Decisions

The lineage of the *Brown v. Topeka Board of Education* Supreme Court case began before the historic decision in 1954 and continued sporadically for the next forty-five years until its resolution in 1999. Regarded by many as the most important Supreme Court decision of the century, historian Juan Williams said, "When you look at *Brown* you are looking at a moment so powerful it is the equivalent of the Big Bang in our solar system."[1] Truly, a Supreme Court decision this significant deserves a thorough review of its legal precursors, discussion of events which led to its conclusion, as well as a review of the significant changes in education that it produced.

The "separate but equal" doctrine first adopted in *Plessy v. Ferguson* "has no place" in the "field of public education" as stated by Chief Justice Earl Warren when he delivered the decision regarding the landmark *Brown v. Topeka Board of Education* case in 1954.[2&3] The *Brown v. Board of Education* case (often referred to as *Brown I*) established that racial segregation in public education is unconstitutional and a violation of the Fourteenth Amendment. The following year, in the decision known as *Brown II*, 1955, the Supreme Court declared that desegregation must begin with "all deliberate speed," indicating that the schools required different remedies for each locality. This decision expressed the expectations that school officials would assess and solve the problems and the court would decide whether the officials were acting in "good faith" and with deliberate speed.[4] The U.S. District Court indicated in 1955 that although the Topeka school district was not fully desegregated, it was making a "good faith effort" toward the established plan of desegregation.[5] The case remained open until the courts believed that full compliance was achieved. No further orders were designated [issued?] by the courts.[6]

The *Brown II* decision in 1955 stated that schools were to begin the desegregation process by permitting children from Kansas, South Carolina, Virginia and Delaware to attend the public schools "with all deliberate speed." This was a victory for the plaintiffs of this case as well as for all children around the country. This case illustrated that the segregation of white and black children had a detrimental impact upon the black children. It should also be noted that prior to that time many schools around the country provided two separate facilities, one for white children and one for black children. By September 1, 1961, "the school board's four-step plan" to comply with the ruling of the 1955 court decision was fully implemented. At no time, however, was there ever a ruling by the court that indicated that the "Topeka Public Schools was (or was not) in full compliance with the Supreme Court's rulings."[7]

In 1974, the United States Department of Health, Education, and Welfare's (HEW) attention was drawn to the Topeka Public Schools. HEW threatened the district with a withholding of federal funds because the "Topeka schools were not in full compliance with the law regarding desegregation…and HEW…was investigating discrimination in all its aspects at all levels of the public school system."[8] The school district contended that they were still under the jurisdiction of the courts and the *Brown v. Board* case was still "an open case."[9]

In 1979, the motion to intervene by individuals was granted by the judge thereby requesting the case which lay dormant for 24 years be revived.[10] This motion gave birth to what became known as the *Brown III* case. A gap in time exists between the motion to intervene and the actual beginning of the *Brown III* case. Beginning in 1987 in the *Brown III* case, a series of litigations took place. They concluded in 1994 with a desegregation plan and a formal ruling resulting in the closing of the case in 1999. There were a number of court decisions and orders handed down between 1987 and 1999 conclusion of the cases, see the following listing.

Detailed listing of the cases collectively known as *Brown III*, as outlined by the Topeka Public School District[11]

671 F. Supp. 1290 (1987) Federal Court Decision

892 F. 2d 851 (1989) Overturns District Court Decision

112 S. Ct. 1657 (1992) Remanded case to 10th Circuit Court

978 F. 2d 585 (1993) Reinstates 1989 Decision and Remands the case to the District Court

Desegregation Remedy is Ordered by Judge Richard Rogers (July 25, 1994) 878 F. Supp. 1430 (Feb. 21, 1995). Orders Payment of Attorneys' Fees

T-316 Unitary Status Granted and Case Closed by the Federal District Court (July 27, 1999)

On July 27, 1999, Judge Richard Rogers granted the Topeka Public Schools motion for a "declaration of unitary status and order of dismissal" bringing to a close the *Brown v. Board of Education* case.[12] There are specific factors which the court examines to determine if a district has met unitary status. Therefore, the school system has complied with the court mandates and is providing an equal education to all children.

The Implications for My Little Daughter, Plaintiff Mrs. Vivian Scales

As we recognized the 50th Anniversary of *Brown* in 2004, it was well-established that the decisions made by the courts in this case were historic and unprecedented. The *Brown* decision essentially called for an end to the segregation of public schools.

There are few remaining plaintiffs of the historic 1954 case. It was indeed fortunate when one of these plaintiffs, Mrs. Vivian Scales, granted an interview to Mrs. Johnnie Sanders on July 30, 2004. A previous interview with Mrs. Vivian Scales was conducted in 1998 by Dr. Judith Lynne McConnell and Mrs. Sanders. Now, six years later, Mrs. Sanders followed the questioning format of the previous 1998 interview. Mrs. Scales is 85 years old and currently living in a Topeka retirement home. Following are some of Mrs. Scales' recollections as a plaintiff in this landmark Supreme Court case.

Interviewer: Hello, Mrs. Scales, you certainly look good!

Scales: No, I don't, look at my hair, it is a mess (she chuckled).

Interviewer: Would you mind if I asked you some questions about the *Brown v. Topeka Board of Education* decision?

Mrs. Scales: No, I don't mind, go right ahead.

Interviewer: What triggered your involvement in what became *the Brown v. Topeka Board of Education* decision?

Scales: Mr. Burnett (president of the local Topeka Chapter of the NAACP) asked, I did not want to, it was not going to be easy. I asked him what would it include and involve. He told me to go to different people and sometimes I would be refused. He told me not to argue. So, I went on because he asked. I asked him if it would be safe. He told me that it would be as safe as I would make it.

Interviewer: The first meeting, what was it like?

Scales: We received instructions, talked about what to do in different situations.

Interviewer: How many people were there?

Scales: Twenty-five to thirty, but only thirteen plaintiffs, there are only two of us left, me and Mrs. Henderson, I don't see her much anymore.

Interviewer: Do you know why there were thirteen plaintiffs?

Scales: Mr. Burnett asked thirteen plaintiffs, thirteen parents considered it and others were not asked.

Interviewer: What did you tell your daughter about attempting to register her in school?

Scales: It was an alphabet system and it was time for the 'S's' to register. I told her it was time to go and register her in school at Parkdale.

Interviewer: How did she feel about going to Parkdale Elementary School, an all-white school?

Scales: She did not care where she went, she was only seven years old. When we went to register Ruth at Parkdale, we were told to go to a room and sit down. We took a rag, bath towel or something to wipe off the seats, they were dusty. Maybe the place they took us to wasn't used much. People would look at us strange, but we were told not to argue. It hurt her feelings when they refused her. She asked me, 'Mom, what did refuse mean?' I told her that they did not accept you to go to school here in the neighborhood. She said, 'Why?' I told her, Well they refused you because we have not gotten that worked out.

Interviewer: Are there any little-known facts or secrets about the development of the case?

Scales: No secrets, when someone comes around to interview, we tell them everything that we know (she then puts on her eyeglasses). I put them (the eyeglasses) on to see whatever it is I am supposed to see (she chuckles).

Interviewer: What was the atmosphere like in Topeka? The environment during the Supreme Court trial?

Scales: It was confusing, items in the newspaper kind of scared us. They knew we were coming to court. It made us wonder what the outcome would be.

Interviewer: What was it like in Topeka when the verdict was announced?

Scales: It was glorious! I remember I was ironing, I left the iron sitting there, it burnt the cover of the ironing board. It was on the television everywhere. Brown recovered! Not exactly but in that order. We all celebrated, it was a glorious day! We got together and said it was over. It took a long time.

Interviewer: How long did it take?

Scales: Quite a while, at least a year anyway. We had to have different meetings along the way.

Interviewer: Were there any repercussions in the African-American community after the decision?

Scales: No incidents at all. No, only a few [people] wanted to rough us up, but it did not last. We ran into a bunch [of people]. One asked, 'Well, what in the hell do you want?' I told him we don't want anything from you, you cannot help us at all! One man said he had to go and see about his children. We told him he would be okay!

Interviewer: How did you feel about the case being named after Oliver Brown?

Scales: It was all right (she laughed). It was incorrectly done, Darlene Brown should have been done first. "D"[for Darlene] comes first [before "O" for Oliver], but we got together and agreed since he [Oliver Brown] was the only man. We let it go, it was a mistake (she chuckled again). We won! No time to argue, we had to get work done. No time for arguments, a few had a few scrabbles but I did not get in any of them. You stay out, then you don't have to get out!

Interviewer: Was your daughter Ruth treated differently or unfairly after the decision?

Scales: I did not know of any unfair treatment, if so we would have went back to court. Every day we had a little conference. I taught her to tell me what went on at school. You know my daughter, she is a big girl now, her name is Ruth, but we call her Toodie. Everyone calls her Toodie.

Interviewer: It has been fifty years since the decision, how do you think the decision has impacted Topeka?

Scales: Fifty years is a long time.

Interviewer: Was your involvement in the case worth it?

Scales: Oh yeah, I kind of would not want to go through it again. I would if I have to. I think we have opened quite a few doors. Have you seen this place (the retirement home where she resides)? I am called a celebrity. I am just me. People are very nice.

Interviewer: Did you participate in the 50th Anniversary ceremony of the *Brown v. Topeka Board of Education* here in Topeka, and, if so, what did you do?

Scales: I did not get to go, too big of a crowd. I walk with a walker, it is hard. I told Toodie (her daughter Ruth) I did not want to go. My daughter kept me up on most of it. I just like to hear about my church, Antioch Missionary Baptist Church. My daughter said she will take me to the Monroe School. I have been to the White House three times.

Interviewer: Oh my goodness, I have not been inside the White House, which presidents did you meet?

Scales: Clinton ...Oh, I can't remember (she chuckles).

Interviewer: Jimmy Carter?

Scales: Yes, President Carter and the one that died.

Interviewer: Ronald Reagan?

Scales: Yes, that's him.

Interviewer: What do you think of the magnet schools here in Topeka?

Scales: I have not been to any of them. My daughter will probably take me around.

Epilogue: Mrs. Scales talked briefly about her deceased husband, Deacon George Scales, and said, "I miss him so much, he never caused me a speck of trouble, and I took him everywhere that I went." It was lunch time for Mrs. Scales and I did not want to disrupt her routine. She invited me to visit her anytime. As I was leaving, we hugged and using her walker to steady herself, she walked me to the elevator.

Reverend Oliver Brown's Daughters, Memories of Growing Up in Topeka

The adults involved in the 1954 Supreme Court case have strong memories of what happened in the 1950's, and so do their children. The struggles faced by one little girl in Topeka, Kansas was multiplied by many children across the country. We are not able to listen to every child's recollection of growing-up in segregated schools or the lifelong ramifications this decision had on their lives and the lives of their families. We are fortunate that many of the plaintiffs' children are alive and they have poignant recollections from their childhood. To better understand the impact of this historic decision, it is necessary to listen to the voices of the children of the Brown case.

Remembrances of Childhood and Realities for Our Grandchildren

In September 1998, Dr. McConnell and some of her undergraduate students interviewed Cheryl Brown Henderson and later her sister, Linda Brown Thompson. These women, two of the three daughters of Reverend Oliver Brown who died in 1961, are some of the original plaintiffs' children affected by this case. The Brown sisters were guest speakers in Dr. McConnell's "Introduction to Early Childhood Education" course at Washburn University. Both sisters provided prepared written questions which included their responses and, in addition, graciously allowed students to ask them questions. The following are three of the questions and responses from those in-class interviews.

Interviewer: From a child's standpoint, how did you feel being singled out for such a test case?

Thompson: Because I was a minor (eight years old), I played a very limited role in what happened at the time. I did appear in court but did not have to testify. My father, of course, provided the testimony about my circumstances (instead of being able to attend the neighborhood elementary school four blocks away, she had to attend Monroe

Elementary School, which was two miles away from her home).

Henderson: The most I remember is that when the parents involved tried to enroll us in the all-white school and we were denied, my mother explained that it was because of the color of our skin. As a child, I did not comprehend what difference that could possibly make.

Interviewer: Why did your parents think the school you attended wasn't equal to others in Topeka? Can you give specific examples?

Thompson: The Topeka case was not about inequality. It was about equal access. The schools for black children were built by the same companies as those for white children. The teaching staff and materials were also equal with regard to their education and of subjects taught. In fact, one of the all-black schools, Washington Elementary School, had more teachers with masters degrees than any school in the city.

Henderson: The issue for black parents was the distance their children had to travel to attend school when there were schools in their neighborhood. Neighborhoods in Topeka were integrated. People lived where they could afford to live.

Interviewer: What improvements in education today do you feel are a result of your parents' willingness to stand up for your rights?

Thompson: We believe for our parents and others it took courage to get involved and to agree to participate. They ran the risk of losing jobs or personal injury. They believed what they were doing was right. This was a case put together by the NAACP and attorneys who then asked parents with elementary-age children to participate.

Henderson: We believe the results have been seen more in other areas of society, such as public accommodations, which were some of the most segregated situations. Education has been slow to comply. The greatest improvement is an understanding of all people by learning about cultures different than our own. Multi-cultural education was unheard of before this took place.[13]

Brown III Decision, Impact for Public Education in Topeka

What actually occurred during the years between the *Brown II* decision in 1955 and the reopening of the case known as *Brown III* in 1979? The following is a detailing of the events which are named *Brown III*, and ultimately led to the closing of the *Brown v. Board of Education of Topeka* case in 1999.

Two cases and an investigation predated *Brown III*. On September 10, 1973, *Johnson v. Whittier, T-5430* case was a class-action suit filed with a complaint that concentrated primarily on the "equality of facilities" rather than the "distribution of students" as was the case in *Brown I*. The *Johnson v. Whittier* case was eventually settled in December of 1978. However, the filing of this case led to an investigation by HEW into the practices of the Topeka Public Schools regarding race discrimination. The HEW investigation suggested that the Topeka schools were not in full compliance with the law regarding desegregation and the agency attempted to cut off federal funding to the district. The school district argued that they were still under the supervision of the courts and this case was still "open." The judge granted a preliminary injunction to the school district on August 23, 1974. The HEW investigation led to the filing of another case titled *U.S.D. 501 v. Weinberger, No. 74-160-C5*. The Weinberger case was dismissed on October 20, 1976.[14] However, in that case an opinion was rendered by the judge which stated that "this court is open and available to hear any charges or claims that legal requirements have not been met by the school district as it relates to racial discrimination."[15] Therefore, there were still some unmet requirements needing remedy and the judge was reminding the Topeka school district, as well as the public, that there must be compliance.

In 1979, the "motion to intervene" was granted by the judge, thereby requesting that the case which lay dormant for many years, be revived. A group of African-American parents filed the complaint on behalf of their children who attended the Topeka Public Schools. Linda Brown, now grandmother Linda Brown Smith, had two of the children named among the seventeen complainants in this case. The parents believed that the Topeka Public School District continued to promote segregation by requiring their children to attend neighborhood schools. So, despite the victory of the 1954 decision, their children were denied a quality education. The litigation that occurred during the next twenty-plus years is collectively known as *Brown III.*

The case which was revived in 1979, went to trial in 1986 and by 1987 a ruling was determined by Judge Rogers in the U.S. District Court in Topeka. The school district stated that the "separate school systems for black and white children were eliminated many years ago" and they had moved effectively toward desegregation and a unitary system.[16] The plaintiffs' case contended that the policies of the school district continued to preserve racially identifiable schools. This was primarily due to the fact that the school district established an open attendance policy around this time that allowed students to freely transfer among schools. The plaintiffs said that consideration was given to school-site locations, optional attendance zones, boundary locations and faculty/staff assignments. Judge Rogers ruled that the school district "provides a high-quality educational opportunity to its students on a nondiscriminatory basis…The court is convinced after reviewing a multitude of factors that the vestiges of past segregation in the district have been dissolved…This case has reached an appropriate denouncement. The district has a unitary system of education."[17]

During the next five years litigation bounced back and forth beginning with the 10th Circuit Court's decision in 1989 to overturn the District Court's ruling in the 1987 case. These five years of litigation concluded in 1993 when the U.S. District Court entered a court-ordered desegregation plan to remedy any of the remaining vestiges on July 25, 1994. In the fall of 1993, the school district gathered a team of educators who examined literature, sought district and community input, visited related sites and heard from experts on procedures to better desegregate the Topeka Public Schools.

After considerable investigation the school district developed a very detailed desegregation remedy plan. The plan included the closing of eight elementary schools, constructing and opening two new magnet schools (one with a technology focus and one with a science and fine arts focus), construction of a new "state-of-the-art" traditional elementary school, changes in elementary school boundaries and monitoring of staff assignments to assure an adequate balance of majority/minority ratios.[18]

Finally on July 27, 1999, Judge Richard Rogers (in T 316) granted the Topeka Public Schools motion for a "declaration of unitary status" and order of dismissal bringing to a close the forty-five-year-old *Brown v. Board of Education* case.[19] There are specific factors which the court examines to determine if a district has met unitary status, the school system has complied with the courts' mandates and is providing an equal education to all children. It was determined that the Topeka school system had met these mandates and thus the case was closed.

Integration at Last, the Topeka Magnet Elementary Schools

A key portion of Topeka Public Schools' remedy plan was the development of two magnet elementary schools. Mrs. Johnnie Sanders, a teacher at the Elisha, John and Charles Scott, Sr. Computer Magnet Elementary School, shared her perceptions about the magnet school concept with Dr. McConnell on July 27, 2004. The following passages come from the record of this interview.

Interviewer: Tell me a little about yourself.

Sanders: I am an African-American woman, married, forty-one-years-old and been a teacher for two years at Scott Computer Magnet School. I have one daughter who is a sophomore at Washburn University and active in my church and I teach children at every opportunity that is presented to me.

Interviewer: Can you tell me what magnet schools are in Topeka and the purpose of each one?

Sanders: There are only two, Meadows Elementary is really not a magnet school, it doesn't have a specialty like the other two, but Meadows Elementary does exist [Meadows is named after Kay E. Meadows, the first black woman ever elected to the Topeka Board of Education in 1985 and then in 1989 the first black woman to serve as president of the Board]. There's Scott Computer Magnet School located on the east side of Topeka and named after Elisha, John and Charles Scott, Sr. who were the attorneys in the famous *Topeka v. Board of Education* case of 1954. The purpose was to provide technology to students from all ethnic backgrounds, each classroom has at least a dozen computers so each child is given training, lessons and writing and math using computers. And I should say, reading, writing and math. Williams Magnet is a fine arts magnet school. It was named after Mamie Williams who was a teacher, counselor and principal for forty-five years in segregated elementary schools in Topeka and then, after 1954, in 'integrated' Topeka elementary schools. Williams Magnet is unique because it has a full aquarium, a rain forest, a space center and a full art design center for students. Williams Magnet has over five hundred students, and I believe each pod (section of the school) has about one hundred and sixty students and each magnet school has four pods.

Interviewer: What is it like teaching at Scott Computer Magnet School?

Sanders: It is very busy, very demanding, very fulfilling and I don't want to say it's tough, but it is hard work.

Interviewer: What grade do you teach and what is the diversity of your students?

Sanders: I teach kindergarten with a class of about twenty-five and my students are 50% Hispanic, 25% African-American and 25% are white.

Interviewer: How many of your students live in the neighborhood of the school and how many would you say are bused or driven to the school each day?

Sanders: I would say...let me think about my standing lines of students...75% of my students live in the neighborhood. Let me change my mind, because a lot of my children are picked up by their parents. So, with that, I would say 50% live in the community, 25% are driven in by their parents and 35% are part of the bus system.

Interviewer: What do you see as the purpose of having a magnet school? Do you believe Scott Magnet School is fulfilling that intent?

Sanders: I believe the purpose of having the magnet school is to provide the opportunity and the resources to children and their families who might not otherwise get it. There's a lot of technology, a lot of resources, there are a lot of experiences at the magnet school that if it wasn't in their community they wouldn't have it...financially, it wouldn't be affordable.

Interviewer: How is it decided what students will attend a magnet school?

Sanders: They have a waiting list. The first child that gets a place is one which lives in the neighborhood and then there's a certain amount of children in the community who are bused in and then there are a group of students outside the school district who are given an opportunity to come into the magnet schools. The population of each magnet school is around five hundred students, ours is five hundred and seventy-five students.

Interviewer: If children live in the Scott School neighborhood and want to attend a different magnet school, can they? Are they put on a list?

Sanders: Yes, then they are put on that waiting list, like with Williams.

Interviewer: Would they get bused to a different magnet school?

Sanders: Yes, if they met the criteria of living within two and one-half miles from the school they would be bused for free. Otherwise, their parents would drive them to the school.

Interviewer: As you know, the intent of the *Brown III* decision was to finally integrate the Topeka Public Schools, do you believe that the development of the magnet schools has met that intent? If so, why? If not, why not?

Sanders: I don't think it perfectly integrated the public schools because families still moved their children farther out into the suburbs. The poor children can't go anywhere. And then, because the magnet schools are located in the urban area, they get a bad reputation because of where they are located. Some people are afraid of bringing their children there. If there is a crime report it is usually in that part of Topeka. The neighborhood continues to get a bad reputation. So, those families who would like to give their children the opportunities available in the magnet schools are too afraid to send their children there. And some parents don't like to have their children on a bus for forty-five minutes a day...by the time the drop-offs are completed.

Interviewer: So, Johnnie, what is the solution to fulfill the promise of the original *Brown* decision?

Sanders: I think every school should be given enough resources so there won't be a shortness of supplies, administrators. Of courses getting the families involved so they can feel comfortable there, to be part of the school.

Interviewer: If that were to happen would it help integrate the schools?

Sanders: No, people would still have a choice. There's still competition, still racism.

Interviewer: So does the establishment of magnet schools, in your opinion, help lessen racism in Topeka?

Sanders: I think to a certain degree it does. Because you have children from three different backgrounds, like I teach and others in the school teach. To love one another, to do the right thing, to be an asset to their communities, so I think the magnet schools provide an opportunity to mold children to change things…or if they (the magnet schools) weren't there things would remain the way they use to be in the past.

Student Diversity in Topeka

During the 2003-2004 school year, the minority enrollment in the Topeka Public Schools District was approximately 51%. This figure is based on a total student enrollment in the district of 14,058 students. The specifics include 49% White, 22% African-American, 15% Hispanic, 11% Multiracial, 2% Native American and 1% Asian-American. The district indicated that "the multiracial designation was used for the first time during this school year and resulted in a substantial increase in minority student designation, moving [Topeka Public Schools] to a majority minority population for the first time."[20]

School Reform Initiative, The Comer School Development Program

The Comer School Development Program (SDP) is an effective school reform initiative implemented by the Topeka Public Schools in 1989 and identified as part of the remedy to desegregate the schools on June 16, 1994. Dr. James A. Comer, a child psychiatrist at the Yale Child Study Center and founder of the SDP, reminds teachers and parents to keep the focus on the child and do "what is best" for the child. He also suggests that a significant component of a child's school success is based upon the relationships he/she has developed with parents and teachers. The main goal of bringing the School Development Program to Topeka was "to create a whole school model that focused on the social needs of the young people and broad-based parental involvement and resulted in higher student achievement."[21]

Although not a mandate by the courts, the school district firmly believed in the merits of the SDP. "Based on an analysis of fall 1993 student enrollment data, 13 of the 35 regular schools are racially identifiable with respect to student assignment. Seven schools are 'racially identifiable minority schools,' meaning that the percentage of minority students enrolled is more than 15 percentage points above the district average. Six schools are 'racially identifiable majority schools,' meaning that the percentage of minority students enrolled is more than fifteen percentage points below the district average."[22]

The federal district court ordered a desegregation remedy on July 25, 1994. The remedy included the SDP as one of the features which would be implemented in the two new magnet schools which were to be built as part of this plan. Of these thirteen schools which were racially identifiable, six were implementing the SDP and three others would eventually implement it in their schools before the final ruling in 1999.

First implemented in two elementary schools in 1968 in the New Haven, Connecticut School District, SDP improved achievement in schools located in low socioeconomic neighborhoods. SDP is a research-based school improvement process that is grounded in the principles of child development and provides the organizational, management and communication framework for mobilizing the support of teachers, parents and other caring adults to encourage the academic, social and emotional well-being of children and youth.[23]

The primary emphasis of the SDP is to provide an effective school governance structure where relationships between staff and parents are established and leadership is developed. The SDP consists of three guiding principles, three teams and three functions. The guiding principles include collaboration, no-fault problem-solving and consensus decision-making. These principles are used throughout the school by staff, administration, parents and students. The three teams include the parent team, the school planning and management team, plus the student and staff support team. The parent component has always been an important element and one which the schools continue to focus upon.

The three functions of SDP include staff development, comprehensive school plan, plus assessment and modification. These three functions are the elements which establish the curriculum, social goals and sharing of information between the schools and the community. When all nine of the elements of this process are working effectively the schools can run like a well-oiled machine. By the 2003-2004 school year, fourteen elementary schools in the Topeka Public School District have implemented the SDP.[24] Within this document, these schools are often referred to as "Comer schools."

The Topeka Public Schools first implemented SDP in 1989. Washburn University began its partnership with the Topeka Public Schools and Yale University in 1992 under the guidance of the chair of the education department. The department chair's leadership, dedication and commitment to this program provided the basis for the education department's further involvement. Since 1992, several department of education faculty members have been trained in the SDP. It is an important aspect of the education department's mission to provide services to the schools and to teach undergraduate and graduate students about the SDP in teacher education courses. The education department faculty liaison, Dr. Gloria A. Dye, in collaboration with the school district liaison, Dr. Larita Owens, continue to provide support and organize in-service teacher training to these Comer schools. The basic principles and collaborative relationships fostered by the SDP have assisted the Topeka Public Schools in their compliance with the court's order.

History Stays Alive in Landmark Monroe Elementary School

Monroe Elementary School, the all-African-American elementary school which Linda Brown attended, has been designated a national historic site. In 1999, rehabilitation and permanent exhibit development funds for this, one of the four former segregated all-African-American schools in Topeka, were appropriated by Congress through the line-item construction program. The Brown Foundation for Educational Equity, Excellence and Research, headed by one of Reverend Oliver Brown's daughters, Cheryl Brown Henderson (president), led the development and completion of the Monroe Elementary School remodeling project. The city of Topeka and its citizens have made a concerted effort to remember their history. These renovation projects, which add to the beautification of Topeka, were finished in the spring of 2004. On May 17, 2004, President George W. Bush commemorated the 50th Anniversary of the *Oliver L. Brown, et al., v. Board of Education of Topeka, Kansas Supreme Court* decision by dedicating the Monroe School, now referred to the *Brown v. Board National Historic Site.*

A host of other dignitaries participated in the Grand Opening of the *Brown v. Board of Education National Historic Site*, including Reverend Fred L. Shuttlesworth, Reverend Jesse Jackson, Kansas Governor Kathleen Sebelius, Secretary of the Interior Gale Norton and director of the National Park Service, Fran Mainella. As Stephen E. Adams, park superintendent, said in the *Brown v. Board of Education National Historic Site Commemorative Program*, "Few realize that segregation in education was only a forum for the NAACP and the Legal Defense and Educational Fund, Inc. to challenge segregation and exclusion in all walks of life…not just for African-Americans but for all Americans. Regardless of who you are, the story of *Brown* is also your story."[25] The *Brown v. Board of Education National Historic Site*, and the corresponding park, are now open for visitors.

Conclusion: Listening to the Voices of *Brown*

In order to better understand this historic court decision, the most precise information comes from original sources. Unfortunately, there are many who were involved in *Brown v. Board of Education, Brown II and Brown III* decisions who have died and whose voices are forever silent. It is imperative to listen to the stories of those who remain and "lived the history of Topeka" in the early 1950's.

What is important for educators is also important for other academicians, historians, civil rights leaders and legislators who care about aspects of the *Brown* decision. Interviews from original sources provide important recollections which can be utilized by researchers and others interested in influencing educational and/or societal change. In addition to the interviews shared in this chapter, the resources of government agencies [such as the Library of Congress and the National Park Service] and organizations bring artifacts and documents to those who want to further the promise of *Brown*. Although not mandated by the courts, the Comer SDP was identified as part of the remedy to desegregate the Topeka Public Schools. The influence of this well-known school reform program within the Topeka Public School Desegregation Plan needs further research and documentation. It is imperative that *Brown v. Topeka Board of Education*, and subsequently, *Brown II* and *Brown III* decisions be studied, not only for their revelations about the past, but for their relevance to the future.

Chapter 3

SOUTH CAROLINA: WINNING THE BATTLE OVER DE JURE SEGREGATION, LOSING THE WAR OVER DE FACTO SEGREGATION

Jackie R. Booker

South Carolina African-Americans were the first to challenge *de jure* segregation in public schools. Beginning with a petition in Clarendon County in 1949 and with the assistance of Thurgood Marshall and the National Association for the Advancement of Colored People (NAACP), the *Briggs v. Elliott* case became the first formal legal attack on public school segregation in the South. Due to some political maneuvering by the governor of South Carolina, the *Briggs* case was folded into *Brown v. Board of Education*. These key cases forever changed public school education in South Carolina. More than fifty years later, we can revisit these decisions and evaluate their impact on public schooling.

This chapter begins with a brief history of public school segregation in South Carolina, analyzes conditions in Clarendon County which led to the *Briggs* case and examines the legacy of public school education in light of the *Briggs*, *Brown* and other important cases.

Background

The drafting of a new Constitution in 1895 marked a dramatic turning point in South Carolina history. This Constitution, established one year before *Plessy v. Ferguson*, created a system of segregated schools: "separate schools shall be provided for children of white and colored races and no child of either race shall ever be permitted to attend a school provided for children of the other race."[1] The 1895 Constitution also increased public school funding. White students in majority black counties like Clarendon, Orangeburg, Georgetown, Charleston and others generally had their education financed by blacks who attended substandard schools.[2] These two issues, inadequate funding for public schools in South

Carolina and its system of segregated schools would plague and retard development in the state well into the twentieth century.

Although black public schools in South Carolina were grossly inadequate, the illiteracy rate declined, perhaps due to the sheer dedication of its black teachers. By 1900, the illiteracy rate dropped to 52.8 percent, three times that of whites, but a significant reduction nonetheless.[3] Spending for public school children, black and white alike, continued to lag behind other southern states and the nation. In 1920, South Carolina had the lowest per-pupil expenditure in the nation.[4] The low expenditure even prompted civic, business and educational leaders to support a tax increase to aid the segregated public school system. The General Assembly responded by passing the 6-0-1 Act in 1924. The General Assembly would support six months of school while counties would fund one month. The zero indicated that counties were encouraged but not legally required to pay for one month of education.[5] While white public schools were generally underfunded and sometimes overcrowded, they at least had running water and indoor bathrooms.

In 1919, black delegates at a statewide convention denounced their lack of voting rights and the segregated system of public schools. Blacks demanded better schools and representation on the county school boards that determined spending priorities.[6] Educational facilities were especially miserable for African-Americans attending rural county schools.

For example, Clarendon County classrooms were always overcrowded; only a few schools could boast of having an auditorium and a library. If the latter existed, it was usually comprised of books passed down from white schools. Black schools had no lunchrooms, no playgrounds and no indoor plumbing.[7] Students in rural counties like Clarendon had no buses. Some walked ten miles or more to attend schools. Although frequently requested, the all-white county school board always refused to provide school buses.[8] Poverty further compounded the already-dismal conditions for blacks seeking an education. Since many school-age blacks worked alongside parents in sharecropping, less than half of all Clarendon County blacks during the 1920s had a fourth-grade education. Another 25 percent had never attended school.[9] A longitudinal study of blacks attending South Carolina public schools was even more revealing.

According to some research, of the 85,691 blacks enrolled in public schools in 1934-35, only 35,925 were second-graders a year later, a decline of 58 percent.[10] Five years later in 1938-39, the original class now totaled 21,393 and further declined to only 21,393 seventh-graders two years later. By 1941-42, only 7,960 remained. In 1944-45, the class, now in the eleventh grade, had been reduced to only three percent of its original size or 2,689 students.[11] For the few black students reaching high school, attending an accredited institution was even more problematic. In 1926, blacks comprised only 0.3 percent of all high school students. By 1936, the figure had risen to 11.8 percent. In 1939, of the 17,163 black high school students, only 51 percent were enrolled in accredited high schools.[12] In 1933, the state had only one public accredited high school for blacks, Booker T. Washington in Columbia, the state capital. Even as late as 1939, many counties did not have an accredited high school for African-American students. The lack of bus transportation prevented most from ever attending high school, accredited or not.[13] Clearly, "separate but unequal" facilities existed throughout the public school system. Nowhere were these conditions more obvious than in Clarendon County.

According to statistics from 1948-49, the county school board spent $149 annually educating a white child but only $43 for each black one. Although there were 61 black public schools in the county, they had an aggregate value of $194,575 while the 12 white schools had an approximate wealth of 673,850.[14] Two years later, county officials spent more money on white students, $166.45, but expenditures for blacks barely rose to $44.33 per child.[15] White schools were constructed of brick or stucco and were stocked with paper and books. Black schools in the county were either clapboard or ramshackle shanties often without adequate supplies. Moreover, although blacks like whites paid taxes, the money was not used to purchase supplies for black schools.[16] White students in the county were transported to school on one of thirty buses while black children walked before reaching their segregated schools. Once they arrived, most black schoolhouses had wooden stoves, kerosene lamps and no running water.[17] While these were glaring inequities in the separate educational facilities, the lack of buses prevented most of the best and brightest students from advancing beyond the fifth or sixth grade in Clarendon County.

Black parents in Clarendon County decried the lack of transportation for their children. A group of parents drafted and submitted a petition to the school board asking for school buses. R.W. Elliott, chair of the school board, responded: "We ain't got no money to buy a bus for your nigger children."[18] In 1948, one parent, Levi Pearson, at the urging of Reverend Joseph A. DeLaine, filed a lawsuit seeking buses for black students. Thurgood Marshall filed the brief which asked for an injunction "enjoining the defendants (Clarendon County school board) from making a distinction on account of race or color" in supplying buses for African-American students.[19] The case was eventually dismissed due to a technicality.[20]

With the failure of the lawsuit, DeLaine, a Clarendon County teacher, preacher and parent, became more involved in the effort to address inequalities in the public school system. DeLaine began working with Marshall and other members of the NAACP.[21] Marshall had, by 1948, earned a reputation as a successful trial lawyer and was already lobbying for equal spending on black and white schools.[22] Thus, Marshall and DeLaine began an attack on an unequal treatment basis, not an assault on the legality of segregated schools. Marshall would need the strong support of Clarendon County blacks. During a November 1949 meeting, Marshall asked DeLaine to find 20 black parents willing to sign a petition which would become part of the impending lawsuit. By December 20, DeLaine had surpassed the goal of 20 petitioners; he had garnered support from 25 parents.[23] Marshall arranged the signers in alphabetical order and Harry Briggs, a World War II Navy veteran, had his name listed first in the suit against the chairman of the Clarendon County schools.[24] The case, which was filed in the United States District Court for the Eastern District of South Carolina, eventually became known as *Briggs et al., v. Elliott et al.*[25]

Briggs v. Elliott

Federal district Judge J. Waties Waring called the attorneys together for a pretrial hearing in November 1950. Waring wanted the desegregation case heard in his court. He had previously ruled in favor of the NAACP and an attack on the South Carolina Democratic Primary in 1947. Marshall argued that segregated public school facilities, as outlined in the 1895 South Carolina Constitution and adopted as part of the South Carolina Code of 1942, were unconstitutional.[26] Marshall claimed that black students in Clarendon County District Number One (formerly number 22) were denied due process in violation of the Fourteenth Amendment in the United States Constitution. Marshall pointed out that the school facilities used by black and white students were markedly different and caused a sense of black inferiority.[27] Joined by two segregationist judges, John J. Parker and George B. Timmerman, Judge Waring was outnumbered from the outset. The federal district panel issued a ruling which surprised few observers.

The court ruled that the 1895 South Carolina Constitution and the South Carolina Code of 1942 were constitutional; that is, the statutes which called for the separation of black and white students in South Carolina public schools were legal. The court, therefore, by a vote of 2 to 1, denied Marshall's request for admission of black students to the county's white schools, continuing the dual school system. Judges Parker and Timmerman did, however, agree that the black and white schools were unequal.[28] Judge Waring offered a strong dissent in the *Briggs* case. His opposition to racial segregation would help form the appeal used by Marshall to the U.S. Supreme Court. Waring believed that the system of segregation was unconstitutional, referring to the gross inequalities of black and white schools in Clarendon County and even mentioning how he had driven past black schools which were little more than shacks. Waring said that "Segregation in education can never produce equality... Segregation is per se inequality."[29] In contrast to Waring, Judge Parker, who cast the deciding vote, wrote his now-famous dictum which said: "The Constitution... does not requite integration. It merely forbids discrimination."[30] These opinions formed the foundation for segregationists and integrationists for decades to come. The *Briggs* decision was not a complete loss or defeat for Marshall, the NAACP or the thousands of black students in Clarendon County.

The federal judges found that "separate but unequal" facilities did exist. They ordered the school board to begin the process of equalizing educational facilities. Governor James F. Byrnes embraced equalization as a way to prevent more dramatic intervention by federal courts or even the Supreme Court.[31] Byrnes argued that if the General Assembly failed to support his equalization programs, he would ask the legislative body to stop funding public education. He once said: "Segregation came before education."[32]

The General Assembly supported a $75 million dollar bond issue and a sales tax of three (3) percent.[33] Led by Byrnes, South Carolina undertook its most ambitious school construction program since Reconstruction. Money went into improving not only black schools but also the equalization of black and white teacher salaries and the state assumed control of transporting white students to school. Blacks still did not receive school buses.[34] In a December 1951 report to Judge Parker, Clarendon County school officials boasted that a contract had been issued to build a new black high school in Summerton and black teacher salaries had been raised to the level of whites. Moreover, four years after Reverend DeLaine had requested, buses were finally provided for black students.[35] Judge Parker asked for and received another report on equalization in March 1952. After reading the report, Parker concluded: "There can be no doubt that as a result of the program which the defendants (Clarendon County school board) are engaged, the educational facilities and opportunities afforded Negroes within the district… will be made equal to those afforded white persons."[36]

Despite the millions spent on upgrading black schools, especially those in the rural areas, they remained substantially behind white schools. Black school buildings, for the most part, remained in stark contrast to white facilities. In addition, Governor Byrnes reaffirmed the position of most whites in Clarendon County and the state: "South Carolina will not now, nor for some years to come, mix white and colored children in our schools."[37] This prophetic prediction by Byrnes would ring true for most South Carolina public schools well after the famous *Brown v. Board of Education* decision was handed down.

Although the NAACP initially supported equalization in southern states and most school districts made some effort to improve facilities, the organization remained troubled by the psychological impact segregation had on black students. According to the NAACP, equalization could not make up for decades of neglect.[38] Based on consultations with Marshall, Robert Carter, his co-counsel Boulware and others, the NAACP decided to appeal the *Briggs* decision to the Supreme Court. There, Marshall and his team took on the system of segregation, not just equalization. They would have to disprove the court's famous decision in *Plessy v. Ferguson*. Thus, *Briggs* became the seed for the most important case concerning public school education during the twentieth century.

South Carolina's Rigid System

Despite the overwhelming joy and jubilation expressed by most blacks, the backlash to *Brown* came quickly. Segregationists in the South promised to resist and fight against desegregation at every turn. In all southern states which formerly had *de jure* racial segregation in its public school system, South Carolina had perhaps the most rigid system. Ten years after the initial ruling in Jim Crow public schools, only ten black students throughout South Carolina attended school with whites. By fall 1964, that percentage had risen to 0.1 percent and in 1965, just 1.5 percent of all black students were enrolled in desegregated schools. Two years later, the figure rose to six percent.[39] Charleston public schools were desegregated in 1963 but a year later, only five of the 46 South Carolina counties had implemented orders from 1954's *Brown I* and 1955's *Brown II* decisions. Full desegregation began in the 1965-66 school year with a minimum mixing of black and white students in 16 school districts, approximately 14 percent of all public school districts.[40]

Clarendon County schools were among the state's slowest to desegregate. Due to a lack of enforcement by federal courts, dual school zones were not abolished until 1964.[41] Ten years after the *Brown* decisions, Clarendon County schools were still segregated. Finally in 1965, the county school board implemented a limited freedom of choice plan. This option, however, still separated the vast majority of black and white students in the county. Even with token desegregation, white flight from Clarendon County public schools, at first a trickle, increased dramatically between 1965 and 1969. Moreover, the division of the county into three districts in 1962 resulted in two which were mostly white and one which was nearly all black. New school boards in the majority black districts gave African-Americans some control over schools but funding to replace the Jim Crow schools became a co-issue with desegregation. The state constructed a high school just outside of Summerton which attracted some white students from the many private academies in the county. Scott's Branch, the new high school, was constructed of brick, had a computer lab, a library, numerous pictures of African-American leaders adorned the hallways, encouraging students to succeed.[42] Despite the modern facility, the vast majority of white students still attended Clarendon Hall and other all-white private academies.[43] Years removed from the initial *Brown* decision, the site of the original court case challenging Jim

Crow schools in the South remained largely segregated. As evidence that all was not well in South Carolina, a white mob in Lamar attacked and overturned two school buses with black elementary students.[44] It would take another full decade and longer before signs of more racial mixture would emerge in South Carolina public schools.

In 1960, black plaintiffs in Clarendon County filed a lawsuit challenging the freedom of choice plans employed by county school boards. The case became known as *Brunson v. Clarendon County*. The suit was finally heard in 1970 before federal Judge Simon Sobeloff of the Fourth Circuit Federal Court of Appeals. Sobeloff accused the school board of delaying and other wise refusing to abide by the spirit of the original case, not *Brown* but *Briggs v. Elliott*. The judge believed that the defendants still used racial inferiority as their justification for not desegregating the Clarendon County schools.[45] Freedom of choice failed in Clarendon County as it did in most other parts of the South. Blacks feared racial attacks and whites were reluctant to engage in social mixing. Both groups attended schools in which they were the overwhelming majority. The Supreme Court further reaffirmed the *Brown* decisions in the next most important case, *Alexander v. Holmes County Board of Education*.

In *Alexander v. Holmes County Board of Education*, the Supreme Court finally addressed the issue of "all deliberate speed" raised in *Brown II*. The Court ruled that school districts still maintaining dual zones had to move at once to eliminate black and white districts. The Justices also stated that "No person is to be effectively excluded from any school because of race or color."[46] Finally, the Court put teeth into *Brown II* some fourteen years after its famous dictum concerning speedy desegregation.

The Decreasing Emphasis on *Brown* and Its Goals

But, ending freedom of choice plans and adding speed to desegregation did not always work. White flight during the 1960s created mostly white school districts in the suburbs, leaving many inner cities segregated. Since the 1970s, both the federal government and the Supreme Court, have withdrawn from the concerted effort to desegregate our public school systems. During the 1980s and into the 1990s, presidents such as Ronald Reagan and George Bush, Sr., combined with a more conservative Congress, Supreme Court, and greater public indifference to desegregation, has led to less emphasis on *Brown* and its goals. Federal agencies cut programs and research intended to measure the degree of desegregation.

The Justice Department brought even fewer cases against school districts which still refused to abide by court-ordered decrees issued, sometimes 40 years earlier.[47] In 1995, the Supreme Court again signaled its more conservative approach to *Brown*. Ruling in the case *Missouri v. Jenkins*, the Court allowed new school districts in the suburbs to take money from urban schools rather than share or split money with city schools. As a consequence of that decision, urban districts, mostly black or minority, became underfunded, further locking students of color into second-rate school systems.[48] The narrow decision in *Jenkins* also reduced the remedies school districts could use including building up inner-city schools to attract whites. The Court had already in *Board of Education of Oklahoma City v. Dowell* (1992) permitted school districts to drop their desegregation plans without having achieved their goals.[49] The *Dowell* and *Jenkins* decisions further distanced the Court from the goals inherent in *Brown*.

Conditions in Clarendon County also demonstrated the lost cause in support of mixing black and white students. The slow, sleepy town of Summerton is now home to about 1,000 people. Most are dependent upon a local manufacturing plant for jobs. The majority of black children still attend Scott's Branch High School. Most whites are either home-schooled or attend Clarendon Hall. Little interaction takes place among blacks and whites in an educational setting.[50] The impact of *Brown* on this community probably peaked in 1968 when the decision from the *Green v. New Kent County* case was handed down. Dual school zones ended and although the attempt was made, desegregation, not integration, was achieved. There was not in most school districts enough whites to achieve real integration or any meaningful interaction between blacks and whites. More than fifty years after the *Briggs* and *Brown* decisions, as the Clarendon County example illustrates, integration in education throughout the South remains tenuous.

Today, the primary issue concerning desegregation continues to be race and racism, but equally important is school funding.[51] School officials in Clarendon have joined forces with seven other mostly-black rural counties to sue the state of South Carolina for adequate school funding. Called *Abbeville v. South Carolina*, the case addresses the old issue of "separate but equal." This time, however, it involves blacks seeking equal funding for schools which are barely desegregated. *Brown*'s original goal of integration has largely failed; desegregation took place throughout the country but now resegregation and funding issues are the twin challenges facing blacks and other minorities seeking a quality education for their children. Without massive support for public education and a recommitment on the part of everyone, the gains made under *Briggs*, *Brown* and other landmark cases will be further diminished.

Chapter 4

BROWN AND GENDER DISCRIMINATION

Elizabeth Davenport

The women's liberation movement in the United States owes much of its progress to the *Brown v. Board of Education of Topeka* decision. Like the disenfranchisement of blacks, the legalized inequality of women in American classrooms, communities and workplaces helped to create a sexual, rather than racial, caste system. In a 1970 article called "Women as Nigger," which popularized the term "sexism," Gayle Rubin wrote that "people are more sophisticated about blacks than they are about women; black history courses do not have to begin by convincing people that blacks are not in fact genetically better suited to dancing than to learning."

Brown and its progeny became the mechanism by which women could work to change sexual misconceptions and achieve equal rights. *Brown* opened the discussion for inequalities experienced by female students. Coupled with the feminist movement's demands for equal rights, Congress passed Title IX of the Education Amendment Act (1972), a comprehensive measure that addressed the many forms of sex discrimination in education including school admission policies, scholarships, sexual harassment, employment practices and discriminatory employment procedures. Title IX applies to any educational program in an institution that receives federal funds (from elementary school through college). Even private schools are covered if they receive federal funding through financial aid programs. If institutions are found to violate Title IX, federal funding can be withdrawn.

Prior to the enactment of Title IX, schools often expelled girls who became pregnant and refused to allow these students to enroll. They required pregnant and parenting students to enroll in special educational programs that were often not the same quality of classes and schools available to other students. Girls and boys were restricted from taking classes which were considered gender-specific (i.e., boys could not take home economics and girls could not take mechanics). Interestingly, during the decades prior to the enactment of Title IX, women were about 41 percent of students admitted to colleges and universities across the country and less than 30 percent of students admitted to the most selective schools.[1] In fact, women during this period earned only 37 percent of master's degrees and 16% of the doctorate degrees.

Initially, Title IX was an amendment to Title VII of the Civil Rights Act (1964) and part of Executive Order No.11246 (1965), which prohibited contractors from discriminating in employment on the basis of race, color, religion or national origin. It was amended in 1968 to include discrimination based on sex and became law in 1972.

In 1975, the Department of Health, Education and Welfare (HEW) promulgated regulations, clarifying facets of Title IX, which applied to intercollegiate athletic programs.[2] Moreover, HEW mandated additional guidelines in 1979 which clarified the obligations imposed by Title IX on recipients of federal financial aid. Although courts have tended to focus on effective accommodation issues when analyzing Title IX cases, equal treatment issues are also relevant when analyzing compliance issues. Title IX became more viable in 1980 when the Department of Education was established and given supervision of Title IX through its Office for Civil Rights.

Since the 1990s, the government has favored an overall approach to evaluating an institution's compliance with the requirements of Title IX. In *Grove City College v. Bell* (1984), the U.S. Supreme Court held that Title IX was program-specific, meaning that the statute applied to a specific program within an educational institution receiving federal funds. However, Congress passed the Civil Rights Restoration Act (1988) which expressly overturned *Grove City College v. Bell* (1984), and reestablished the effectiveness and vitality of Title IX. In 1996, the Department of Education again issued a Title IX policy clarification, incorporating the analytical system of the early 1990s cases.

Considerable progress has been made in the thirty years since the enactment of Title IX, including increased opportunities for women and girls in athletics, access to higher education, more career training and development, employment opportunities, math and science education. Today, women make up the majority of students in American colleges and universities, earning 56 percent of bachelor's degrees and 57 percent of master's degrees. Women also receive 42% of all doctorate degrees.[3] Minority women, for example, experienced substantial gains in professional degrees as well as doctorates earned during the past twenty years. By 2000, minority women earned the majority of professional degrees and doctorates among minorities.[4]

Title IX has also made a profound impact in the area of athletics. Since 1971, women's participation in sports has increased fourfold. More than 100,000 women participate in intercollegiate athletics and 2.4 million (39%) participate in high school athletics. Title IX prohibits schools from suspending, expelling or discriminating against pregnant high school students in educational programs and activities. Finally, from 1980 to 1990, dropout rates for pregnant students has declined to thirty percent, which has a definitive effect on the entire society because women who are forced to drop out of school are unable to support and care for their children.[5]

Conclusion

Yes, we have come a long way, baby! However, there is much more work to be done. According to *The Big Payoff: Educational Attainment and Estimates of Work-Life Earnings*, a publication of the U.S. Department Census Bureau, women still lag behind men economically. On average, a man with a high school education will earn about $1.4 million from ages 25 to 64 years. This compares with about $2.5 million for men completing a bachelor's degree and $4.8 million for men with a professional degree. In contrast, men with less than a high school education will earn an average of $1.1 million. Women who have completed high school will earn an average of $1 million, while women with a bachelor's degree will earn an estimated $1.6 million. Although the work-life payoffs for women with professional and doctoral degrees are substantial, $2.9 and $2.5 million respectively, these earnings are markedly behind those of men with the same educational background.[6] According to Marlene Kim, "Women are more likely to be low-paid if they are young, single or less educated, or if they are employed in service occupations, retail trade, agriculture or personal services."[7] Furthermore, women holding the 59 percent of the low-wage jobs in America today are still more likely to earn a lower wage than their male counterparts.[8]

In July 2003, the Bush Administration announced a new policy where colleges and universities would no longer prove "substantially proportionate" participation of men and women in athletic activities covered by Title IX. At that time, the administration created the Commission on Opportunities in Athletics to analyze the effects of Title IX. Some proponents of this action assert that this Commission was packed with opponents of Title IX as its final recommendations include allowing: 1) schools to possibly misrepresent both the number of opportunities and slots for men and women sports by not counting all students; 2) students to use "interest surveys" to determine whether more men than women are interested in sports; 3) the use of private funds that could increase the financial support for men's teams at the expense of women's teams; and 4) the Secretary of Education to identify additional ways of demonstrating compliance with Title IX that could enable high schools and colleges to avoid the equal opportunities mandate. These changes have the potential of devastating girls' and women's sports, as well as equal opportunities in other facets of American life.

As long as there is gender discrimination, disenfranchised women will use *Brown* and its progeny along with the 14th Amendment of the United States Constitution to obtain full and equal treatment.

Chapter 5

THE JURISPRUDENTIAL IMPACT
OF BROWN V. BOARD OF EDUCATION*

Kevin H. Smith

That *Brown v. Board of Education* had a profound–if not necessarily immediate–impact on American society is universally acknowledged. Legal scholars have focused their attention on *Brown*'s impact on the desegregation of public K-12 schools. Their emphasis is understandable. *Brown* established a fundamental and unambiguous constitutional principle: Separate public K-12 educational facilities are inherently unequal and violate the equal protection provision of the 14th Amendment. And *Brown*'s immediate effect was to spark an intense, decades-long legal struggle over the methods and speed of implementing public K-12 school desegregation.

Legal scholars also have examined *Brown*'s significant impact on desegregation jurisprudence beyond the sphere of public K-12 education. *Brown* can be read as being limited to public K-12 education. For example, the Court stated:

> We conclude that in *the field of public education* the doctrine of "separate but equal" has no place. Separate *educational facilities* are inherently unequal. Therefore, we hold that the plaintiffs and *others similarly situated* for whom the actions have been brought are, by reason of *the segregation complained of*, deprived of the equal protection of the laws guaranteed by the Fourteenth Amendment.

However, *Brown* also contains language that can be read more broadly. For example, the Court stated:

> "Whatever may have been the extent of psychological knowledge at the time of *Plessy v. Ferguson*, [the *Brown* Court's] finding [concerning the negative impact of state-

---

*A version of this essay appears in the North Dakota Law Review, Volume 81, Issue 1 and is reprinted with the permission of the North Dakota Law Review.

mandated segregation] is amply supported by modern authority. Any language in *Plessy v. Ferguson* contrary to this finding is rejected." In the years immediately following *Brown*, the Court's new understanding of the negative psychological impact of state-mandated segregation was used by federal and state courts to strike down numerous forms of state-mandated segregation that previously had been permitted under *Plessy*'s "separate but equal" doctrine. It is now well-settled that *Brown* overruled *Plessy* and eviscerated the constitutional authority for any government-mandated segregation based on the principle of "separate but equal." As a result, legal scholars have come to identify *Brown* with those aspects of American jurisprudence that relate to the end of the "separate but equal" doctrine in its many forms and applications.

Whether *Brown* has had a more pervasive influence, an enduring influence on American jurisprudence that extends beyond the abolition of the "separate but equal" doctrine, is at once less studied and more uncertain. If *Brown*'s legacy is to be completely understood, the full extent of its impact on American jurisprudence must be examined.

The remainder of this chapter is divided into four parts and a conclusion. In Part I, I briefly observe that an examination of cases decided since *Brown* indicates that courts routinely cite *Brown* other than for abolishing the "separate but equal" doctrine. In Part II, through Part IV, I examine three purposes not directly related to desegregation for which *Brown* repeatedly is cited: (1) *Brown* as an explicit recognition of the negative psychological, emotional, and social impacts of discrimination in its many forms; (2) *Brown* as an example of when it is proper for a court to overrule a long-standing and deeply rooted legal precedent; and (3) *Brown* as an example of a court's ability to use social science evidence in legal decision-making. And, finally, I conclude that *Brown* continues to exert an important influence on American jurisprudence in addition to its influence on the issue of racial desegregation.

I. The Changing Nature of Courts' Use of *Brown*

The purposes for which courts cited *Brown* changed over time. In the years immediately after *Brown* was decided, courts cited *Brown* primarily in cases involving desegregation issues. In the last several decades, however, courts frequently cited *Brown* in cases that do not involve desegregation issues. *Brown* now enjoys an influence on American jurisprudence that extends beyond its core holding.

Brown has been cited in approximately 2,000 cases. I began by reviewing approximately the first 250 cases to cite to *Brown* (which covers the period from 1954 to 1963) and approximately 140 of the most recent cases to cite to *Brown* (which covers the period from 1997 to 2003). I adopted this strategy in order to determine whether the attributes of cases citing *Brown* had changed over time. And, indeed, this examination revealed distinct and changing patterns in the contexts in which, and the purposes for which, courts cited *Brown*.

In the first set of cases, *Brown* was cited mainly by lower courts in the context of public school desegregation cases and for the purpose of reiterating the unconstitutionality of state-mandated racial segregation in public K-12 school education. *Brown* also was cited in striking down state-mandated racial segregation in public facilities such as swimming pools, parks and golf courses, and with respect to services such as public transportation. In these latter cases, courts either (1) held that *Brown* directly overruled *Plessy* and outlawed all forms of discrimination based on "separate but equal" or (2) reached their decision through reasoning by analogy that state-mandated segregation of the type at issue in the particular case was unconstitutional because it produced the same types of harmful effects about which the Court had been concerned in *Brown*.

The pattern of use to which *Brown* was put during this period is understandable. *Brown* provided the legal basis for the many suits challenging the constitutionality of segregated public K-12 schools in particular school districts. In these cases, *Brown* was cited in that part of each opinion in which the court set forth the case law that governed its decision. And *Brown* also was cited, directly or by analogy, in cases in which courts struck down various forms of state-mandated segregation.

Brown's core holding was never subjected to serious challenge. A unanimous Supreme Court decision saw to that. Opponents of segregation framed their arguments in terms of the speed at which, and the methods in which, desegregation of public K-12 schools should occur. And before too many years, the applicability of *Brown* to other forms of state-mandated segregation also was too entrenched to be seriously questioned. *Brown* had served its original purpose.

More recently, courts have had little reason to cite *Brown* for its core holding (regarding public K-12 schools) or for its broader holding (striking down the "separate but equal" doctrine and state-mandated segregation). *Brown* continued to be cited in school desegregation cases, but only in historical context, as part of the procedural overview of the case. Courts cited *Brown* in contexts outside of racial segregation, drawing upon elements of the opinion distinct from its core holding. Three categories of citation usage were evident: (1) *Brown* as an explicit recognition of the negative psychological, emotional and social impacts of discrimination; (2) *Brown* as an example of when it is proper for a court to overrule a long-standing and deeply rooted legal precedent; and (3) *Brown* as an example of a court's ability to use social science evidence in legal decision-making.

These preliminary findings suggested that *Brown* has had a pervasive and enduring impact beyond its core holding. Left unanswered, however, were the questions of the extent to which, and the manners in which, courts cited to *Brown* in each of the three non-desegregation categories. I returned to the Westlaw database and performed three searches, each search being designed to identify the set of cases belonging to a specific category. In Parts II-IV, I report the results of these searches.

II. *Brown* as an Explicit Recognition of the Effects of Discrimination

The *Brown* Court minced no words about the negative psychological, emotional and social effects of state-mandated racial segregation. The Court categorically and explicitly stated that state-mandated racial segregation of school children "generates a feeling of inferiority as to their status in the community that may affect their hearts and minds in a way unlikely ever to be undone." The Court found that the short-term effects of this sense of inferiority was "to [retard] the educational and mental development of Negro children and to deprive them of some of the benefits they would receive in a racial(ly) integrated school system." And the Court determined that in the long-term "it is doubtful that any child may reasonably be expected to succeed in life if he is denied the opportunity of an education" as a result of state-mandated racial segregation.

The Court, at least implicitly, acknowledged that any form of state-mandated racial segregation had negative psychological, emotional and social effects when it declared that its determination regarding the effects of racial segregation undermined *Plessy*. The Court stated: "Whatever may have been the extent of psychological knowledge at the time of *Plessy v. Ferguson*, this finding is amply supported by modern authority. Any language in *Plessy v. Ferguson* contrary to this finding is rejected."

The Court's statements in *Brown* and my initial review of recently decided cases suggested that courts might apply *Brown* by analogy to state-mandated actions other than racial segregation that they perceive as creating a sense of inferiority. To investigate this possibility, I used Westlaw to generate a list of all federal and state cases that include the quotation from *Brown* concerning the sense of inferiority created by state-mandated racial segregation. I removed all cases dealing exclusively with racial segregation and examined the remaining cases.

Brown's influence extends beyond racial segregation and is pervasive. First of all, the quotation from *Brown* has been cited at all levels of the federal court system, that is, by the United States Supreme Court, courts of appeal,[1] and district courts;[2] and the quotation also has been cited by at least one judge on two state Supreme Courts.[3] In addition, courts have cited the quotation from *Brown* with respect to a wide variety of legal issues other than state-mandated racial segregation, including law school affirmative-action admissions programs, denial of admission of an all-black high school to a state athletic association, suspension from school of a student with behavioral and emotional problems, segregation from the general student body of students with AIDS, the constitutionality of a city-mandated road closure at the border between a white neighborhood and a black neighborhood,[4] treatment of a trust intended to benefit only white people, the constitutionality of a rule prohibiting coeducational teams in high school contact sports, treatment of minority principals when schools close as a result of a plan to end desegregation, racial discrimination as a form of unfair labor practice, employment discrimination, housing discrimination, denial of supplemental social security income benefits to patients of public mental hospitals, treatment of children benefitting from aid to families with dependent children, and a state statute criminalizing miscegenation.

The *Brown* Court's finding that state-mandated racial segregation in public K-12 schools produces harmful effects has been extended in at least three ways. First, the principle has been extended to actual, physical state-mandated separation based on factors such as gender, emotional and behavioral illnesses, and medical illness. Second, the principle has been extended to state-mandated actions which do not physically segregate, but which have a stigmatizing effect, such as the denial of supplemental social security income benefits to patients of public mental hospitals. Third, the principle has been used to recognize that the psychological and emotional harm that results from discrimination is a compensable form of injury.

None of these courts cited *Brown* for its core holding; therefore, *Brown* did not serve as the primary legal authority for these decisions. Instead, the courts appeared to view *Brown* as establishing a general legal principle regarding the importance of promoting human dignity and self-esteem or, at a minimum, a general legal principle restricting governmental activities that undermine human dignity and self-esteem. In either event, *Brown* served a facilitative function by providing the courts with an open-ended principle that could be applied in a variety of legal contexts.

III. *Brown* as an Example of the Operation of *Stare Decisis*

Brown was a jurisprudential sea change, a sea change made possible only by a court overruling a long-standing precedent that had both a profound importance to existing constitutional jurisprudence and a profound impact on society. The *Brown* Court acted, however, without discussing either its authority to overrule a prior Supreme Court decision or the circumstances in which it would be appropriate to do so. Despite this lack of discussion, numerous courts have cited *Brown* both as authority for the general power of a court to overrule itself and to illustrate the circumstances in which it is appropriate to do so. Before I examine these cases, I begin with a brief description of relevant jurisprudential concepts.

A.   *Stare Decisis* and Precedent

Courts at all levels are influenced by the related doctrines of *"stare decisis"* and "precedent." *Stare decisis* provides that a legal issue decided by a court of competent jurisdiction remains settled unless the decision is overruled by the deciding court or the deciding court is overruled by a higher court of competent jurisdiction. Thus, for example, any legal issue properly decided by the United States Supreme Court is deemed settled unless and until the Supreme Court overrules itself, that is, unless and until the Supreme Court changes its decision regarding the proper resolution of the legal issue. Disagreement exists regarding the circumstances under which a court is permitted to "change its mind" and overrule a previous decision. It is well-settled, however, that the doctrine of *stare decisis* embodies a strong presumption against overruling a prior decision.

Once a court has decided a legal issue, the doctrine of precedent applies. The doctrine of precedent provides that a court is bound by its own prior decisions and by the decisions of any higher court in its vertical chain of authority. For example, the United States Supreme Court's interpretation of the Fourteenth Amendment is binding on all other federal and state courts because the United States Supreme Court is the highest court in the land with respect to the proper interpretation of the United States Constitution. On the other hand, the United States Supreme Court's interpretation of the Fourteenth Amendment is not binding on a state court that is interpreting a similar provision of its state constitution. Rather, the decision of the United States Supreme Court is merely "persuasive authority."

B.   *Brown* and *Stare Decisis*: The Cases

My initial review of recently decided cases revealed instances in which courts cited *Brown* in conjunction with discussions concerning whether to overrule a prior decision. To investigate the possibility that courts might regularly cite to *Brown* in this context, I used Westlaw to generate a list of federal and state cases in which *Brown* had been cited in a court's discussion concerning whether to overrule a prior decision. I eliminated those cases that simply referred to the fact that *Brown* had overruled *Plessy*. An examination of the remaining cases revealed that *Brown* has been used to frame judicial debates concerning whether a particular decision should be overruled.

Brown's pervasive influence may be measured by the range of courts that have cited *Brown*, the nature of the legal doctrine being considered, and the nature of the legal issues being considered. First of all, *Brown* has been cited at all levels of the federal court system, that is, by the United States Supreme Court, courts of appeal, and district courts; and *Brown* also has been cited by at least one judge on eleven state Supreme Courts. In addition, *Brown* has been cited by courts that considered overruling, or that actually overruled, prior decisions involving the United States Constitution, a state constitution,[5] state legislation,[6] and common law rules. Further, *Brown* has been cited by courts that considered overruling, or that actually overruled, prior decisions dealing with a wide variety of legal issues besides segregation and other forms of racial discrimination, including abortion, the Eleventh Amendment, procedural due process, voting rights for residents of Puerto Rico, defamation in the press, criminal sentencing, insurance, alleged medical malpractice and charitable immunity, sovereign immunity, tolling of statutes of limitation involving personal injury suits against municipalities, worker's compensation, state law forbidding the sale of motor vehicles on Sunday,[7] sale of real property, the initiative and referendum provision of the Mississippi Constitution, and the determination of whether judges are "officers" within the meaning of the Wisconsin Constitution. While these cases suggest *Brown* has had a pervasive impact on American jurisprudence concerning the operation of *stare decisis*, the more specific nature of that impact still remains to be discussed.

Although *Brown* overruled a long-standing precedent, the *Brown* Court did not specifically address the doctrine of *stare decisis*. Rather, after acknowledging that its decision turned on the "effect of segregation on public education," the Court looked at the then-current conditions in society and the then-current state of "psychological knowledge" concerning the impact of state-sanctioned segregation. This line of reasoning implies that the *Brown* Court believed a court may overrule a previous decision if the theoretical underpinnings of the earlier decision no longer are valid and the decision has a harmful effect. In the absence of a clear statement concerning the theory of *stare decisis* on which it was operating, however, *Brown*'s legacy depends upon how courts choose to use these cryptic statements and the general context within which the *Brown* Court chose to overrule *Plessy*.

Broadly speaking, courts use *Brown* in one of four ways. First, *Brown* is sometimes cited with little or no discussion, apparently as a naked example of a court's authority to overrule itself. Because the general authority of a court to overrule itself is so well-settled, one supposes that this use of *Brown* represents both a manifestation of the adage that "one should provide a citation for every legal point" and a means of saying "if the United States Supreme Court recognizes a court's power to overrule itself, that's good enough for this court." This use of *Brown* is content neutral because it permits a court to overrule a prior decision regardless of whether doing so has a "liberal" or a "conservative" impact. Thus, this use of *Brown* is facilitative, only.

Second, courts cite *Brown* as authority for the proposition that a court may overrule itself even with respect to a case that spawned a long-standing line of authority[8] and even where overruling a case may have a significant impact on society. This use of *Brown* also is content neutral because it permits a court to overrule a prior decision regardless of whether doing so has a "liberal" or "conservative" impact. Again, this use of *Brown* is facilitative, only.

Third, courts cite *Brown* as an example of a court involving itself in an issue by overruling a prior case in order to protect a politically powerless group when the political branches had not involved themselves to remedy the problem. This use of *Brown* is not content specific; it may be used with respect to any legal issue. Nonetheless, because of its emphasis on protecting the politically powerless, this use of *Brown* presumably will tend to assist in producing a "liberal" outcome.

The fourth—and most numerous—category of cases cite *Brown* as an example of a court overruling a case that is wrong, that is, in error. Several variations on this theme can be identified. In one subset of these cases, courts view *Brown* as an example of a court overruling itself when there has been a change in the circumstances upon which the initial decision was based. The circumstances might involve some form of societal change[9] or a change in society's understanding of the proper scope of "constitutionally protected civil rights." In another subset of these cases, courts view *Brown* as an example of a court overruling itself when the original case was wrongly decided and produced harmful effects. In a third subset of these cases, courts view *Brown* as an example of a court overruling itself when it came to conclude that the prior decision was somehow wrong or was based on a mistaken concept. Again, the uses of *Brown* falling within this category are content neutral.

The courts' use of *Brown* in each of the previous four broad categories of cases was more or less ad hoc, opportunistic, if you

will. *Brown* was cited when it would advance or facilitate the
argument being made by the particular court or judge. *Brown* was
not cited as part of a comprehensive explication of a philosophy of
stare decisis. In two cases, however, various members of the United
States Supreme Court cited *Brown* as part of an ongoing debate
concerning the proper role of *stare decisis* in the decision whether to
overrule a case that establishes an interpretation of the United
States Constitution. A full discussion of each side's position is far
beyond the scope of this chapter; however, several general
observations are offered.

In *Casey* and *Thornburg*, a number of Justices considered the
proper role of *stare decisis* in their decision whether to overrule *Roe
v. Wade.* In the most recent case, Casey, Justices O'Connor,
Kennedy and Souter authored a joint opinion in which they both
discussed their interpretation of the doctrine of *stare decisis* and
explained the role that *stare decisis* played in their decisions not to
vote to overrule *Roe.* They asserted that a case establishing a
constitutional principle could be overruled only if a "special
reason" existed, such as an alteration in the facts upon which the
original case had been faced; that the prior decision had been
wrongly decided was not sufficient to justify overruling the
decision. In their view, the benefits of adhering to a prior decision
outweigh the costs of allowing a wrongly decided case to
stand—unless there is some additional special reason for overruling
the prior decision. To overrule a case merely because a majority of
the then-current Court believed the prior decision to be wrong
would jeopardize the Court's legitimacy by making the Court
appear to be as political as the other two branches of government.

To illustrate the situations in which they believed special
circumstances would warrant overruling a decision, Justices
O'Connor, Kennedy and Souter analyzed two occasions on which
the Supreme Court had—correctly in their view—overruled itself
with respect to a major constitutional issue. Their analysis included
the following description of *Brown*:

The Court in *Brown* addressed these facts of life by observing
that whatever may have been the understanding in *Plessy*'s time of
the power of segregation to stigmatize those who were segregated
with a "badge of inferiority," it was clear by 1954 that legally
sanctioned segregation had just such an effect to the point that
racially separate public educational facilities were deemed inher-

ently unequal. (citation omitted) Society's understanding of the facts upon which a constitutional ruling was sought in 1954 was thus fundamentally different from the basis claimed for the decision in 1896. While we think *Plessy* was wrong the day it was decided, see *Plessy*... (Harlan, J., dissenting), we must also recognize that the *Plessy* Court's explanation for its decision was so clearly at odds with the facts apparent to the Court in 1954 that the decision to reexamine was on this ground alone not only justified but required.

Brown ... rested on facts, or an understanding of facts, changed from those which furnished the claimed justifications for the earlier constitutional resolutions. [*Brown*] was comprehensible as the Court's response to facts that the country could understand, or had come to understand already, but which the Court of an earlier day, as its own declarations disclosed, had not been able to perceive. As the decision [was] thus comprehensible [it was] also defensible, not merely as the victor[y] of one doctrinal school over another by dint of numbers (victor[y] though [it was]), but as [the] application of constitutional principle to facts as they had not been seen by the Court before. In constitutional adjudication as elsewhere in life, changed circumstances may impose new obligations, and the thoughtful part of the nation could accept each decision to overrule a prior case as a response to the Court's constitutional duty.

The Justices then concluded that no special reason existed for overruling *Roe*.

Chief Justice Rehnquist and Justices White, Scalia and Thomas disagreed and took the position that the Court had the power—indeed the obligation—to overrule a case on a constitutional issue when the case was wrongly decided. No special reason was needed. *Brown* was justified by the simple fact that *Plessy* originally had been decided incorrectly as a matter of constitutional law. They asserted that the Court improves, not undermines, its stature when it overrules erroneous decisions.

The debate in *Casey* is reminiscent of an earlier debate. In *Thornburgh v. American College of Obstetricians and Gynecologists*, the Court examined the constitutionality of a Pennsylvania abortion statute. Justice White, with whom then-Justice Rehnquist joined, dissented from a majority decision that struck down aspects of the statute. Justice White cited *Brown* as an application of the principle that the Court may overrule a constitutional case solely because it was incorrect when originally decided.

The debate in *Casey* and *Thornburgh* about the proper interpretation and application of *stare decisis* likely never will be settled. Yet, the fact that *Brown* is used to frame the debate indicates that *Brown* will continue to play a central role in the jurisprudence regarding the circumstances under which a court may overrule a case consistently with the doctrine of *stare decisis*. The relevance of *Brown* to this debate may be seen by the fact that several lower courts have cited to it. It should be noted, however, that either interpretation of *Brown* is content neutral, that is, does not necessarily lead to liberal or conservative decisions.

Overall, while it appears that *Brown* will continue to be cited as an example of the operation of *stare decisis*, it also appears that *Brown*'s role will continue to be more facilitative than substantive. Courts will continue to disagree about the nature of *Brown*'s relevance to the operation of *stare decisis*. Courts will continue to cite *Brown* to justify a conclusion that a case should or should not be overruled, rather than to provide an objective rule or test either for when a prior decision should be overruled or for what the new rule of law, if any, should be.

IV. *Brown* as an Example of the Use of Social Science

The *Brown* Court's conclusion that separate educational facilities were inherently unequal rested, at least in part, on the Court's determination that such facilities had a negative psychological and sociological impact on minority schoolchildren. The Court stated:

We come then to the question presented: Does segregation of children in public schools solely on the basis of race, even though the physical facilities and other 'tangible' factors may be equal, deprive the children of the minority group of equal educational opportunities? We believe that it does.

To separate [children in grade school and high school] from others of similar age and qualifications solely because of their race generates a feeling of inferiority as to their status in the community that may affect their hearts and minds in a way unlikely ever to be undone. The effect of this separation on their educational opportunities was well-stated by a finding in the Kansas case by a court which nevertheless felt compelled to rule against the Negro plaintiffs:

Segregation of white and colored children in public schools has a detrimental effect upon the colored children. The impact is greater when it has the sanction of the law; for the policy of separating the races is usually interpreted as denoting the inferiority of the Negro group. A sense of inferiority affects the motivation of a child to learn. Segregation with the sanction of law, therefore, has a tendency to (retard) the educational and mental development of Negro children and to deprive them of some of the benefits they would receive in a racial(ly) integrated school system."

The Court's determination concerning the negative effect of segregation was based—at least in part—on social science research. In the text of its decision, the Court stated that its conclusion was based on contemporary "psychological knowledge" concerning the effects of segregation. The Court supported its conclusion with a footnote listing the citations of five social science research projects. Thus, the Court took judicial notice of the results of social science research studies and used that information as a legislative fact, that is, as the foundation for the constitutional principle it established.

The legislative fact regarding the impact of state-mandated segregation was, of course, binding on the Court and on all lower courts in the context of state-mandated racial segregation in public K-12 education. In addition, the Court's determination regarding the psychological and sociological effects of segregation was applied by analogy to strike down the "separate but equal" doctrine as it was being applied to ethnic segregation in public education and in a wide variety of non-educational circumstances, such as parks, beaches and swimming pools, golf courses and public transportation.

These uses of *Brown* and my initial review of recently decided cases suggested that courts might rely on *Brown* as authority to use social science research results in other contexts. In order to investigate this possibility, I used Westlaw to generate a list of such cases.

Brown's influence arguably is pervasive. First, *Brown* has been cited at all levels of the federal court system, that is, by the United States Supreme Court, courts of appeal, and district courts; and *Brown* has been cited by at least one judge on several state supreme and intermediate appellate courts. In addition, *Brown* has been cited by courts to authorize the use of social science research with respect to a wide variety of legal issues other than desegregation of public K-12 schools, including the constitutionality of two prisoners in a single prison cell; the constitutionality of the death penalty; the constitutionality of an affirmative-action admissions program at a public law school; the constitutionality of a state law banning the intrastate advertising of alcohol; the constitutionality of campaign finance limitations; the constitutionality of methods of remedying public school segregation; whether a jury instruction regarding cross-racial identification is constitutionally required in certain criminal cases; whether a state voter-purge statute violated the Voting Rights Act; and the effect of racial discrimination by a labor union.

It is worth noting that these cases do not require that unanimity exists among social scientists in order for a court to take judicial notice of social science research. Some courts made this observation to buttress the use of social science research results in a particular case. For example, in *Cromedy*, the court relied on social science research to support a constitutional requirement that cross-racial identification jury instructions be given in appropriate cases despite recognizing that a snapshot of the literature reveals that although many scientists agree that witnesses are better at identifying suspects of their own race, they cannot agree on the extent to which cross-racial impairment affects identification. The research also indicates disagreement about whether cross-racial impairment affects all racial groups.

To other courts, the observation that social scientists disagree on research results reflects a criticism of basing constitutional principles on social science research. For example, dissenting from a decision upholding the University of Michigan Law School's admissions policy, which employed race as a factor, Circuit Judge Boggs observed: "Even more fundamentally, social science data as to the efficacy in the eyes of one or another researcher of policies of discrimination are themselves of limited utility in resolving the ultimate constitutional issue. At the time of *Brown*..., there were certainly researchers with academic degrees who argued that segregated education would provide greater educational benefits for both races." Such statements not only reflect skepticism about social science research, but evidence a concern that social science evidence might be marshaled to support contradictory constitutional rules. Indeed, Judge Boggs went on to state: "Does anyone think that a factual belief in such analyses would have, or should have, led to a different constitutional outcome in *Brown*? I very strongly doubt it. Similarly, research asserting that Jews and Gentiles in fact interacted more harmoniously under Lowell's Harvard plan would not justify that policy either." And, at least one court attempted to limit *Brown*'s effect by arguing that in the particular case the record of evidence, including social science research, indicated that separate educational facilities did not produce any psychological harm.

Other courts have noted that social science research results may be subject to a variety of conceptual and methodological criticisms. Indeed, even the sociological statements in *Brown* have been criticized, with Justice Thomas, for example, noting that "[t]he studies cited in *Brown I* have received harsh criticism.

Apart from the concerns about contradictory and methodologically questionable research results, some judges have been troubled by the practice of grounding–even in part–constitutional rights on social science research. They believe that constitutional rights exist independently, based, for example, on the original intent of the Framers. Therefore, these courts would be critical of basing constitutional rights on even a well-established, unanimous set of well-designed social science research projects. Typical of statements reflecting this perspective is the following comment offered by Justice Thomas:

> *Brown I* ... did not need to rely upon any psychological or social-science research in order to announce the simple, yet fundamental, truth that the government cannot discriminate among its citizens on the basis of race. As the Court's unanimous opinion indicated: "[I]n the field of public education the doctrine of 'separate but equal' has no place. Separate educational facilities are inherently unequal." [citation omitted] At the heart of this interpretation of the Equal Protection Clause lies the principle that the government must treat citizens as individuals, and not as members of racial, ethnic or religious groups. Segregation was not unconstitutional because it might have caused psychological feelings of inferiority. Psychological injury or benefit is irrelevant to the question whether state actors have engaged in intentional discrim-

ination—the critical inquiry for ascertaining violations of the Equal Protection Clause. The judiciary is fully competent to make independent determinations concerning the existence of state action without the unnecessary and misleading assistance of the social sciences.

While both the sociological approach and the specific social science research results used in *Brown* have not met with unanimous agreement, *Brown* nonetheless serves as the focal point, the organizing case for the debate, at least within the context of the psychological impacts of segregation and discrimination.

Courts have not confined their use of *Brown* to cases involving constitutional issues, however. Several courts have cited *Brown* to support the use of social science research results and scientific techniques in the determination of party-specific, case-specific adjudicative facts. For example, in *Ortiz v. City of Philadelphia, Office of the City Commissioners Voter Registration Division,* Circuit Judge Lewis referred to social science works, including at least one work cited by the *Brown* Court, in dissenting from the majority's finding that a voter-purge statute removing inactive votes did not violate the Voting Rights Act. And in *City of Pittsburgh v. Plumbers Local Union No. 27,* the court based its conclusion in part on social science research regarding "various facets of discrimination such as is here established and its effects upon its victims."

Brown also has been cited to justify the use of hard science in determining adjudicative facts. In *Emerson,* the court took judicial notice of "it would take judicial notice of reliability of both theory underlyings horizontal gaze nystagmus (HGN) test and its technique for purposes of determining whether testimony regarding the HGN test was admissible as expert testimony."

Courts also have used *Brown* as an example of the appropriate use of social science when criticizing courts that have created rules without an empirical basis. For example, in *Flemino,* the court criticized a court-established rule permitting expert testimony for the legal conclusion that a child suffered sexual abuse. The court stated:

> The *Myers* Court cited no sociological studies or identifiable and reliable empirical data to prove that juries in child abuse cases are so hamstrung by the "enormity of the charge," that they are helpless unless experts for the state patiently explain to them that, yes, this minor was

sexually abused and yes, when she described the abuse, she was truthful. There is simply no reliable way to defend this proposition in *Myers*.

And courts have used *Brown* as an example of the appropriate use of social science research while declining to do so in the particular case. For example, in *Brust*, the court declined to resort to social science research while determining whether it would retain a presumption that the mother in a divorce case was better suited than the father to care for children of "tender years."

Overall, it appears that *Brown* will continue to be cited as an example of the role of social science research in judicial decision-making and that *Brown*'s role will continue to be more facilitative than substantive. Courts will continue to disagree about the situations in which social science research is relevant and will continue to cite *Brown* to justify the use of such research. *Brown*, however, does not provide an objective rule or test either for when social science research should be used or what the new implications of its use, if any, should be.

Conclusion

Brown has had a profound and enduring impact on American jurisprudence. *Brown* eviscerated the "separate but equal" doctrine. This is its greatest legacy. But *Brown* continues to exert a broader influence on American jurisprudence.

At its core, *Brown* concerned human rights, human dignity and self-esteem, concepts with no logical boundary on their application. And courts have seized hold of these themes and have applied them in an ever-increasing variety of circumstances.

Brown also represented a monumental break with legal precedent, a break that brought tremendous conflict to the legal system. Despite—or perhaps because of—the Court's silence regarding its theory of *stare decisis*, courts cite to *Brown* as a signal example of when it is appropriate to overrule precedent. The *Brown* Court's silence has meant, however, that courts offer conflicting interpretations of *Brown* and cite to *Brown* opportunistically. As it is likely *Brown* will remain one of a handful of truly monumental cases in which the Court overruled itself, *Brown* likely will continue to be at the heart of any serious discussion of *stare decisis*.

Brown represents a classic example of the use of social science research in judicial decision-making. Once again, despite—or perhaps because of–the Court's silence regarding its theory of when the use of social science research is warranted, courts cite to *Brown* as a signal example of when such use is appropriate. The Court's failure to provide a clear statement of when such use is permissible has resulted in courts citing to *Brown* opportunistically, whenever and however it seems to support the current court's desired outcome.

Part II

ITS IMPACT ON HISTORICALLY BLACK

COLLEGES AND UNIVERSITIES

Chapter 6

TRAPPED IN THE BACK OF THE BUS: BLACK COLLEGES, THE COURTS AND DESEGREGATION RULINGS

Saran Donahoo & Denise O. Green

The stipulations regarding the use of race-conscious policies provided by the Supreme Court in *Gratz v. Bollinger* (2003) and *Grutter v. Bollinger* (2003) affects all public higher education institutions. However, the fact that race receives more consideration at some universities than others suggests that *Brown v. Board of Education* (1954), *Regents of the University of California v. Bakke* (1978) and these latest decisions do not influence all public institutions equally. As state agencies, public Historically Black Colleges and Universities (HBCUs) experience the same legal obligations to desegregate and limitations on the use of race-conscious policies as Predominantly White Institutions (PWIs). Yet, labeled as vestiges of the segregation era, HBCUs must also contend with challenges to their very existence.

The authors examine how legal developments focused on collegiate desegregation affects public HBCUs. To that end, this analysis determines if desegregation and diversity policies, as defined by *Brown, Bakke* and *Grutter,* privilege PWIs by judging and treating HBCUs differently. As such, this chapter offers a brief examination of the varying impact *Brown, Bakke* and their corollaries have had on PWIs and HBCUs.

Early on, *Brown* had no direct impact on the structure or functioning of HBCUs. The fact that many states affected by the decision ignored its mandate because they did not want to desegregate their PWIs prevented *Brown* from having any significant influence on other types of institutions. However, as some states began to accept collegiate desegregation as inescapable, HBCUs remained outsiders, as the institutions rarely received consideration or participated in the higher education desegregation process. Consequently, cases involving HBCUs went to trial not because students felt that the institutions did not comply with *Brown,* rather because students, faculty and others affiliated with HBCUs believed the states deliberately excluded these institutions from the desegregation process. The cases of *Alabama State Teachers Association v. Alabama Public Schools and College Authority (ASTA v. APSACA)* (1968), *Norris v. State Council of Higher Education* (1971) and *Geier v. Dunn* (1972) each illustrates the new marginalization that states imposed on HBCUs, via *Brown*.

In *ASTA v. APSACA*, alumni from Alabama State College sued Alabama's state educational agency to prevent the expansion of Auburn University into the City of Montgomery. Under Act No. 403 of 1967, the state approved funding for the construction of a four-year degree-granting branch of Auburn University. The location for the new campus originally opened as the University of Alabama Montgomery Extension Center, which offered courses similar to those available at a junior college. Insisting that *Brown* called for the desegregation of all public institutions, the plaintiffs in *ASTA* argued that allowing Auburn to develop another campus would limit and prevent white students from enrolling in Alabama State.

Alabama adopted Act No. 403 of 1967 to meet the demand for increased higher education access within Montgomery. Having an existing four-year degree-granting institution already operating in that city, Alabama could have easily used the funds raised in Act No. 403 to expand Alabama State to meet this need. However, the existence of this act indicates that policymakers never considered Alabama State as a viable option for educating white students. Although *Brown* overturned the policy of restricting campuses to students of a particular race, the insufficient guidelines provided in the decision made it easy for states to exclude public HBCUs from the collegiate desegregation process. Indeed, the U.S. District Court for the Middle District of Alabama used *Brown* to uphold the plan to open a new campus of Auburn University, contending that "a new institution will not be a white school or a Negro school, but just a school, as it is to believe that Alabama State would so evolve."[1] Likewise, the U. S. Supreme Court's affirmation of the lower court's decision completely ignored the racial overtones embedded in Act No. 403. The dissenting opinions authored by Justices Douglas and Harlan even disregarded the racial issues affecting this case.[2] Essentially, both the Middle District of AL and the U. S. Supreme Court segregated HBCUs by supporting the interpretation that ending racial policies would be enough to end racial segregation in higher education.

Similar to *ASTA*, *Sanders v. Ellington* (1968) and *Geier v. Dunn* (1972) placed the need to bring more higher education to a large city at odds with the constitutional duty to desegregate. Focused on Nashville, both of these cases challenged the State of Tennessee's treatment of Tennessee State University (TSU). In *Sanders v. Ellington*, Rita Sanders, a faculty member at TSU, sued Tennessee Governor Buford Ellington after the state decided to increase higher education access in Nashville by expanding and remaking the Nashville Center into another campus of the University of Tennessee (UTN). Citing the provisions of the Civil Rights Act of 1964, the United States joined the case as a plaintiff-intervener seeking a court order that would require Tennessee to create and adopt a meaningful collegiate desegregation plan.[3]

Citing and mimicking *ASTA*, the U.S. District Court for the Middle District of Tennessee ruled in favor of the state. Pointing to the very limited desegregation obligations stipulated in *Brown*, the Middle District of Tennessee found that Sanders did not really have a case since the State of Tennessee no longer supported or perpetuated segregation as an official policy. However, the district court did diverge from the *ASTA* decision by issuing an order that required Tennessee to develop and submit a desegregation plan that addressed the specific needs of public higher education in the state.[4]

The participation of the United States in *Sanders* proved to be crucial since the Civil Rights Act of 1964, not *Brown*, offered the best avenue for making Tennessee accountable for addressing the remnants of the segregation era. Indeed, the next phase of this litigation, *Geier v. Dunn*, used the Civil Rights Act of 1964 and the mandate of a desegregation plan issued in *Sanders* to revisit Tennessee's neglectful treatment of TSU. Restating her objection, Rita Sanders Geier sued the State of Tennessee after TSU received no consideration under the state's desegregation plan. Between the 1968-1969 and 1969-1970 academic years, African-American enrollment at all public colleges and universities except TSU increased by 42.2 percent.[5] Despite these efforts, the Middle District of Tennessee held that the state failed to satisfy its full duty to desegregate public higher education since TSU remained a racially identifiable institution. As such, the district court ordered

Tennessee to revise its desegregation plan relative to TSU and mandated that the state consider utilizing more radical measures such as merging TSU and UTN into one institution.[6]

The outcome in *Sanders* and *Geier* clearly demonstrates *Brown*'s inability to offer any significant guidelines in dealing with HBCUs during the early years of collegiate desegregation. Indeed, it was the Civil Rights Act of 1964 not the *Brown* decision that made visible the discrimination HBCUs experienced.

The case of *Norris v. State Council of Higher Education* (1971) afforded the courts an opportunity to decide which approach to desegregating HBCUs should prevail—either *ASTA v. APSACA* or *Sanders v. Ellington.* Similar to the other two cases, *Norris* developed after faculty, current students and prospective students of Virginia State College challenged the State of Virginia's decision to elevate Richard Bland College, a two-year college located within seven miles, to four-year degree-granting status. Established in 1960, Bland began as a feeder school to the College of William and Mary. Over the years, some Bland students also transferred to Virginia State to complete their four-year degrees. According to Ethel Norris and the other plaintiffs, elevating Bland would disrupt desegregation efforts at Virginia State by forcing the two institutions to compete for students.[7]

In deciding *Norris*, the U. S. District Court for the Eastern District of Virginia applied elements of both *ASTA* and *Sanders*. Acknowledging *Sanders*, the Eastern District of VA found that escalating Bland would inhibit desegregation at Virginia State by eliminating the need for Bland students to transfer to complete their degrees. As such, the district court ordered that Bland remain a two-year institution. However, emulating *ASTA*, the Eastern District refused to require the State of Virginia to develop a collegiate desegregation plan since the United States, the party with the authority to make such a request, failed to join the lawsuit.[8]

Just as the limited directives provided in *Brown* made it easier for states to avoid desegregating PWIs, the same decision also hurt HBCUs by failing to offer any guidelines or stipulations regarding their participation in the collegiate desegregation process. Contrary to cases that focused on desegregating PWIs, the fact that the Supreme Court issued *Brown* in two phases neither helped nor harmed HBCUs. Indeed, *Brown* had very little influence on the way states viewed or addressed racial issues involving these institutions.

Much like the African-American students they serve, individual HBCUs were forced to fight for inclusion and desegregation.

Moreover, the collegiate desegregation cases at both PWIs and HBCUs reveal one key shortcoming of *Brown*–institutional racial identifiability. Giving African-American students the right to attend PWIs did not have an immediate impact on the landscape or environment of HBCUs. Likewise, eliminating racial restrictions at HBCUs was generally not enough to attract students from other races.

Bakke and A Remedy of Retreat

It was not until *Regents of the University of California v. Bakke* (1978) that the Supreme Court offered any meaningful clarification regarding the process or constitutional obligations related to collegiate desegregation.[8] Even so, *DeFunis v. Odegaard* (1974) planted the seed that made *Bakke* possible. Mimicking African-American student plaintiffs of the 1930s, 40s, 50s and 60s, Marco DeFunis, Jr.- a white Jewish applicant- sued the University of Washington Law School arguing that the institution violated the Equal Protection Clause of the Fourteenth Amendment by refusing to admit him because of his race. Challenging the law school's admissions process, DeFunis contended that students who identified themselves as members of certain minority groups received an unfair advantage since they were not held to the same academic standards as students of other races.[9]

Unlike other challenges to institutional admissions policies, DeFunis gained access to and enrolled in the UW Law School long before his case received final adjudication. Somewhat prematurely, the King County Superior Court issued the writ of mandamus DeFunis requested allowing him to enroll as a law student in 1971.[10] Essentially, DeFunis had already achieved the remedy he requested when his case attained Supreme Court review. As such, the Supreme Court labeled *DeFunis v. Odegaard* (1974) moot and refused to deliberate the racial/constitutional questions involved in the case. In doing so, the high court temporarily evaded clarifying the application of *Brown,* the use of race-conscious policies, or the validity of affirmative-action programs to achieve collegiate desegregation.

Directives From *Bakke*

By itself, *DeFunis* had no real impact on the legal obligations or limitations colleges experienced in considering race in their admissions process. However, the dissension in the *DeFunis* decision ensured that the high court would have to address the racial and constitutional issues left unresolved in that case. After more than two decades of avoiding these issues, *Regents of the University of California v. Bakke* finally forced the Supreme Court to offer more guidelines than those provided in *Brown*.

Contrary to *Brown*, *Bakke* directly confronted constitutional and racial issues at colleges and universities. Similar to *DeFunis*, Alan Bakke, a prospective white student, accused the University of California at Davis Medical School of discrimination by selecting students on the basis of their race. Correspondingly, *Bakke* improved on *Brown* by offering a more limited definition regarding the applicability of race-conscious policies. For institutions, *Bakke* officially made achieving a racially diverse student population constitutionally permissible and acceptable.[11] Nevertheless, this decision actually retreated away from the sentiment expressed in *Brown* by removing the constitutional requirement that states and institutions actively pursue students from traditionally under-represented racial groups by making collegiate desegregation (campus diversity) optional.

Impact on PWIs

The combination of *Bakke*, *Wygant v. Jackson Board of Education* (1986) and *City of Richmond v. J. A. Croson Co.* (1989) severely limits the conditions under which a state can legally justify utilizing race-conscious policies. The requirement that states "narrowly tailor" racial initiatives to achieve a specific diversity goal[12] and the additional requisite that such states and institutions pass the "strict scrutiny" test[13] by providing specific evidence to prove that such programs are needed now makes it very difficult to demonstrate that diversity is indeed a "compelling interest"[14] in any state. Indeed, cases such as *Hopwood v. Texas* (1994, 1996, 2000); *Gratz v. Bollinger* (2003) and *Grutter v. Bollinger* (2003) depicts the negative impact that *Bakke* and its subsequent limitations have on the policies utilized to help students of color gain access to PWIs.

The *Hopwood v. Texas* case applied the limitations on the use of race-conscious policies that resulted from *Bakke*, *Wygant* and *Croson*. In *Hopwood*, four white students filed suit against the University of Texas School of Law accusing the institution of using a racial quota system in its admissions system and illegally giving an advantage to students from some minority groups.[15] By erroneously applying the standards regarding the use of race outlined in *Bakke*, *Wygant* and *Croson*, the Fifth Circuit held that any use of race in college admissions is now illegal and unconstitutional. Moreover, the Fifth Circuit also ordered that UTX allow the plaintiffs to reapply to the law school free of charge and instructed the lower court to reconsider awarding damages to the prevailing litigants. Later, the Fifth Circuit reiterated its original decision, finding that UTX would not have accepted *Hopwood* and the other plaintiffs as law students even if the institution used an exclusively race-neutral admissions process in 1992 and ordering UTX to abandon its use of race-conscious policies for any reason.[16]

Based on the Fifth Circuit's reading of *Bakke* and other subsequent cases, race-conscious policies are no longer valid under the Constitution. As such, the *Hopwood* rulings effectively repeal *Bakke* by eliminating any compelling state interest as a justification for the use of race in the State of Texas. During this same period, voters in both California (Proposition 209) and Washington (Initiative 200) passed legislation that also nullified race-conscious policies.[17] Furthermore, the Eleventh Circuit Court of Appeals' decision in *Johnson v. Board of Regents of the University of Georgia* (2001) also had an impact on the use of race by public colleges and universities in states under its jurisdiction. Specifically, *Johnson* overturned the use of race-conscious policies in Georgia and provided the impetus for Governor Jeb Bush to develop the One Florida Initiative, which had the same impact on that state.[18] As such, *Hopwood* created a rippling effect whereby some states and lower federal courts now choose to reinterpret Supreme Court decisions or simply evade them altogether. But, historically, this strategy is not new. States and lower courts have historically reinterpreted or circumvented Supreme Court decisions to avoid remedying racial discrimination against African-Americans. Under *Hopwood*, PWIs are no longer allowed to consider the race of their applicants in spite of the impact this limitation will have on their ability to achieve a diverse student population.

Although the Fifth Circuit offered a constitutional interpretation of race-conscious policies that directly confronted *Bakke*, the Supreme Court declined to use *Hopwood* as an opportunity to review its standing opinion on the issue. It was not until *Gratz v. Bollinger* and *Grutter v. Bollinger* that the high court chose to reenter this debate. Rather than bring a final resolution to the controversy surrounding race-conscious policies in public higher education, the Supreme Court decisions in the Michigan cases simply upheld the arrangement established in *Bakke* by transferring responsibility for final adjudication to another generation of the court.

The cases of *Gratz v. Bollinger* and *Grutter v. Bollinger* challenges the University of Michigan's use of race in determining admissions decisions in the College of Literature, Science and Arts and the Law School, respectively. In both cases, white students accused the university of practicing racial discrimination after the university rejected their applications.[19] Reviewing these cases simultaneously, the Supreme Court invalidated the application of race as used by LSA arguing that the point system employed by the university unfairly advantaged minority students.[20] However, the high court, by a 5 to 4 vote, did not completely abolish the use of race in the Law School case, since the law school applications underwent individualized consideration, with race being only one of many factors considered in admissions' decisions.[21] The result of *Gratz* and *Grutter* is that PWIs retain the right to use race-conscious policies, yet institutions are not allowed to use any type of formulaic or mathematical system that assigns a predetermined value to a student's race. As such, *Bakke* remains intact with the Michigan cases collectively, providing a refined explanation of what the Supreme Court regards as a quota. Essentially, *Gratz* and *Grutter* serves to discourage many large institutions from considering race because it becomes more costly for them to review the high volume of applications received, especially for undergraduate admissions.

Impact on HBCUs

Rather than resolve the debate over race-conscious policies, *Hopwood*, *Johnson*, *Gratz* and *Grutter* encourage states, PWIs and voters to abandon diversity as a compelling interest. Consequently, PWIs now experience little or no obligation to ensure that students of color gain college access. On the other hand, HBCUs remain the targets of judicial review, political scrutiny and interference because many campuses still find it difficult to enroll non-African-American students. Sagas such as the *Geier* cases and the *Ayers* decisions demonstrate that HBCUs receive disparate treatment when racial issues at these institutions come before the courts.

The resolution to *Geier v. Dunn* required the State of Tennessee to devise a practical remedy for bringing TSU into its desegregation plan. Despite directions from the district court to consider "radical" remedies to this situation, the State of Tennessee argued that having "an 'open–door' admissions policy" was enough to fulfill its duty in this case.[22] Dissatisfied with the state's lack of effort, the Middle District of Tennessee ordered that TSU and UTN merge into one institution.[23] In the next phase of the case, the Sixth Circuit Court of Appeals affirmed the lower court's decision finding that the State of Tennessee does have a legal duty to desegregate all of its public higher education facilities including its public HBCUs and that the court-ordered merger is within the discretion and jurisdiction of the court.[24] Acknowledging the state's role in creating this problem, the court held that TSU could not "attract a 'white presence' to its campus because of the competition of UTN for students in the Nashville area. This competition would not have been so formidable if UTN had remained a nondegree-granting extension center."[25] In essence, the State of Tennessee brought the entire *Geier* situation down on itself by creating the conditions that made it almost impossible for TSU to desegregate on its own.

As noted by the court, the State of Tennessee made the merger between TSU and UTN necessary. However, it is also important to note that the merger is one of the remedies originally proposed by the plaintiffs in *Sanders v. Ellington*. Even though *Geier* and the other plaintiffs ultimately achieved the remedy they sought, the application of this remedy to the *Geier* cases demonstrates a major departure from the judicial experience of PWIs that had similar problems with race-conscious policies. Indeed, UTN ceased to exist as an independent institution in order to help the state fulfill its constitutional duty to desegregate TSU.

Moreover, *Geier v. Alexander* reveals another difference between the way the courts address desegregation at PWIs and HBCUs. In these two most recent cases, the courts attempted to resolve the racial issues affecting higher education in Tennessee by assigning each public institution a specific enrollment goal for increasing racial diversity on each campus. While the State of Tennessee contends that these percentage goals are not quotas,[26] the use of percentages required under the *Geier* settlement are very similar to the percentages overturned as quotas under *Hopwood v. Texas.*

In addition, the percentages stipulated in the *Geier* settlement also places a greater burden on Tennessee's HBCUs than required of its PWIs. Originally set in *Geier v. Alexander*, the Middle District of Tennessee required each public college and university to achieve a specific integration percentage by the 2000-2001 academic year. The settlement required PWIs to achieve increased minority student enrollment percentages generally ranging from 2.79% to 21.06%. Larger PWIs such as Austin Peay State University and UT-Knoxville had goals of 19.08% and 11.03%, respectively. The University of Memphis received the highest-goal percentage among Tennessee's PWIs at 39.18%. Conversely, the district court ordered TSU to increase its non-African-American student enrollment percentage to 50% *(see Table 1 below).*[27]

TABLE 1
Tennessee Institutional Racial Integration Percentages

INSTITUTION	Minority Student Enrollment, 1996[1]	Enrollment Goal for 2000-2001	Minority Student Enrollment, 2002[2]	Difference Btwn Enrollment Goal & Actual 2002 Enrollment
Austin Peay	18.36%	19.08%	28.30%	+ 9.22%
TSU	24.5%	50.00%	19.10%	-30.90%
U of Memphis	27.35%	39.18%	38.00%	- 1.18%
UT-Knoxville	4.59%	11.03%	11.10%	+ 0.07%

Clearly, the settlement places a greater burden on public HBCUs by insisting that TSU attract and enroll a larger proportion of white

[1]   1996 enrollment data adapted from "Tennessee System Fails Diversity Test" (1997). For TSU, minority student enrollment refers to all non-African-American students.

[2]   2002 enrollment data adapted from NCES (n. d.). For PWIs, this column does not include students for whom race was unknown or nonresident aliens.

students, even at the risk of turning away many African-American students.

Simultaneously, there are much greater disparities between early integration percentages and the court-ordered goals set for TSU than for Tennessee's PWIs. In 1996, after twelve years of working to satisfy the court order, Austin Peay had a minority student enrollment of 18.36%, less than 1% away from its goal percentage. During that same year, UT-Koxville and U of Memphis still needed to increase minority student enrollment by 6.44% and 11.83%, respectively. On the other hand, TSU had an enrollment disparity of 25.5% *(see Table 1)*.[28] Furthermore, TSU has actually lost ground in this area since the institution enrolled only 19.1% non-African-American students in 2002.[29] Such an increasing disparity might not exist at TSU had the court order set a goal that more closely resembled its demonstrated progress.[30] In this way, TSU once again experienced differential treatment compared to PWIs in Tennessee, especially since the courts did not require any other institution to make such significant gains in less time, less time than the entire state had to implement *Brown*.

Mississippi's HBCUs. Similar to the *Geier* cases, *Ayers v. Fordice* (1995) and other related decisions signify a long battle to force a state to improve and equalize its public HBCUs. Originating in the State of Mississippi in 1975, the *Ayers* cases began as an effort to force the state to truly dismantle the dual higher education system adopted during the segregation era.[31] To this end, *Ayers* attempted to force Mississippi to implement practical and effective desegregation efforts that addressed the three historically black institutions in the state–Alcorn State University, Jackson State University and Mississippi Valley State University.[32] However, the *Ayers* cases basically stagnated until 1992 when the Supreme Court ruled that Mississippi was still operating a dual higher education system and ordered the state to develop a desegregation plan.[33]

The desegregation plan ordered in *United States v. Fordice* (1992) did have an impact on Mississippi's post-secondary landscape. First, the intervention by the courts forced Mississippi to adopt universal standards for all of its public institutions. In addition, the United States District Court for the Northern District of Mississippi also ordered Mississippi to provide additional financial resources to its public HBCUs to improve the resources and educational offering at these campuses.[34] As a result, the financial settlement in the case promises to dedicate close to $500 million to remedying the continued elements of *de jure* segregation in Mississippi's public higher education institutions over a seventeen-year period.[35]

Beyond the requirement to equalize standards and increase funding for public higher education in Mississippi, the *Ayers* settlement includes a provision obliging each of the public HBCUs to "achieve and maintain ten percent other-race enrollment before receiving its share of the endowments."[36] Comparing minority student enrollment before and after the Supreme Court ordered Mississippi to develop a post-secondary desegregation plan in 1992, Alcorn State and Jackson State actually enrolled fewer non-African-American students than the number who attended these universities before the plan began to take effect *(see Table 2 below)*.

TABLE 2
Mississippi Institutional Racial Integration Percentages

INSTITUTION	Minority Student Enrollment, 1988[3]	Minority Student Enrollment, 1997	Minority Student Enrollment, 2002[4]	Enrollment Difference Between 1988 and 2002, +/-
Public 4-Year HBCUs				
Alcorn State	8.38%	4.95%	5.10%	- 3.28%
Jackson State	5.13%	6.32%	1.70%	- 3.43%
MVSU	0.68%	2.84%	2.90%	+ 2.22%

[3] Data for 1988 and 1997 adapted from Roach (1998). For Mississippi's HBCUs, Minority Student Enrollment for all years includes all non-African-American students.

[4] 2002 enrollment data adapted from NCES (n.d.) and does not include students for whom race was unknown or non-resident aliens.

TABLE 2   **(Continued)**
Mississippi Institutional Racial Integration Percentages

Public 4-year PWIs

Delta State University	20.43%	30.18%	33.40%	+12.97%
Mississippi State University	17.28%	21.67%	20.90%	+ 3.62%
Mississippi University for Women[5]	18.31%	30.25%	30.00%	+11.69%
Ole Miss	12.23%	18.07%	15.40%	+ 3.17%
University of Southern Mississippi	16.92%	22.55%	27.70%	+ 10.78%

As such, the "ten percent" stipulation represents yet another element of maltreatment perpetrated against Mississippi's public HBCUs. Outside of the fact that it appears to create a quota system similar to that overturned in *Hopwood*, the settlement also requires these same institutions to make themselves more attractive to their under-represented populations while denying them the funds needed to accomplish this goal. The *Ayers* funds are designated to help remedy the lingering vestiges of *de jure* segregation found in Mississippi's HBCUs. Requiring these institutions to remedy this problem *without* these funds perpetuates Mississippi's practice not redressing racially segregated post-secondary education.

Conclusion

The judicial experiences of HBCUs in Alabama, Mississippi and Tennessee clearly demonstrate that the courts do not apply collegiate desegregation mandates to all institutions equally. Recent decisions in *Hopwood*, *Grutter* and other cases have virtually freed PWIs from any specific constitutional obligations to use race-conscious policies to improve college access for students of color. Conversely, the *Geier* and *Ayers* rulings contradict the decisions in cases that directly focused on PWIs by blaming HBCUs for their inability to attract non-African-American students. In this way, the

---

[5] Became co-educational as a result of *Mississippi University for Women v. Hogan*, 458 U.S. 718 (1982) in the Supreme Court ordered the university to start admitting male students.

courts erroneously view and treat HBCUs negatively simply because these institutions generally do not enroll a high proportion of white students.

Moreover, the courts are more likely to favor the use of "radical" remedies to address collegiate desegregation issues at HBCUs than when addressing these same issues at PWIs. Since *Brown*, courts have repeatedly assumed control over elementary and secondary school districts to enforce school desegregation mandates and address other racial issues.[37] On the other hand, the legal history surrounding collegiate desegregation indicates that these same judiciaries are generally reluctant to assume this level of control over post-secondary institutions, choosing to give deference to educational leaders. Nevertheless, the decisions in *Geier* and *Ayers* suggest that courts do not have the same confidence in the administrators of public HBCUs. Rather than require educational experts to assess and address the diversity issues affecting these campuses, courts treat HBCUs more like K-12 school districts by setting specific benchmarks and policies for desegregating these institutions. By treating these institutions as elementary and secondary school districts, judiciaries send the message that HBCUs are more on par with K-12 schools rather than predominantly white colleges and universities.

As Young argues, legal equality does not guarantee practical equality.[38] The equality mandated to HBCUs under the law can only develop if the courts uniformly apply the legal mechanisms and obligations of collegiate desegregation to all institutions in a like manner. If *Grutter* is indeed the prevailing decision regarding race-conscious policies, then HBCUs should suffer no greater obligation to admit non-African-American students than PWIs experience to bring students of color onto their campuses. In the future, rather than punish HBCUs, courts should recognize them for their long-standing history of serving students of color by adopting one standard for collegiate desegregation that may be applied equally to all types of public institutions.

Chapter 7

AN EXAMINATION OF THE STRUGGLE FOR EQUITY IN HIGHER EDUCATION: LITIGATION IN THE *AYERS V. FORDICE* CASE IN MISSISSIPPI

Andrew Ann Dinkins Lee

Black people have to bear the burden for changing conditions in Mississippi.
—Jake Ayers[1]

Walking in the venerable steps of Myrlie Evers, the late Betty Shabazz and Coretta Scott King, Lillie Ayers carries on the legacy of her late husband, Jake Bertram Ayers, the architect of the *Ayers v. Fordice* case. According to Lillie Ayers, it was Emmett Till's brutal murder that spurred her husband into political activism.[2] As a result of this impetus, Ayers joined the *Delta Ministries, The Child Development Group* (the forerunner organization to Head Start in Mississippi) and the *Children Defense Fund* and, subsequently, traveled tirelessly throughout the South to states such as Alabama, Louisiana, Arkansas and Mississippi wherein he had many opportunities to see the inequalities in the public schools, colleges and universities.[3] Stirred by what he saw, Ayers believed he had a personal obligation to help change the system. Operating under the auspices of *Black Mississippi Council on Higher Education*, Ayers, on behalf of his son, Jake Ayers, Jr., and 20 other African-American, "college-bound" students, filed a lawsuit charging the Mississippi system of public higher education of discriminatory practices.

Making a Case for Equity in Higher Education

The *Ayers* suit charged that the Governor of Mississippi, the Board of Trustees of State Institutions of Higher Learning and other state education officials, maintained and perpetuated a racially dual system of public higher education in violation of the Fifth, Ninth, Thirteenth and Fourteenth Amendments and Title VI of the Civil Rights Act of 1964.[4] The plaintiffs believed Mississippi's policies on public higher education represented what Frederick Humphries referred to as "the ultimate symbol of apartheid,"[5] and that this very visible expression of racism was embedded in the very laws and statutes of the state. Indeed, that level of racial divide was most evident in the manner in which the state established the protocol for each of its eight public institutions of higher education. Mississippi's system of four-year universities was formally segregated by race from its inception in 1848 through 1962, when the first black student (James Meredith) was admitted to the University of Mississippi by order of the court (*Meredith v. Fair*).[6] Consistently, each institution was established virtually for the sole purpose of keeping the races separate:[7]

- The University of Mississippi (Ole Miss) was chartered on February 24, 1844 and mandated [to] serve white persons only.
- Alcorn State University (Alcorn Agricultural and Mechanical College), the oldest land-grant college for blacks in the United States (founded in 1830) … was purchased by the state and renamed Alcorn University in 1871, and was designated to serve as an agricultural college for the education of black youth.
- Mississippi State University, in 1878, the legislature established the Mississippi Agricultural and Mechanical College; student enrollment in Mississippi State University was restricted to white persons only by an act of the legislature.
- Mississippi University for Women was established by the legislature in 1884 as the first state-supported college established exclusively for the higher education of "white" women in the United States.
- University of Southern Mississippi was established by an act of the legislature in 1910 and student enrollment was restricted to white persons only.
- Delta State University was established by the Mississippi legislature in 1924. For all intent and purpose, it was established to serve a primary white population.
- Jackson State University was established by an act of the legislature on May 6, 1940 for the purpose of training black teachers for the black public schools of the state.
- Mississippi Valley State University was established in 1946 by the legislature for the purpose of educating teachers primarily

for rural and elementary black schools and to provide training for black students.

As late as the early 1970s, Ayers and others noted that all of the state's public institutions of higher education retained their racial markers. Thus, the plaintiffs argued that the discriminatory manner in which Mississippi funded and operated its three public HBCUs, Jackson State University, Alcorn State University and Mississippi Valley State University, rendered them "markedly inferior" to the other five public universities in the state. Because of this, they reasoned that the state had "an affirmative duty" to provide equity in public higher education to all her citizens, regardless of class or color.[8] Informally, Ayers and others pleaded with the state to correct the problem and only after all efforts failed did Ayers decide to challenge the legality of Mississippi's governance of its eight public institutions of higher learning. Although Ayers and the other plaintiffs held guarded hope that the lawsuit would serve as a vehicle to compel the state to grant immediate injunctive relief for black students in the state's three HBCUs, no such outcome was offered. To the contrary, Mississippi resisted any effort to change the status quo. Consequently, not only did the case fail to move at "all deliberate speed," the *Ayers* case did not make its first substantive appearance in court until 1987, twelve long years after the lawsuit was first filed and one heartbreaking year after the untimely death of Jake Ayers in 1986. All in all, from its earliest arrival to the courts, all the way through to its current legal woes, the *Ayers* case has stalled, stuttered and meandered its way through the legal system for nearly three decades.

Ayers Goes to the U. S. Supreme Court

To begin, some might wonder why the *Ayers* case is so compelling and why it has had such longevity in the courts. First, *Ayers* is compelling because it has the potential to become the second landmark case, after the 1954 *Brown* decision, to move the courts closer to racial justice in education. Second, it has enjoyed a long life in the courts because many of the questions *Brown* posed remain unresolved. Indeed, the discriminatory divide that was exposed in *Brown* is reified in *Ayers*. In fact, Mary Connell contends that the road to *Brown* intersects with the road to *United States v.*

Fordice. In particular, Connell traces the steps that eventually set the stage for *Ayers'* Supreme Court debut:

[I]n 1990, the Fifth Circuit Court of Appeals, sitting en banc in *Ayers v. Allain,* held that the standard set forth in *Bazemore* was the appropriate standard by which to measure the desegregation actions of a state with respect to its public higher education institutions. Siding with *Bazemore,* the Fifth Circuit Court sided with the defendants, the State of Mississippi, and found that the state had done all it was constitutionally required to do to achieve desegregation in all of its eight public universities by adopting 'in good faith racially nondiscriminatory admission policies.'[9]

The persistence of the plaintiffs' refusal to accept the Fifth Circuit Court's decision pushed *Ayers* closer to an appointment with the U. S. Supreme Court. Remarkably, their cause was aided when another circuit court countered the Fifth Circuit Court's decision. Connell points out that the Fifth Circuit Court's preference for *Bazemore* placed its findings in direct conflict with the Sixth Circuit Court's ruling in two other cases, *Geier v. University of Tennessee* and *Geier v. Alexander.* In both of these cases the court sided with the *Green v. County School Board of New Kent County* (1968) decision.[10]

Notwithstanding the merits of the substantive pleadings in *Ayers,* these dueling decisions in the circuit courts forced *Ayers* before the Supreme Court. At issue in *U. S. v. Fordice* was whether the state's affirmative duty to end all vestiges of segregation, established in *Brown* (1954), extended to colleges and universities. Inevitably, the *United States v. Fordice* decision found that the mandate to desegregate did apply to colleges and universities and, arguably more importantly, Mississippi was indeed perpetuating a dual education system. Subsequently, the Court remanded the case back to Judge Neal B. Biggers' district court, the original site of the *Ayers* case, and ordered him to find a remedy for Mississippi's unconstitutional practices. Astonishingly, just as the original lawsuit took twelve years to go to trial, the remanded case once again languished, without meaningful resolution, under Judge Biggers' jurisdiction for another twelve years, despite the Supreme Court's orders. In 2003, Judge Biggers finally proposed a 503 million dollar settlement, citing the need to *avoid* lengthy litigation and mounting costs to the taxpayers.[11] What was expected to be the culmination of a bitterly fought case and a pinnacle victory for Judge Biggers detoured once again into another round of litigation. In short, although some of the plaintiffs agreed to the settlement, many contested both the manner in which the settlement was reached and the stipulations of the settlement.

Most noticeably, Lillie Ayers, Jake Ayers' widow, along with others did not accept the settlement in part because they believed it catered too much to the needs of white students. Namely, as a condition of accepting the settlement, the plaintiffs would have to agree to 1) raise admission requirements which could negatively impact the number of black students entering Mississippi's three HBCUs and 2) increase the number of white students enrolled in each HBCU by 10% of the total enrollment, a heavy burden for HBCUs.[12] This level of concession was unacceptable to Lillie Ayers and fellow plaintiffs because, for them, what is at stake is not whether white students mingle with black students but rather whether African-American students enjoy **equal access** to a quality education. To this end, the plaintiffs were certain; the case centered on the question of justice, not just *bricks and mortar.*

The Dilemma

The quest for equity in public higher education within the legal system has presented the plaintiffs in *Ayers* with an unforeseen challenge. Although the courts heralded a change in educational policy, based upon *Brown,* the Civil Rights Act of 1964, and other affirmative-action strategies, the very real possibility that Mississippi's three HBCUs may face mergers or closure haunts the *Ayers* case. Many HBCUs, like Jackson State, Alcorn and Mississippi Valley, face a critical dilemma because the interpretations of "remedial measures" for past discriminatory practices were left to the courts. Regrettably, instead of designing remedies which would address equity and past discrimination, the courts construed injunctive relief into the flawed principle of desegregation. The courts' focus on the latter, without a doubt, circumvented any chance that cases, such as *Ayers,* would realize equity in the truest sense of the word. Tate, Ladson-Billings and Grant argue that "the shortcoming in *Brown* [and inferentially in *Ayers*] is that the court proposed an essentially mathematical solution to a socio-political problem."[13] Unquestionably, as the authors further note, "the ability to transform a mathematical interpretation of equality into social reality has not been realized."[14]

In the same way, Ivory Phillips, President of the *Mississippi Coalition on Black Higher Education*, maintains that the real problem with the *Ayers* case is that District Court Judge Neal Biggers misconstrued the *Ayers* case into a classic *desegregation* case.[15] Contrary to the judge's position, Phillips asserts that Jake Ayers and other plaintiffs never claimed desegregation as their primary focus; instead, they filed the lawsuit in 1975 to compel the state to provide black students with equal access to a quality education in the state's three HBCUs. Phillips contends that any attempt to forecast the case in any other light clearly marks an intentional diversion. In other words, the courts' misrepresentation of the case appears to forecast the socially constructed–engineered–demise of HBCUs, in the name of desegregation.

Unmistakably, Wilton E. Blake admonishes that while it was racism that created the need for HBCUs, if left unchecked, racism will destroy them.[16] Blake's warning calls attention to a disturbing trend. That is, one of the most controversial issues surrounding the question of equity is that plaintiffs of color have invariably undermined the survival of their own institutions of higher learning because they are asked to take a fatalistic approach to advance their cause. Like Phillips and Blake, Darryll Jones questions the presence of "racial considerations" in the context of the educational process. In effect, Jones argues that in order to receive resources from the state, HBCUs were placed in a precarious position because they had to proclaim themselves as obsolete or inferior.[17] Frederick Humphries cautions that the perception of inferiority served as the "hidden frame of reference" in *Ayers* and was used to justify the states, plan to close its HBCUs.[18] Moreover, Humphries contends efforts to achieve desegregation and receive funding allowed "access to white colleges [to become] the defining factor in desegregation cases."[19] Indeed, the quest for proximity to whites as opposed to equity continues to be the Achilles' heel of *Brown* and its related cases. After all, it is not difficult to see that this is the case.

Based upon research findings and critical observations delineated in seminal discourses, such as Cornel West's *Race Matters*, William Bowen and Derek Bok's *The Shape of the River*, James T. Patterson's *Brown v. Board of Education*, the Supreme Court's ruling in *Grutter v. Bollinger* and Gary Orfield and Chungmei Lee's *"Brown at 50: King's Dream or Plessy's Nightmare?,"* a report associated with The Civil Rights Project at Harvard University, each with implications related to the *Brown* decision, it is without question, safe to say that fifty years since the landmark *Brown* decision, African-Americans have not, in large measure, realized equity in higher education.[20] The theme running through virtually all of these critical texts and reports is that equity is still an elusive enterprise. For example, although Bowen and Bok document the success of affirmative action when it comes to increasing minority presence in selective colleges and universities and in the professorate, the necessity for this research suggests continuing disparity in education. Still further, Orfield and Lee's findings point to the eroding gains of *Brown*, primarily because of white flight from public schools which, in turn, creates disparity in education. Moreover, James T. Patterson maintains even though *Brown* struck down a "formidable edifice of racial discrimination in the United States… the complicated issues that *Brown I* tried to resolve in 1954 still torment Americans half a century later."[21]

Interestingly, Mississippi continues to engage in widespread discriminatory practices in higher education, blatantly ignoring the Supreme Court's mandate to remedy the vestiges of discrimination.[22] This lack of adherence to the law gives cause for the plaintiffs in *Ayers* to question the capability of the courts to provide equity in higher education to millions of African-Americans. This is a critical point because, for the plaintiffs, equity encompasses also the question of redress. Even so, such questions as equity and redress are unlikely to receive the attention of the courts. In the latter instance, Elaine R. Jones, former head of the NAACP Legal Defense Fund, notes that the courts have not been receptive to the question of redress. According to Jones, in addition to the historical hesitancy to resolve the issue of redress, recent court decisions have "made it more difficult to implement programs and policies designed to remedy the effects of past discrimination and its aftermath"[23] Even in the face of such long odds in the courts, some of the plaintiffs in the *Ayers* case remain undaunted because they believe unequivocally the courts have some unfinished business.

Conclusion

Despite its unfortunate dilemma of being mired in the throes of a desegregation case, *Ayers'* trajectory encompasses an unavoidable confrontation with the legal system on the question of equity and redress. Indeed, the questions *Brown* put before the courts in 1954 weigh heavily in the *Ayers* case. For this reason, *Ayers* holds much promise in its potential to veer the courts back to these fundamental issues raised in *Brown:* 1) How can race be eliminated from the educational policy? 2) When will the courts transcend *Plessy?* 3) How should state, regional and federal courts mete out justice for generational discrimination against black students? The absence of resolution disturbs the consciousness of a proud democratic society that guarantees equal protection under the law.

While the courts carry on with their mantras, in Pollyanna-like fashion, about the need to end segregation in higher education, the plaintiffs in *Ayers* must struggle mightily to advance the inalienable rights of the disenfranchised. They must heed Jake Ayers' admonition to black people in Mississippi: They must bear the burden for changing their conditions. In order to be successful, the plaintiffs in *Ayers* will need to redefine the case in their own terms—under a new banner. They will need to cast off the labels of desegregation and affirmative action to assist the courts to see the case anew and to reach a very different conclusion than heretofore. The elusive pursuit of equity in higher education must not prevail. Most, emphatically, *Ayers* cannot and must not fail in its *indefatigable* quest to compel the courts to answer *Brown* fifty years later.

Chapter 8

THE IMPACT OF *BROWN V. BOARD OF EDUCATION* ON COLLEGES IN TENNESSEE: THE TRAGEDY OF A DREAM DEFERRED

Amiri Yasin Al-Hadid

There are very salient and powerful questions that must be addressed as the courts, legislative bodies and administrators of HBCUs continue to fulfill the progressive intent and legacy of *Brown v. Board of Education.* Should the same court orders and public policies used to *desegregate* predominantly white public institutions of higher education also be used to *dismantle* the predominantly black HBCUs? Should the same model of desegregation employed at the predominantly white colleges be used at the HBCUs? Or should a different model be employed? What role should African-American culture play in the structuring of the general education core curriculum and the major core of each department, program and discipline at the HBCUs?

In spite of the limited funding and resources, the HBCUs managed to educate generations of African-American intellectuals, scholars and professionals. They have made an enormous contribution to the entry of millions of African-Americans into the American middle class. They never had an official policy or practice of discrimination or segregation against non-African-Americans. As a matter of fact, HBCUs welcomed all qualified students, faculty, administrators and staff without prejudicial regard for their color, ethnicity, gender, language, nationality or race. Some HBCUs had an "other-race" presence during the days of Jim Crow. If this is the case, and indeed it is, why should the cultural identity and predominantly African-American status quo of these institutions be changed by federal courts and state governments?

Ultimately, the question for justice as an artifact of history is, do HBCUs have a right to maintain their predominantly African-American status? Or should they surrender to the white power structure and be transformed into predominantly white HBCUs?

Martin Luther King, Jr., a proud graduate of Morehouse College, addressed the issue from this perspective:

There is no contradiction in believing in integration and supporting the Negro College Fund. You must remember that although Negro colleges are by and large *segregated institutions [emphasis added]*, they are not *segregating institutions [emphasis added]*. If these colleges are properly supported they will serve in an integrated society. Many of these colleges already have white students. It is not true to feel that as soon as integration becomes a thoroughgoing reality, the so-called Negro private colleges will close down. In supporting these Negro colleges we are only seeking to make sure that the quality and caliber of these schools are of such nature that they will be appealing to all people.[1]

King's Affirmation of HBCUs Applied to Both Segregated and Integrated Society.

However, the dominant thrust of many of the court cases that seek to "desegregate" the HBCUs are really trying to force them to demographically mirror a predominantly white society. In other words, the HBCUs should become "racially non-identifiable" and have no cultural identity, dignity or historical traditions. Thus, desegregation becomes the negation of African-American culture, history, identity, thought and values; and the affirmation of white culture, history, thought and values.

Some conservative African-Americans assert that, "black colleges will always be HBCUs." What they mean in their wishful thinking is, African-Americans should be consoled by the fact that, no matter what happens to black colleges in the present and the foreseeable future, they shall always be known in the annals of history as "black colleges." Therefore, white students, teachers, administrators and staff can be given as much authority, privilege and power as the courts mandate at HBCUs; this legal engineering can never eliminate the culture and history of the HBCUs. Hence, African-American students, faculty, administrators, staff and alumni of HBCUs should not resist court ordered desegregation of their beloved institutions. "The world is changing" and they must adapt and have no anxiety, fear or grief; in time, the transformed HBCUs will be better institutions because they will have more money and resources to develop their departments, programs, buildings and facilities.

On the other side of the great debate many defenders see these institutions as a case of "arrested development." From their very inception, these institutions were underfunded, marginally supported and expected to fail. The defenders of HBCUs have come to link their future existence, growth and development with the case for reparations for centuries of chattel slavery and colonization. The essential argument is African-Americans were not given their promised "forty acres and a mule" after the end of chattel slavery. Therefore, the creation of the HBCUs by Southern states, certain border states, missionaries and philanthropists is fundamentally a down payment on reparations. Given this line of argument, it is historically just and culturally fair for the HBCUs to maintain their predominantly African-American status in perpetuity. For it is more than obvious that institutionalized racism, which in reality is a form of colonization, is not likely to disappear and give birth to a culture and society that measures up to Dr. Martin Luther King, Jr.'s dream.

King clearly understood the dialectical relationships between education and legislation as instruments of social change. He stated:

> Through education, we seek to change attitudes; through legislation and court orders, we seek to regulate behavior. Through education, we seek to change internal feelings (prejudice, hate, etc.); through legislation and court orders, we seek to control the external effects of those feelings. Through education, we seek to break down the spiritual barriers to integration; through legislation and court orders, we seek to break down the physical barriers to integration. One method is not a substitute for the other, but a meaningful and necessary supplement.[2]

Ideally, a color-blind and not a color-conscious society, will produce a nation that can see, feel, think and work in a world where differences of color, ethnicity, gender, language and nationality do not give rise to prejudice, discrimination and violence. America is fundamentally a multi-ethnic democracy striving to create one people out of the strengths of her cultural and ethnic diversity.

The Great Debate of the Curriculum at HBCUs

HBCUs were established to provide an educational experience that would help the descendants of African slaves make the transition from the impediment of human bondage to the bounties of human freedom. In this regard, these institutions had to first teach literacy because it was illegal for African slaves to learn the skills of reading, mathematics and writing during the period of their enslavement from 1619-1865 in the United States of America. Once this objective was achieved then they could matriculate in a curriculum that was designed to give them marketable skills in an economy and labor force that was defined by industrial capitalism. In order to craft a curriculum that would meet the needs of the labor force, a great debate took place in the early stages of the development of African-American colleges.

The issue was whether the curriculum should be based on the liberal arts or industrial education. W.E.B. DuBois eloquently presented the case for a liberal arts education in *The Souls of Black Folk*.[3] Booker T. Washington presented the case for industrial education in *Up From Slavery*.[4] As these two philosophies engaged in dialectical debate, the private colleges came to adopt the liberal arts philosophy espoused by DuBois and the public colleges came to adopt the industrial education model espoused by Washington because they were primarily land-grant colleges created by the 1890 Morrill Act.

What both men failed to realize is that they were both right. DuBois' liberal arts philosophy was designed to produce what he called a Talented Tenth that would provide race leadership in the professions of business, education, law, politics and religion.[5] A closer and less critical examination of Washington's philosophy will reveal a type of economic nationalism based on self-sufficiency. DuBois' philosophy was congruent with the aim and goals of the National Association for the Advancement of Colored People (NAACP) of which he was a founding member. Washington's philosophy was more compatible with the Universal Negro Improvement Association (UNIA) led by Marcus Garvey.

A careful reading of W.E.B. DuBois' *Black Reconstruction*[6] suggests that after emancipation African-Americans shifted from chattel slavery to colonization. Moreover, this colonization persisted from 1865-1965; from the Emancipation Proclamation to the 1965 Voting Rights Act. So in a certain way, African-American colleges and universities have been engaged in an academic process of de-colonizing the minds, bodies and souls of African descendants in the African-American region of the African Diaspora. Implicit in the general philosophy of African-American education are the ideals of democracy, equality, freedom and justice. Historically, HBCUs were established based on an assimilation model. Rather than restoring the African prisoners of war back to the cultures, religions, names and nationalities that their ancestors bequeath them, the vast majority of these Africans, willingly or unwillingly, chose to make "America their home" away from their homeland. Albeit "strangers in a strange land," "a long ways from home" assimilation into the post-Antebellum American society appeared to be an option. Especially since the American government offered restitution in the form of the 13th,14th and 15th Amendments. Never mind the economic fact that America reneged on the promissory note of forty acres and a mule, which would have given the liberated prisoners of war or chattel slaves some land and the ability to cultivate that land for food, clothing and shelter, which in time would have set the stage for the possibility of economic self-sufficiency and self-determination.

While most Africans settled for the possibilities of assimilation into the American society and culture, a small number of the captives decided to return to Sierra Leone after the American Revolutionary War (1775-1783), and another small group decided to return to Liberia before and after the American Civil War (1861-1865). In their efforts to build Liberia and Sierra Leone, African-American colleges were also established in these colonial territories. Accounts of how formal American slaves helped to build the educational systems can be found in the works of Edward Wilmot Blyden and Alexander Crummel.

The typical curriculum at an HBCU is almost identical to the curriculum at the PWI. African-American culture finds it most fully articulated expressions in extracurricular activities such as theater, concerts, dance, lectures by famous African-Americans, Black History Month programs; Homecoming activities, Step Shows, pledging Black Greek-Lettered organizations, Martin Luther King, Jr.'s Birthday observances and other celebratory and episodic events. It is extremely rare to find African-American culture, history, thought and values canonized in the general education core curriculum at HBCUs as required courses. It is atypical to find departments at the HBCUs that have African-centered courses required in the major core of their discipline. Moreover, a number of HBCUs, such as Clark Atlanta, Florida A & M, Grambling State, Morgan State, Morehouse and Tennessee State Universities have degree granting departments/programs in Africana/African-American Studies. If education is the inter-generation transmission of culture, then the 117 HBCUs should be the world's leading transmitters of African and African-American culture. Otherwise, it will be extremely difficult for African-Americans to overcome the barrier of cultural dislocation and historical amnesia. At most HBCUs, when African-centered courses exist, they are usually taught in the traditional departments such as art, English, history, music, philosophy, political science and sociology as electives rather than required courses in the general education or core curriculum.

Given this unfortunate state of affairs, it seems as though the Africana Studies departments and movement have discovered a culturally relevant liberal arts curriculum that is worthy of serious study by the leadership of the HBCUs.[7] As long as the assimilation/integration paradigm continues to dominate the purpose, mission, curriculum and thought patterns of administrators, faculty and students, it shall become increasingly more difficult for the HBCUs to compete in the global marketplace. The paradigm has already shifted from "race relations" to ethnic relations. As the cultural, economic, political and social fabric of the American society increasingly comes to be defined by its multi-cultural heterogeneity, it is very important for the national African-American community to take its rightful place in the new paradigm and configuration of the emerging American society. The HBCUs must adapt to these new contingencies in the academic, cultural, economic, political and social environments.

The Brain and Talent Drain

In 1950, approximately 90 percent of African-Americans enrolled in college were educated at the HBCUs.[8] This enrollment pattern changed dramatically after the assassination of Dr. King on April 4, 1968 and the creation of Black Studies Programs and Black Cultural Centers at the PWIs in the 1960s and 1970s. These concomitant events stimulated desegregation activities at the PWIs and accelerated the migration of African-American students, faculty, administrators and staff to the PWIs. As African-American enrollments increased at the PWIs, the national percentage of African-Americans enrolled at the HBCUs decreased. It is significant to note that the absolute number of African-Americans enrolled at the HBCUs has increased over the period from 1950 to 2004, however, the percentage has decreased from 90 percent in 1950 to about 18 percent in 2004.

As early as 1968, scholars suggested that HBCUs were experiencing a "brain and talent drain." Scholars at the HBCUs were lured to the PWIs by offers of higher salaries, lower teaching loads, opportunities to conduct funded research and publish books and articles in scholarly journals. In contrast, it is extremely difficult to engage in scholarly activities at the HBCUs because of the heavy teaching loads.[9] Also, many students come to the HBCUs from high schools that did not adequately prepare them for the rigorous demands of college-level education. Therefore, remedial education and mentoring on the part of professors and designated staff consume a lot of time, energy and resources. (This underscores the fact that busing and desegregation have not significantly improved the academic skills of African-Americans, a problem that *Brown v. Board of Education* intended to eradicate.) As such, professors cannot fully engage in the intellectual mode of production through research and publication. When professors are fortunate to secure research grants their salaries do not significantly change nor do their departments fully benefit from the influx of new revenue streams. Most of the funds are consumed by indirect cost and the university sees grant money as another form of fund-raising for the institution.

With so many structurally induced constraints on scholarly productivity, it becomes fairly easy for the PWIs to entice talented professors and students to leave the HBCUs and join the PWIs. Similarly, lucrative scholarships for students and athletes provide incentives to lure them to the PWIs. In reality, the HBCUs cannot compete with the offers that are being made by the PWIs. The brain and talent drain on the HBCUs are directly related to the impact of *Brown v. Board of Education* on higher education, particularly with efforts to desegregate and diversify the composition of the student body, faculty, administrators and staff.

Tragedy of a Dream Deferred: Two Case Studies

HBCUs are currently being desegregated and merged out of cultural and historical existence. This miscarriage of justice is occasioned by the racist and reactionary interpretations and application of legal statutes and legislation. Rather than interpreting the laws to grant reparations to African-Americans, it is easier for legal institutions, governing boards administrators to operate within an a historical existential framework. By so doing, historical justice is jettisoned into suspended animation and mergers, stipulations of settlements and consent decrees become hallow substitute for moral justice. Dr. King recognized and defined two types of laws: just laws and unjust laws. According to King, "Any law that uplifts human personality is just. Any law that degrades human personality is unjust. All segregation statues are unjust because segregation distorts the soul and damages the personality. It gives the segregator a false sense of superiority, and the segregated a false sense of inferiority."[10] The strategies and tactics used to desegregate HBCUs have been blatantly unjust. In reality, many actions against HBCUs have been hostile attempts to transform them into white institutions.

This observation shall be demonstrated by a brief analysis of two cases in point: (1) Bluefield State, an HBCU that is now a predominantly white institution; and (2) Tennessee State University, an HBCU that merged with University of Tennessee at Nashville, a predominantly white institution, under its authority and name. These two desegregation outcomes exist at polar opposite on the continuum of HBCU desegregation. Bluefield State represents the dream denied and Tennessee State represents the dream deferred.

Case # I: Bluefield State College

Bluefield State College was founded in 1895 in Bluefield, West Virginia; the same year that Booker T. Washington gave his Atlanta Exposition Speech and one year before the Supreme Court ruling in the *Plessy v. Ferguson* case. This area of the country is known for its coal mines and many of the early students were the sons and daughters of coal miners. In the glorious years of BSU, white veterans attended the college on the G.I. Bill. In this respect, Bluefield State was ahead of the *Brown v. Board* decision, which would accelerate the desegregation process in higher education. Dr.

Albert L. Walker, current president of Bluefield State, explained the problem at BSU in this context: "When the coal mining started to decline, families started to migrate from Bluefield and the enrollment at BSU declined dramatically.[11] For example, in 1964 the enrollment was as low as 609.[12] This dramatic decline in enrollment caused state officials to assess the future of the college. The issue was whether to close the college or keep it open and try to develop it.

Cox, Gentry and Spence suggested a correlation between *Brown v. Board of Education* and the declining enrollment at Bluefield State. "As was the case with many black colleges, the Supreme Court ruling began a new difficult era for Bluefield State as it struggled to maintain a quality program for its clientele. Two primary factors had a significant influence on what many term the decline of Bluefield State. First, new opportunities were opened to black students as formerly restricted colleges and universities began not only to accept qualified blacks, but actively recruit them. Further, this recruitment did not end at the student level; qualified black teachers were likewise lured away from black institutions."[13] This was the beginning of the "brain and talent drain" from the HBCUs to the PWIs.

At West Virginia State College, the impact of *Brown v. Board of Education* was slightly different, but the net result for African-Americans was the same. The 1996-97 catalog reports an increase in total enrollment due to *Brown* and a decline in the percentage of African-Americans:

> In 1954, when the U.S. Supreme Court in *Brown v. Board of Education* ruled that segregated schools were unconstitutional West Virginia State College had an enrollment of 837 students. Within the next few years, the enrollment increased dramatically and West Virginia State College was transformed to a racially integrated institution. It gained nationwide recognition as a "living laboratory of human relations." [14]

Today, with an enrollment of about 5,000 students, the college maintains its reputation of academic excellence. It continues to be known as a model for human relations with a student body that averages about 88% white, 11.5% black and .5% Asian, Hispanic and others."[15] While the total enrollment increased, the percentage of African-Americans declined to 11.5%. In 1964, ten years after *Brown v. Board of Education*, the college was predominantly African-American with a student enrollment of 2,636.[16]

Case #II: Tennessee State University

Tennessee State University was founded on June 19, 1912. It is an HBCU by virtue of the fact that it was created by the 1890 Morrill Act, which established land-grant colleges for African-Americans. Also, the university came about as a result of a 1909 Act of the Tennessee General Assembly. Today, TSU defines herself as a comprehensive urban land-grant university.[17] The university has an enrollment of about 10,000 students. Undergraduate enrollment is approximately 81 percent African-American and 16 percent Caucasian. Graduate enrollment is 49 percent African-American and 42 percent Caucasian.[18] These statistics demonstrate the impact of *Brown* on TSU.

In 1964, Tennessee State University was predominantly African-American with an enrollment of 4,200 students.[19] Four years later in 1968, the history of Tennessee State University would start moving in a different direction. Dr King was assassinated in Memphis, Tennessee in 1968. He came to Memphis to support the efforts of the sanitation workers, who were predominantly African-American, to form a union and improve their salaries and working conditions. The University of Tennessee established a campus in Nashville, which came into sharp competition with TSU for white students. At San Francisco State University and other predominantly white universities, African-American students were waging a protracted struggle to establish Black Studies programs, Black Cultural centers, increase the enrollment of black students and the number of black faculty and administrators. This parallel development would advance the cause of civil rights and increase African-American representation at the PWIs. The victories won by African-American students to increase their numbers at the PWIs would precipitate collateral damage at the HBCUs in the form of the "brain and talent drain." This is why today the 117 HBCUs educate only 18% of African-Americans in colleges and universities as indicated above.

Nashville, the capital of Tennessee, is the home of four HBCUs, American Baptist College, Fisk University, Meharry Medical College and Tennessee State University. TSU was under a federal court order to create a white presence. However, this was difficult with the University of Tennessee at Nashville being in the same city. Similarly, UTN was expected to have a black presence. Both state institutions were unable to meet their goals of an "other race" presence. The issue went to court and Judge Frank T. Gray put forward a proposition that would become the legal driving force behind the efforts to desegregate TSU. He said the "heart of the matter of eliminate[ing] the dual system of higher education in the state of Tennessee is the existence of *black Tennessee State University*" [*emphasis added*]. He subsequently ordered the two universities to merge under Tennessee State University's name. This was the first time in American history that a predominantly black university had disenfranchised a white university and incorporated all of its buildings, facilities and assets.[20] At the time of the merger in 1977, there were 5,000 white students at UTN and 5,000 students at TSU. If the white students had remained stationary, the merged institution would have had 10,000 students. As expected, there was "white flight," about 2,000 students, which reduced the student body to 8,000.

Faculty, administrators and staff from UTN were offered jobs at the new TSU. As incentives to prevent "white flight" in the ranks of faculty, administrators and staff from the former UTN, employees were given tenure, increases in rank and salary raises. This, of course, did not go well with the African-American faculty, staff and administrators because their salaries were already among the lowest in the state of Tennessee. This obvious discrimination, in the name of desegregation, was resented by the faculty (black, brown, red, yellow and white) already at TSU.

In a short period of time, some former UTN faculty went back to court and alleged that TSU was becoming "resegregated" because each freshman class remained predominantly African-American. The federal court granted these faculty persons plaintiff-intervener status in the ongoing case. However, the court refused to grant the same status to the TSU Alumni Association, which obviously had a compelling interest in the outcome of the court litigations. The allegation was not proven in court, however, Judge Thomas Wiseman negotiated a Stipulation of Settlement in 1984 and ordered TSU to become 50 percent white and 50 percent black by 1993.[21] During the Stipulation of Settlement period, the administration at TSU was given strict orders by the Tennessee

Board of Regents (TBR) not to project the image of TSU as a black university. TSU must be presented to the public as a "racially non-identifiable" university. The court order was so absurd that Miss Tennessee State University was not permitted to be featured in *Ebony* magazine in the annual The Black College Queens issue. Miss TSU retained a lawyer to protest the injustice and her right to be featured as a Black College Queen in *Ebony* magazine was quickly reinstated.

The 50:50 black/white quota unfairly imposed on TSU was not met. Nor were the quotas stipulated for the state's other PWIs under the jurisdiction of the Tennessee State Board of Regents. Their quotas ranged from 6 to 15 percent. None of them reflected the sociological fact that African-Americans comprise about 20 percent of the population in the state of Tennessee. In the Memphis area, African-Americans are more than 20 percent of Shelby County, however, the University of Memphis was not ordered to become 20 percent African-American. Consequently, the issue was taken back to court. And a third ruling was decreed.

In the third round of litigation the quotas were eliminated, and a Consent Decree was agreed upon on by all parties on January 4, 2000. The Consent Decree targets improvements in the infrastructure of TSU such as funding, buildings and facilities. However, the goal of making TSU a PWI is still a real possibility. White students are given minority scholarships from high school with a 2.4 grade point average. The counterpart to the minority scholarship does not exist for African-American students at the PWIs.

Jeffrey Lehman provides an excellent summation of the cases that were cited and analyzed:

> The racial composition of some African-American colleges has changed dramatically; some of these colleges now have a predominantly white student body. Mandated by court orders to raise its white population to 50 percent, the enrollment at Tennessee State University in 1998 was about 30 percent white. Those historically African-American institutions with predominantly white enrollments by 1998 are Lincoln University in Missouri (72 percent white) Bluefield State College in West Virginia (89 percent

white), and West Virginia State University (85 percent white).[22]

Indeed, these statistics represent the tragedy of a dream deferred.

Lehman's research reveals some more enlightening data on HBCUs:
> In 1964, over 51 percent of all African-Americans in college were still enrolled in historically African-American colleges and universities. By 1970, the proportion was 28 percent; 16.5 percent by the fall of 1978 and 6.2 percent by 1998. Yet despite the decline in percentages, as recently as 1999-2000, 24 percent of all African-Americans received baccalaureate degrees earned at HBCUs.[23]
>
> Clearly, HBCUs are still having a significant impact on the production of baccalaureate degrees among African-Americans nationwide.

Canon, Curriculum and Paradigm

In his famous poem, *"Harlem,"* Langston Hughes raised a rhetorical question that speaks clearly to the arduous struggle of historically African-American colleges and universities. "What happens to a dream deferred? Does it dry up like a raisin in the sun? Or fester like a sore—and then run? Does it stink like rotten meat? Or crust and sugar over—like a syrupy sweet? Maybe it just sags like a heavy load. Or does it explode?"[24] Some HBCUs are more than one hundred years old. Others, if they are not desegregated out of cultural and demographic existence, or bankrupted, will hopefully celebrate their centennial anniversary in the 21st century. HBCUs have accomplished miracles under the tyranny of institutionalized white supremacy with limited funds, facilities, buildings and resources. And now that Kwanzaa (harvest of the fruit of our collective labor) is fast at hand, it is either too late or too soon to celebrate the marvelous accomplishments that the ancestors (faculty, students, administrators and staff) accomplished through culture, knowledge and skills motivated and driven by enormous sacrifice.

Charles J. Ogletree, Jr. makes a strong case along these lines:
There has been no clearer example of the
failure to ensure equal educational facilities than
the treatment of Historically Black Colleges and
Universities (HBCUs). Of the 103 currently
existing HBCUs, it was reported in 2003,
"fifteen percent are on warning or probation
status with accreditation agencies. Many can
barely meet their payrolls. Two–Morris Brown
in Atlanta and Mary Holmes College in West
Point, Mississippi–have lost their accreditation... In *United States v. Fordice*, the court found
that Mississippi continued to discriminate
against HBCUs in such areas as admission
standards and that such discrimination was
traceable to the *de jure* segregation of the Jim
Crow era."[25]

Thurgood Marshall, a graduate of two HBCUs: Lincoln University
and Howard University Law School, and his associates never
intended for HBCUs to be culturally and demographically disman-
tled by the legal branches and permutations of *Brown v. Board of
Education*. However, the white power structure strongly believes
that the transformation of predominantly black institutions into
predominantly white institutions is the most practical, equitable and
just remedy to the complex cultural, economic, political and social
problems created by the vestiges of chattel slavery and the dual
system of higher education. However, when one looks at the racist
and reactionary legal and political battles that are being fought to
circumvent affirmative action at the PWIs, it becomes clear what
will happen if African-American colleges and universities became
predominantly white HBCUs. On a more concrete level, when one
examines the cases of Bluefield State and West Virginia State, the
stark reality of what happens when an HBCU is transformed into
a PWI becomes crystal clear. African-Americans need more access
to higher education and not less. The HBCUs represent a safety net
for those students, faculty and administrators that are locked out
of the PWIs because of the stiff resistance to affirmative action.

Now is not the time to surrender HBCUs to the hypocrisy of
desegregation and diversity. Now is the time to shift the cultural

paradigm of these precious institutions of higher education and make them African-centered. The mission statement for the HBCUs in the 21st century and beyond should be economic self-sufficiency and self-reliance. Booker T. Washington had the right infrastructure, but the wrong superstructure. W.E.B. DuBois had the right superstructure, but the wrong infrastructure. The synthesis of the thesis of Washington and the antithesis of DuBois seems to be the final solution to the de-colonization of the African-American community in the 21st century.

We currently have 117 HBCUs and they are the only institutions in America where African-Americans truly can get affirmative action, simply because we have the permission, authority and power to affirm ourselves. It is not a case of making HBCUs equal to PWIs by using legal and political strategies of desegregation and integration. Simply put, the case for the continued existence of predominantly African-American colleges and universities is one of reparations. In point of historical fact (the mother of justice), the creation of HBCUs by the Freedmen's Bureau, missionaries, philanthropists and state governments was but a down payment on reparations. Now is the time to collect the unpaid balance by demanding adequate resources from state, public and private institutions that clearly benefitted from the enslavement and colonization of millions of Africans.

Chapter 9

THE IMPACT OF *BROWN* ON PUBLIC HBCUS: A NORTH CAROLINA CASE STUDY

Mickey L. Burnim

With more public HBCUs than any other state, North Carolina was one of the original *Adams v. Richardson* states. Through its subsequent legal entanglements with the federal government, North Carolina became an early example of the impact of the *Brown* decision. Using available data from the University of North Carolina system and interviews of a number of persons who played key roles in the changes to the state's higher education policies, this chapter will examine the changing role of HBCUs as a result of *Brown*. Further, I will discuss the impact of the decision on resource allocation decisions of the public HBCUs and explore the future of such institutions. Questions to be addressed will include the changing characteristics of the student body, the faculty and the operating procedures (particularly with respect to recruitment and enrollment management practices).

Since 1972, the University of North Carolina has been comprised of sixteen public constituent institutions, including five HBCUs–Elizabeth City State University (ECSU), Fayetteville State University (FSU), North Carolina Agricultural & Technical State University (NCA&T), North Carolina Central University (NCCU) and Winston-Salem State University (WSSU). With its five public HBCUs in a higher education system that had evolved from a foundation of segregation, North Carolina became one of the targets of the *Adams v. Richardson* lawsuit that was filed by the NAACP Legal Defense and Educational Fund in 1970. In the lawsuit, the plaintiffs charged the U.S. Department of Health, Education and Welfare (HEW) with failing to enforce Title VI of the 1964 Civil Rights Act against "states that operated dual segregated public systems of higher education."[1] The *Adams* case continued for almost ten years before North Carolina's higher education history took a different turn.

In March of 1979, the Office of Civil Rights (OCR) within HEW filed a lawsuit contending that the University of North

Carolina[2] had failed to eliminate vestiges of its *de jure* segregation era. Subsequently, in April of 1979, the state of North Carolina filed a lawsuit against the U.S. Department of Education to enjoin the federal government from discontinuing its federal financial assistance. These matters were settled with the two parties signing a *Consent Decree*[3] in 1981 after eleven years of disagreement. Through the provisions of the *Consent Decree* for enhancing the HBCUs and increasing their enrollment of white students, the foundation was laid for the growth and development of these institutions over the ensuing twenty years.

The *Consent Decree* covered a five-year period and contained two sections of commitments. Section VI contained commitments to increase minority presence enrollment and employment where "minority presence" meant African-Americans in the PWIs and whites in the HBCUs. Execution of the commitments in this section by the HBCUs led to changes in their student recruitment practices and, arguably, marked the beginning of the dramatic transformation to today's enrollment management procedures. New recruitment publications were developed and distributed, closer relationships were forged with the state's public schools through workshops for their guidance and counseling staffs, and extensive high school visitation programs were established. Additionally, each HBCU was required to employ a white recruiter to help recruit white students. Likewise, each PWI was required to employ African-American recruiters to help recruit African-American students. These and numerous other provisions in this section of the decree defined the path that higher education desegregation efforts in North Carolina would take.

Section VII of the *Consent Decree* described the commitments made for the further development of North Carolina's public HBCUs. These commitments included equitable state funding for operations, financial support for capital improvements, professional development for faculty and administrators, and new degree programs.

These commitments and the other terms of the *Consent Decree* were honored and, upon its expiration in 1986, the UNC system unilaterally decided to continue to abide by its provisions for another five-year period. By 1991, then, North Carolina's public HBCUs had ten years of experience in modern student recruitment practices, more equitable state funding and qualitative improvements in their faculties, administrations and facilities.

Viewpoints from Some Key Participants

Sometimes the full story of a significant occurrence cannot be told with numbers alone. Eyewitness accounts and impressions from the people involved can often be quite revealing and insightful. Accordingly, the author has recently interviewed several persons who were present and involved in the North Carolina desegregation effort in very significant ways. Some of their words, thoughts and recollections are recounted below.

President William C. Friday.[4] William C. Friday served as president of the University of North Carolina from 1956 until 1986. After the North Carolina General Assembly made all sixteen public institutions of higher education in North Carolina constituent institutions of the University of North Carolina in 1971 the heads (chancellors) of these institutions, including those of the five HBCUs, reported to him. President Friday was perhaps the central figure in the long years of contention leading up to the signing of the *Consent Decree* and through its first five-year run.

President Friday believes that the *Brown* decision expedited what was going to happen anyway. In his view, the decision "changed the culture of the South." His intent was to strengthen the HBCUs by enhancing their quality and thereby make them more attractive to all students. He and his administration sought to broaden the curricular offerings at the HBCUs, particularly in the arts and sciences. Another part of the enhancement strategy was to place new attractive programs on the HBCU campuses. One example was the evening law program at North Carolina Central University at the time when five other institutions in the system wanted law schools. In President Friday's view, these qualitative improvements helped to counteract what could have been a very serious "brain drain" for the HBCUs. He did not see any crippling migration of the HBCUs' traditional clientele to the PWIs.

President Friday also recalled that there was little raiding of HBCU African-American faculty members by the PWIs in the system. Though he did remember one instance of a faculty member being hired away from an HBCU in another state, within the university system there was great sensitivity to the harm and ill will that this could create. Collaboration across institutions such as the exchange of faculty in some departments, or joint appointments in the NCCU and UNC-Chapel Hill law schools was more the rule.

Dr. Raymond H. Dawson.[5] Dr. Raymond H. Dawson served as the senior vice president and vice president for the University of North Carolina from the early 1970s until the mid-1980s. His perspective on the impact of the *Brown decision* in the UNC system also extends to the mid-1960s and is shaped by his role as one of the principal architects of that change. Dr. Dawson notes that the Friday administration generally recognized that the HBCUs would have had to change as the system grappled with the challenge of desegregation. He observed that the competition for well-prepared African-American students began in the 1960s, and by the late 1960s there were intense efforts by the PWIs to recruit African-American students and faculty. The HBCUs simply would not be able to survive this competition if they did not change, so the Friday administration set about the task of facilitating those changes.

The principal approach that they would take was to strengthen the arts and sciences of the HBCUs. If the academic programs of these institutions included expanded choices for students and these programs were of high quality, then the HBCUs would be able to compete for well-prepared African-American students and some white students. Dawson noted that a real effect of the *Brown decision* was to place the HBCUs and their leaders on the "horns of a cruel dilemma." The question was "how to embrace the Civil Rights movement that called for desegregation as well as protection for the HBCUs, which had been founded to serve a need that existed because of racial segregation." They needed to say, "We want to serve African-American students, our traditional clientele," and say, at the same time, "We want to attract and serve students of other ethnic backgrounds, including whites." This was not just an intellectual conundrum. Some politicians within the state were calling for changes on the higher education scene like closing the NCCU Law School and the HBCUs and sending their students to community colleges.

Dr. Charles Lyons[6]

Dr. Charles Lyons worked in several key education roles during the years after the *Brown* decision was being felt in North Carolina. From 1959 through 1962, he served as dean of the college at Elizabeth City State Teachers College (now Elizabeth City State University), executive secretary of the North Carolina Teachers Association from 1962 to 1964 and from 1969 through 1987, he was the last president and first chancellor of Fayetteville State University. During some of these years, Dr. Lyons also served as chairman of the Board of Directors of the National Association for Equal Opportunity in Higher Education (NAFEO). This was an organization founded by HBCU presidents and chancellors to advocate for African-American interests in American higher education. Through the efforts of this organization, Dr. Lyons worked with the federal government in trying to develop the criteria and guidelines which would be used to guide states in dismantling their segregated systems of higher education.

When asked whether he had been concerned about desegregation of higher education having a negative impact on enrollment in HBCUs, Dr. Lyons quickly responded that he had not. In fact, through his work with NAFEO, he had been actively working for the desegregation of higher education. He had anticipated and expected that more white students would enroll in the HBCUs as a result of the changes taking place. He and his colleagues at NAFEO felt that enhancing the quality of the HBCUs would enable them to attract more students of all races and ethnic backgrounds, including whites.

Dr. Lyons indicated that he was not concerned about the diversification of enrollments at HBCUs changing the fundamental character of these institutions in North Carolina because of the population mix of the state. North Carolina had a significant African-American population and he felt that their ties to the HBCUs would remain strong for the foreseeable future. On the other hand, he foresaw the loss of some African-American students to the PWIs, but did not believe that those institutions would admit enough of these students to pose a serious threat to the HBCUs.

Similarly, Dr. Lyons did not fear or anticipate any serious loss of African-American faculty members to the PWIs. At both Elizabeth City State Teachers College and Fayetteville State, his big challenge was finding enough qualified teachers to deliver the curriculum. In fact, sometime in 1959 or 1960, he persuaded the president of ECSU to petition the Board of

Trustees for a change in the institution's hiring policy that would permit the hiring of non-black faculty members. The board relented and authorized the hiring of non-black faculty, "except Anglo-Saxons."

With respect to the effect of desegregation on the marketing and recruiting activities of ECSU and FSU, Dr. Lyons noted that the primary means used to attract good black and white students was to place emphasis on the quality of their degree programs. Their teacher education curriculums were broadened to include the liberal arts and new degree programs were added. This perspective leads to the danger that Dr. Lyons sees for HBCUs today and in the future: failure to achieve acceptable levels of quality will lead to declining enrollments and a more tenuous existence.

Dr. Albert N. Whiting[7]

Dr. Albert Whiting served as chancellor of North Carolina Central University from 1967 until 1983. Dr. Whiting expected some HBCUs to close in the wake of the *Brown* decision because of a loss of students due to competition. In general, he felt that desegregation forced the HBCU leadership to become more creative in their efforts to attract and retain students. He led NCCU, for example, in establishing the evening program for the Law School and a program in Early Childhood Librarianship. Other new initiatives included the offering of extension courses for credit in the Research Triangle Park and the establishment of the Evening College. These and other programs attracted new students, many of whom were white.

Because of the approach that was taken there, Whiting believes that the overall quality of students at NCCU improved as a result of the *Brown* decision. As the graduate and professional programs were successful in attracting well-prepared white students, the overall quality in those programs increased. He did not perceive much change in the quality of students at the undergraduate level. Similarly, Dr. Whiting did not see much change in the socioeconomic characteristics of the student body at NCCU. Once funds became available, a very high percentage of students at NCCU received federal financial aid and he believes that remained fairly constant throughout his tenure.

With respect to faculty, Dr. Whiting did not observe much shifting of faculty from NCCU to PWIs at all. In part, he attributes this to his success in supplementing faculty salaries with grant funds from foundations.

Dr. Whiting noted that one effect of the *Brown* decision was to lead him to direct NCCU's recruiting efforts to attract white students even before the *Consent Decree* was negotiated and implemented. It was not the kind of marketing and recruitment that is prevalent today, but the emphasis on student recruiting was broadened to include white students with additional money put into student recruitment activities.

Dr. Cleon F. Thompson, Jr.[8]

Dr. Cleon Thompson was another important participant in North Carolina's desegregation movement during the critical years of its unfolding. He was an advisor to President William Friday during the years of conflict and negotiation with OCR and later provided leadership for two different constituent institutions in the UNC system. His work experience with the University of North Carolina began in 1974 when he was hired by Friday to serve as director of Special Programs with a portfolio of advocacy and support of the system's HBCUs. From 1975 until 1985, he served as Friday's vice president for Student Services and Special Programs. In 1981, Dr. Thompson accepted a special assignment of serving as interim chancellor at NCA&T. He was elected chancellor of WSSU in 1985 and served in that role for ten years.

Dr. Thompson believes that the integration of the public schools forced by the *Brown* decision served as a catalyst for increasing the demand for college education for African-Americans. He saw that an integrated public school experience led many African-American students to believe that they were better prepared for college and raised their expectations as to possible careers that were coming open to them as a result of the integration movement taking place in the country.

Although he believes that PWIs did indeed "siphon off" a lot of the better-prepared African-American students in the early years after the decision, HBCUs persist until this day as "mosaics." By this, he refers to the HBCUs continuing to serve students with a wide range of academic ability and preparation. Thompson noted that to counter this "siphoning" of African-American students, the HBCUs employed a strategy of recruiting nontraditional white students. These were adult students who typically had family obligations, needed a college education for career advancement, and for whom convenience was highly valued. This strategy was reinforced, if not initiated, by the terms of the *Consent Decree*, which provided for the use of "minority presence" grants to encourage white students to enroll in HBCUs and African-American students to enroll in PWIs.

Dr. Thompson stated that the PWIs did not raid the African-American faculties because they were not interested in hiring them. To illustrate the point, he recalled that he had worked with President Friday and others to establish an intra-UNC faculty exchange program to encourage inter-institutional collaboration and cooperation. Under the provisions of the program, a PWI and an HBCU would exchange faculty members for a year and the president's office would pay the faculty members' expenses associated with the temporary relocation. He remembers only one exchange, and the program was subsequently discontinued.

According to Thompson, President Friday and his staff recognized that if the HBCUs were to survive and progress, they would have to be improved. More and better equipment and modern facilities were needed, and faculty salaries needed to be increased. They also believed that more care and attention would have to be given to the selection of chancellors and chief academic officers for the HBCUs. The leadership that these institutions would need for the intensified competition and sophisticated challenges would be different from those who might have been chosen to lead in an earlier era.

Finally, Thompson voiced his assessment that North Carolina has been more successful in its desegregation of public higher education than most other states with HBCUs because of the HEW/OCR experience. The very factor that made North Carolina more vulnerable to attack also worked to its advantage in effecting new remedies and strategies to eliminate vestiges of a segregated system of higher education. That factor was its Board of Governors structure. With a single governing board for the university system, the federal government could bring pressure to bear more effectively. Likewise, the governing board had the concentrated power to influence the legislature with respect to funding and other policy decisions.

Themes from the Interviews

Three themes emerged from the interviews. First, all of the interviewees believed that qualitative improvement of the HBCUs would be a key to their successful transition to a post-*Brown* world. To achieve this, they saw the need for expansion and enhancement of academic programs, items critical to attracting students.

Second, there also seemed to be general agreement among the interviewees that there was little adverse impact on the ability of HBCUs to attract and retain African-American faculty members. The primary factor in this belief is the fact that the numbers of such faculty members was very small to begin and so there were few to raid.

Third, the interviewees were unanimous in their belief that diversification of the enrollments in the HBCUs was a desirable approach. The most salient feature of this strategy was the effort to enroll larger numbers of white students. For various reasons, the interviewees did not believe that there was a danger of reaching a racial tipping point that would fundamentally change the mission of these institutions.

Enrollments During the 70s, 80s and 90s

(part 1) Table 1 Undergraduate Enrollment: North Carolina's Public						
	1976		**1980**		**1986**	
	Total	*White*	*Total*	*White*	*Total*	*White*
NC	14,458	760	14,982	1,384	15,769	1,932
All HBCU w/o UT-Nashville	123,262	12,666	123,402	16,197	118,008	18,729
	1997		**1998**		**1999**	
	Total	*White*	*Total*	*White*	*Total*	*White*
NC	19,569	2,718	18,976	2,367	19,444	2,315
All HBCU w/o UT-Nashville	143,402	19,043	141,387	18,022	142,265	17,572

*UNC-GA Planning/Enr. REF/06--28-04
Source: HEGIS Fall 1976 - Fall 1984, IPEDS Fall 1986 and thereafter

As Table 1 shows, from 1976 to 2003 total undergraduate enrollment in North Carolina's public HBCUs grew 70 percent. During the same period, total undergraduate enrollment in all public HBCUs grew 30 percent, less than half that for HBCUs in North Carolina. Similarly, for these same years white undergraduate enrollment in North Carolina's public HBCUs grew 239 percent versus 37 percent for all public HBCUs. As a percentage of total enrollments, whites grew from 5.3 percent in 1976 to 16.5 percent in 2003 for North Carolina's public HBCUs. For all HBCUs, the percentage of white students grew from 10.3 percent in 1976 to 10.9 percent in 2003. Between 1976 and 2003 they attracted much larger percentages of African-American and white students. With respect to undergraduate enrollment, it appears that the North Carolina strategy worked.

(Table 1 part 2) and All Public HBCUs — 1976–2003*									
1988		**1990**		**1992**		**1994**		**1996**	
Total	*White*	*Total*	*White*	*Total*	*White*	*Total*	*White*	*Total*	*White*
15,910	1,995	16,801	2,223	18,982	2,848	19,662	2,861	19,371	2,863
126,964	19,923	138,842	21,709	154,396	23,414	152,173	21,853	147,507	19,929

2000		**2001**		**2002**		**2003**	
Total	*White*	*Total*	*White*	*Total*	*White*	*Total*	*White*
19,479	2,181	20,592	2,183	22,601	2,474	24,647	2,573
142,412	16,747	147,607	16,493	153,636	16,822	159,964	17,377

Note: In 1978, UT-Nashville was merged with Tennessee State University doubling its size and creating a 50/50 black/white racial composition. This table excludes data from UT-Nashville

Table 2 shows that the total for both graduate and undergraduate students in North Carolina's public HBCUs grew from 12,742 in 1972 to 23,693 in 2003, an increase of 86 percent. Clearly, this growth was dominated by the increase in African-American student enrollment. Though the numbers were much smaller, total non-black enrollment grew from 651 to 5,267 over this period, an increase of 709 percent. The growth in non-black student enrollment was dominated by an increase of 2,916 white students for growth of 517 percent.

Table 2							
University of North Carolina Fall Headcount Enrollment - HBCU Total							
1972, 1983–2003*							
Year	Black	White	Am. Indian	Asian	Hispanic	Other/ Unknown	Total	%Minority (% White)
1972	12,091	636	12	0	0	3	12,742	4.99%
1983	14,455	2,247	43	54	45	555	17,399	12.91%
1984	13,606	2,440	41	66	60	444	16,657	14.65%
1985	14,233	2,620	47	61	53	360	17,374	15.08%
1986	14,753	2,887	69	70	45	306	18,130	15.92%
1987	14,676	2,854	52	100	55	206	17,943	15.91%
1988	14,945	3,009	64	99	75	186	18,378	16.37%
1989	15,593	3,300	54	102	74	182	19,305	17.09%
1990	15,729	3,529	67	123	76	153	19,677	17.93%
1991	16,390	3,846	88	164	121	121	20,730	18.55%
1992	17,340	4,155	96	195	133	134	22,053	18.84%
1993	17,869	4,250	85	198	160	167	22,729	18.70%
1994	18,240	4,082	96	207	153	173	22,951	17.79%
1995	17,753	3,953	114	196	189	177	22,382	17.66%
1996	17,804	4,051	119	250	268	167	22,659	17.88%
1997	18,265	3,862	135	285	291	160	22,998	16.79%
1998	18,054	3,458	118	241	267	264	22,402	15.44%
1999	18,491	3,421	121	237	264	297	22,831	14.98%
2000	18,479	3,182	111	225	261	345	22,603	14.08%
2001	19,703	3,297	132	230	304	412	24,078	13.69%
2002	21,590	3,785	145	281	324	462	26,587	14.24%
2003	23,693	3,927	151	296	383	510	28,960	13.56%

*ProgAssess/Enr. AT003.U/11-4-03
Source: OCR (Compliance Report of Institutions of Higher Education)

Indicators of the academic characteristics of students in the UNC system that would permit a comparison of African-American students in the HBCUs and the PWIs over a substantial portion of the period since *Brown* were not available to the author. Ideally, one would have been able to compare SAT scores and high school grade point averages over the last thirty or so years. Freshmen SAT scores, however, were available for the UNC constituent institutions for the period 1993-2003. Those data show that the combined averages SAT scores for entering freshmen at the HBCUs declined 51 points, or 5.6 percent, over this period. The combined average SAT scores for entering freshmen in all of the constituent institutions remained virtually unchanged over this period. Though it would be improper to draw conclusions about the 50-year trend since *Brown* on the basis of data from a single ten-year period, these SAT comparisons hint at the possibility that, as time passes, HBCUs are indeed enrolling larger percentages of students with lower SAT scores. Even that inference is tenuous since this is not a comparison of SAT scores for African-American freshmen at the two types of institutions. It is quite possible that these results could be obtained even if the SAT average for African-American freshmen in the PWIs were declining faster than that for the HBCUs since African-Americans comprise such a very small percentage of freshmen at the PWIs. Finally, it should be noted that the SAT score is, at best, an imperfect proxy for gauging a student's ability or likelihood for academic success.

The author was also unable to find useful data for comparing the socioeconomic characteristics of African-American students at the two types of universities. Chart 1 below shows the percentage of Pell Grant recipients for a seven-year period. Pell Grants are federal awards granted to students on the basis of financial need. In general, the poorest students have the greatest need. The data reveals a slight upward trend in the percentage of African-American Pell Grant recipients in each of the HBCUs and for the UNC system as a whole for this period. The data also shows that the percentage of African-American students receiving Pell Grants at the HBCUs is consistently larger than the percentage receiving them for the system as a whole, except for NCA&T. So for this period of time, at least it appears that the HBCUs had larger percentages of poor African-American students and the percentage of such students was trending upward throughout the system.

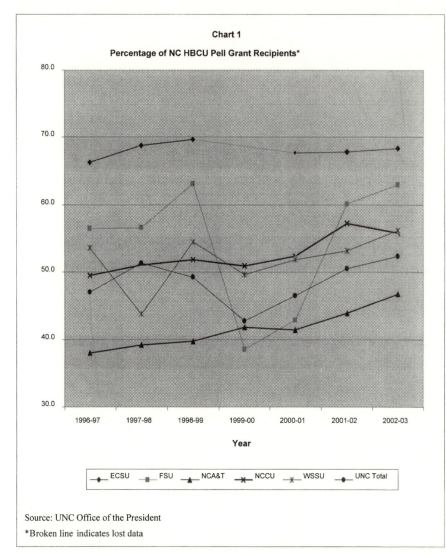

Chart 1

Percentage of NC HBCU Pell Grant Recipients*

Source: UNC Office of the President

*Broken line indicates lost data

There is a paucity of data regarding the credentials of faculty by race, so it was not possible to track the change in African-American Ph.D.s at HBCUs versus PWIs. Table 3 shows the number of faculty by highest degree held by UNC constituent institutions. At the time of the restructuring of the University of North Carolina, the HBCUs had very low percentages of their full-time faculty holding doctorates or first professional degrees. Significant improvement was shown by 1980 with three of the HBCUs moving beyond 50 percent. By 2003, NCA&T recorded 84 percent, NCCU had almost 77 percent and the others were well above 60 percent. These numbers suggest, then, that the quality of the faculty at these institutions increased markedly during the post-*Brown* era.

TABLE 3 Percentage of Full-Time Faculty Holding the Doctorate or First Professional Degree			
INSTITUTION	**1972**	**1980**	**2003**
ECSU	27.2	52.6	64.6
FSU	32	53.8	69.5
NCA&T	36.2	56.1	84
NCCU	35.3	49.2	76.8
WSSU	33.6	38.7	64.2
Sources: Statistical Abstract of Higher Education of N. C. 2003-04; *Consent Decree*			

Efforts to Expand Enrollments (Marketing & Recruiting)

It seems quite clear that changes to the American higher education landscape, many of them emanating directly from *Brown*, have led to increased pressure on the enrollments of public HBCUs. The obvious direct link between enrollments and funding for these institutions is pushing them to become more aggressive and creative in efforts to stabilize and grow their enrollments. Without students, no university can survive. In North Carolina, this reality has led to a significant investment of resources in activities that fall under the rubric of "enrollment management."

According to Garlene Penn, "enrollment management" was "the buzzword of student affairs professionals throughout the

1980s."[9] Citing other authors, she writes, "Enrollment management is an organizational concept and systematic set of activities whose purpose is to exert influence over student enrollments."[10] Further, its goals are to define and market the institution, incorporate the various relevant constituencies into the marketing plans and activities, and bring to bear the appropriate human, fiscal and technical resources.[11]

In various ways, public HBCUs in North Carolina have established enrollment management structures and systems to accomplish these goals. The UNC President Board of Governors requested funds from the state legislature to help prepare these institutions to accommodate a disproportionate share of the dramatic growth in enrollment for the system that was expected for the period 1998 to 2008. With the resulting allocations, North Carolina's public HBCUs hired enrollment management firms to assist them with developing enrollment management plans and then proceeded to implement those plans. In most cases, the plans called for adding admissions recruiters, data technicians, financial aid counselors and new software packages to manage communications flow. Plans called also for significant increases in expenditures for recruitment and marketing. Since these plans were funded and implemented, enrollment at these five institutions has grown 28 percent. This rate of growth overshadows that for the entire system of 9.5 percent as anticipated by the system's plan.

The enrollment data depicted in Chart 2 below reveals a dramatic increase in the rate of growth for the HBCUs beginning in 2000. Since the trend line for African-American enrollment is virtually parallel to the trend line for total enrollment, it seems reasonable to conclude that this growth acceleration is fueled by African-American student enrollment. This conclusion is reinforced by the observation that the trend line for white student enrollment shows only a slight increase in its rate of growth. This suggests that the new marketing and enrollment management techniques are having a disproportionate impact on African-American students.

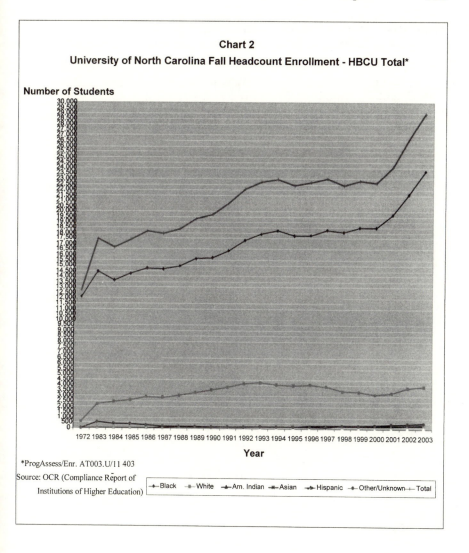

Chart 2

University of North Carolina Fall Headcount Enrollment - HBCU Total*

Number of Students

1972 1983 1984 1985 1986 1987 1988 1989 1990 1991 1992 1993 1994 1995 1996 1997 1998 1999 2000 2001 2002 2003

Year

*ProgAssess/Enr. AT003.U/11 403

Source: OCR (Compliance Report of
    Institutions of Higher Education)

Black   White   Am. Indian   Asian   Hispanic   Other/Unknown   Total

Implications for the Future of Public HBCUs

Since the 1970s, North Carolina's public HBCUs have grown faster as a group than all other public HBCUs. They are also growing more rapidly than public PWIs in North Carolina. Similarly, the North Carolina public HBCUs, as a whole, have been more successful in diversifying their enrollments than have all public HBCUs. The *Brown* decision provided the impetus for the HBCUs to change, aided by the North Carolina approach, which appears to have been very successful.

There would seem to be some reasonably direct implications of the North Carolina case for public HBCUs in other states. First, it is possible to find circumstances in which the desegregation strategy of strengthening HBCUs to make them more attractive to all students can succeed. Based upon the interviews that informed this study, such circumstances would include a real commitment on the part of higher education governing bodies in other states to encourage and facilitate the establishment of new degree programs. These circumstances would also include the willingness of state legislatures to appropriate funding needed for the enhancement of programs and facilities. Currently, such circumstances may not exist in every state that has public HBCUs.

The data and interviews of this study also suggest that the strategy of enrollment diversification for public HBCUs does not inevitably lead public HBCUs to abandon their historic mission of providing an effective higher education option for African-American students. Fifty years after *Brown*, North Carolina's public HBCUs are growing rapidly, increasing their diversity and still serving their historic mission. It is possible to negotiate the horns of the public HBCU dilemma.

Due in significant part to *Brown*, HBCUs today have to function in a highly competitive market for students. Based on the North Carolina experience, a third implication is that systematic and aggressive marketing and recruitment can be very effective for public HBCUs. Enrollment in North Carolina's HBCUs has grown 28 percent versus 12 percent in all HBCUs. While some of this difference might be explained by faster population growth in North Carolina, not all of it is. For the period 2000 to 2003, the U. S. Census Bureau estimates that North Carolina's population grew by only 4.5 percent, and three of the HBCU states (Florida, Georgia and Texas) had considerably higher (> 6%) estimated growth rates for this period.[1]

The final implication of this study derives from the fact that the public HBCUs are growing in their enrollments. This is happening, in part, as a result of some of the factors discussed in this chapter. The point, however, is that they are showing long-term growth even though thoughtful people might have expected them to experience declining enrollments which would lead ultimately to their extinction. The fact that this has not occurred reveals that the public HBCUs are serving a critical public service. Because college graduates, on average, have significantly higher earnings than do non-college graduates, broadening the pool of students going to college will mean that more African-Americans will be productive, high-income-earning citizens than would be the case otherwise. Beneficiaries of our market-driven economic system have a stake in the promulgation of the American way of life. This is important because our experiment in democracy is not guaranteed to succeed. It is in the best interest of this nation to make sure that more and more people of all ethnic backgrounds feel that they stand to benefit from maintaining American democracy and its companion market-based economy.

As a final note, I offer some personal observations and thoughts regarding the specific impact that *Brown* has had on one of North Carolina's five public HBCUs, Elizabeth City State University. My tenure as chancellor began fourteen years after the signing of the *Consent Decree* but the momentum for change that it created has continued apace and perhaps even accelerated. ECSU's rich history as an HBCU is still recognized and celebrated, but today the institution is increasingly viewed and treated by citizens of the state, prospective students, legislators and UNC system officials as a valuable higher education resource that performs a critical role as a constituent institution of that system. Just within the last five years, ECSU's Division of Academic Affairs has been reorganized into four schools, each headed by a dean, and several new degree programs have been added. Several of the programs added since the *Consent Decree*, such as marine environmental science and music industry studies, are very distinctive. Three of them represent the university's first stand-alone graduate programs.

ECSU has also experienced a significant improvement to its facilities over the last twenty years. We are currently in the midst of a $60 million new construction and renovation program that will transform for the better what is already an attractive college campus. $46.3 million of this is our share of the $3.1 billion bond referendum passed by the citizens of North Carolina in 2000.

We continue to emphasize student-centeredness in all university operations and have reallocated some existing resources to use along with new allocations to provide better service in key areas such as financial aid and business operations, develop and implement a modern enrollment management plan, develop and execute a comprehensive marketing plan for the institution and build an effective institutional advancement division to raise more private funds to support the institution's mission.

The HBCU dilemma created by *Brown* about which Drs. Dawson and Thompson spoke directly remains a formidable challenge. In spite of this, ECSU's enrollment has grown by more than seven percent in each of the last two years, and similar growth is expected for the third year in a row. It also has the largest percentage enrollment of white students among the HBCUs. That ECSU and its sister public HBCUs in North Carolina are growing and diversifying their enrollments in the current highly competitive environments attests to the possibility of a resolution to the dilemma these universities face.

Chapter 10

THE *BROWN* DECISION IN LOCAL CONTEXT: RACE AND PUBLIC EDUCATION IN NORFOLK, VIRGINIA

Jeffrey L. Littlejohn

Thurgood Marshall's "Proper Sense of Perspective"

Almost two decades ago, Americans celebrated the bicentennial anniversary of the U.S. Constitution. The commemoration was a festive affair with parades and picnics, concerts and colloquiums. Local civic groups and national organizations joined with law professors and Supreme Court Justices as the nation praised what Thomas Jefferson once called "the text of civil instruction–the touchstone by which to try the services of those we trust."[1] And yet, one of the lone critics of the commemoration was Thurgood Marshall, the brilliant civil rights lawyer and constitutional expert. As the only African-American Justice on the Supreme Court, Marshall was keenly aware of "the suffering, struggle and sacrifice" that the nation's black community had endured during two centuries of constitutional government in America. Rather than simply paper over these past struggles–and the document that made them necessary–Marshall called for a "proper sense of perspective" on the past. He encouraged Americans to give up their "complacent belief" in the "wisdom, foresight and sense of justice exhibited by the framers." In its place, Marshall called for a more "sensitive understanding" of the original Constitution, its defects and "its promising evolution through 200 years of history."[2]

As we commemorate the Fiftieth Anniversary of *Brown v. Board of Education*, we would be wise to remember Justice Marshall's admonition. Although the *Brown* decision signaled the way to greater equality and opportunity in America's public schools, its legacy has often proved as complicated as the Constitution's.

As we attempt to contextualize *Brown*–to place it in perspective–there are numerous methodological avenues open to us. The one that I have chosen here is a local history approach, focusing on Norfolk, Virginia. Although often overlooked, Norfolk was one of the oldest and most important cities involved in the desegregation struggles of the last century. As such, it witnessed three major educational battles which may help us frame the *Brown* decision in the long-developing and complex series of events that have defined the relationship between race and public education.

The first pivotal showdown began in Norfolk during the era of "separate but equal," years before the *Brown* decision in 1939. By that time, sixty-eight years of segregation had created tremendous inequality in the city's white and black schools. In response, Aline Black and Melvin Alston, two African-American teachers at Booker T. Washington High School, joined with the National Association for the Advancement of Colored People (NAACP) and lawyer Thurgood Marshall to file suit against the City of Norfolk so that they might win salaries equal to those of their white counterparts. Although Black lost her case and was unable to secure an appeal, Alston won his—the first such equalization victory in the state of Virginia. Although Alston's success had no immediate impact on segregation itself, the NAACP's victory in cases like his paved the way for a switch in legal strategy that would soon challenge the entire idea of "separate but equal."[3]

The second educational showdown began in Norfolk soon after the *Brown* decision, in 1956, as several of the city's African-American families sued the school board for its failure to desegregate public schools. What followed was a hard-fought three-year legal battle, pitting Mayor W. F. Duckworth, local segregationists and Governor J. Lindsay Almond, Jr. against local African-American families and the NAACP. The tides turned many times during the struggle, but in the summer of 1958, District Court Judge Walter Hoffman ordered that Norfolk begin integrating its previously all-white schools. In response, Governor Almond shut down the six schools that were to be immediately integrated, displacing almost 10,000 students in the largest district in the state. It took two further judicial decisions—one by the Virginia Supreme Court of Appeals and the other by the Federal District Court in Norfolk—to re-open the schools in February 1959. The six previously all-white schools were then open to the "Norfolk 17," and these few African-American students were soon in classes with nearly 10,000 white students. Although massive resistance had been defeated, the school closings represented how difficult the road ahead would be for supporters of integration and equality.[4]

The third educational showdown began in Norfolk during the early 1980s, as the city's leaders considered ending cross-town busing for elementary schoolchildren. Court-ordered busing for desegregation had begun in 1971, but by 1975, the city achieved "unitary" status, which meant that the federal courts no longer considered Norfolk a segregated public school system. Although crosstown busing continued, the next ten years produced a dramatic transformation in the racial composition of Norfolk's public schools. White children were leaving the district in large numbers and the system was becoming increasingly African-American. As a result, in 1982, the school board sponsored six public forums to consider a proposal to end the crosstown busing of elementary schoolchildren which many people believed to be a major cause of "white flight" from the district. Parents and community leaders immediately took sides in the debate, which resulted in the school board's approval of the proposal to end cross-town busing. The fight was not over, however. Within a month, several African-American leaders filed suit in *Riddick v. School Board of the City of Norfolk*. The case was not decided until 1986, when the Fourth Circuit Court of Appeals issued the first federal opinion permitting a school district to dismantle its integration plan. Norfolk would no longer bus its elementary schoolchildren.[5]

Had Norfolk's struggle for educational equality come full circle since *Brown v. Board of Education*? It is my hope that by looking at the *Riddick* case and the earlier educational battles in Norfolk, we may begin to place the *Brown* decision within the larger struggle for educational rights in America—that we may gain what Thurgood Marshall called a "proper sense of perspective" on the past.

Before Norfolk's Three Educational Battles: The City and Its Early Public School System

Norfolk, Virginia was founded in 1682, seventy-five years after the first English colonists landed at Jamestown. Blessed with a deep natural harbor and easy access to the sea, the town grew into one of the most active maritime ports in British North America. Although Norfolk was burned during the American Revolution, and was again the scene of conflict during the Civil War, the city remade itself in the twentieth century, becoming one of America's preeminent centers of international trade and defense.[6]

Public education in Norfolk has been a source of conflict throughout the city's history. Although local community leaders worked to establish free public schools as early as 1761, it was not until 1853 that the city council determined to set up a permanent public school system. After four years of intense work, Ashland Hall, the first white public school in Norfolk, was established in 1857. Then, the following year, Superintendent Thomas Tabb and an elected school board established four new public schools, giving Norfolk one of the first public school systems in the state of Virginia.[7]

Of course, Norfolk's schools functioned under Virginia law, which prohibited the education of black children. This fact had been clearly established in Norfolk only a few years earlier when Margaret Douglass, a white woman from South Carolina, was imprisoned for a month in the city jail for teaching free black children to read the Bible. Douglass was apparently unaware that, after Nat Turner's Rebellion in 1831, Virginia outlawed not only the teaching of slaves, but the teaching of any black person to read or write.[8]

The Civil War changed this. When Norfolk fell to the Union in May, 1862, Northern generals closed the city's public schools to white children and opened them to blacks. At the close of the war, however, the city government regained control of the buildings and returned the schools to the white community. No public schools were opened for black children until 1871 when Virginia's state government opened its Department of Education, and the Norfolk City Council established a segregated black public school in each of the city's four wards. The black schools were then incorporated into the existing white establishment, and they were governed by one superintendent as part of the Norfolk Public School system.[9]

Between 1871, when the Norfolk school system came under the formal control of the Virginia Department of Education, and 1939, when the first of our educational battles began, Norfolk underwent a terrific transformation. The city's population exploded, from roughly 20,000 in 1870 to almost 144,000 in 1940. Immigration, urbanization, two world wars and the establishment of the Norfolk Navy Yard helped to propel the city's growth.[10]

As Norfolk grew, so did its public school system. By 1896, twenty-five years after the district was established, the city had twelve schools, including one high school, with sixty-two teachers and a paid full-time superintendent, Richard A. Dobie.[11] Yet, Norfolk's white city leaders had not waited on the Supreme Court's *Plessy* decision to segregate their schools, which were anything but equal. Although white and black students made up almost equal proportions of the 3,000 students enrolled in 1896, white children attended ten of the city's schools with fifty-one teachers while black students attended only two of the city's schools with eleven teachers.[12] The student-teacher ratio was thus much higher for blacks than it was for whites—figures for 1886 place the ratio at 74 students per black teacher and 42 children per white teacher.[13]

As the Norfolk school system developed, the inequities between white and black schools became more pronounced. Although public schools made great strides in the city with "electric lights (1899), telephones (1901), school libraries (1902), art courses (1904), physical education classes (1908), high school athletics (1909), lunch programs (1911), free textbooks (1915) and kindergarten (1919)," these signs of progress were always more abundant in white schools.[14] Despite the fact that the first five decades of the twentieth century saw an increase in support for public schools, state and local funding actually expanded the disparity between white and black schools. In 1925, for instance, "state and local governments [in Virginia] spent an average of $40.27 per white pupil and only $10.47 per black student."[15] This terrible gap in per-pupil expenditure meant that white students attended newer facilities, read from better books, benefitted from a lower student-teacher ratio, attended longer school sessions, experienced less classroom crowding and had better lab, library and gymnasium equipment.

This was not the end of the inequality, though. In Norfolk, as in the rest of the South, black teachers faced the same sort of discrimination as their students, which resulted in the first major educational battle in Norfolk: the struggle to enforce the "separate but equal" doctrine for teacher pay.

The First Educational Battle: The *Black* and *Alston* Cases, 1939-1940

From the beginning of segregated public schooling in Norfolk, black teachers made less than their similarly trained white counterparts. By the late 1930s, the disparity in pay was pronounced, with black teachers earning roughly 56 to 72 percent of what their similarly skilled white colleagues made. Dissatisfaction with the situation was high. As trained professionals, African-American teachers wanted the same level of respect and status that white teachers had in the community. As a result, in 1937, with new pressure from the NAACP, the Norfolk Teachers Association (NTA), the city's all-black union, joined with its statewide body, the Virginia Teachers Association (VTA), in a legal effort to challenge the discriminatory pay scale established by the City of Norfolk.[16]

The first real step in the effort was taken by a volunteer, Ms. Aline Black, a young chemistry teacher at Booker T. Washington, Norfolk's only black high school. On October 27, 1938, Black petitioned the Norfolk School Board for pay equal to that of her comparably trained white counterparts. At the time, she earned roughly two-thirds of the "white salary" she requested, and the white janitor at her school made more than any black teacher on the staff. Still, the school board denied her request, and in 1939, Black was forced to file suit in state court.[17]

Obviously, this course of action had been anticipated by the VTA and the NAACP, whose lawyers represented Black in court. The hope was that if Norfolk's white leaders would not willingly equalize the salaries paid to the city's white and black teachers, then the state courts might be used to force them. The argument against Norfolk's discriminatory pay scale was clear enough: it violated Black's constitutional rights under the due process and equal protection clauses of the Fourteenth Amendment. And yet, the City of Norfolk mounted a powerful defense in court, arguing that Black had no right to a higher salary since she had willingly signed a yearly contract to work at her current rate of pay. Furthermore, Norfolk's counsel argued the city government had the sole right to set personnel standards, and the court could not interfere in its decisions.[18]

In the end, Judge Allan R. Hanckel found for Norfolk, writing that the court had no power to overturn the personnel decisions of the city's school board or to interfere in a contract legally entered. Although Black's attorneys quickly filed an appeal with the Virginia Supreme Court, her case was abandoned when the city failed to renew her teaching contract for the following year. This meant that although Black had worked for the City of Norfolk for 12 years, she could not continue as a litigant in the case since she now had no legal relationship to the body that she was trying to sue.[19]

Still, the NAACP did not give up on Norfolk. On Sunday, June 25, 1939, Thurgood Marshall joined with the organization's executive director, Walter White, in a public protest of Black's treatment. Organized by P.B. Young, editor of the *Norfolk Journal and Guide*, the public meeting included hundreds of children who marched through the streets of downtown Norfolk carrying signs lambasting the school board and its decision to let Black go. When the marchers reached their destination, St. John's African Methodist Episcopal Church, Marshall and White assured the crowd that the battle for equalization would continue.[20]

Indeed, within a few short months, Black's colleague, Melvin Alston, a commerce teacher at Booker T. Washington, had initiated a new pay equalization suit. This time, Thurgood Marshall joined the NAACP legal team, including Leon Ransom, William Hastie and Oliver Hill as the civil rights organization took the case to court. There was another difference as well. As head of the Norfolk Teachers Association, Alston had convinced the NTA to join the suit as a co-litigant, which meant that any decision in the case would have a widespread impact.[21]

Initially, Alston's case proceeded as Black's had. Although the NAACP lawyers argued that Norfolk's pay schedule violated their client's Fourteenth Amendment equal protection rights, Circuit Judge Luther Way found that Alston had voluntarily entered a contractual relationship with the City of Norfolk and that he had no right to contest the rate of pay he was receiving. Again, the NAACP was forced to appeal. This time, Marshall pushed on to the Fourth Circuit Court of Appeals where Norfolk's salary schedule was put under the microscope. The court record shows that first-year black elementary schoolteachers made $611 a year while first-year white elementary schoolteachers made $937 a year, a difference of $326. At the high school level, the salary was $699 for black teachers and $970 for white teachers, a difference of $271. These facts, when presented with Marshall's constitutional argument, persuaded Judge John J. Parker and his colleagues that "the school board's use of a racially discriminatory salary schedule was a 'condition' that violated black teachers' rights under the equal protection clause [of the Fourteenth Amendment]." This decision overturned the previous opinion written by Judge Way and although the City of Norfolk appealed to the Supreme Court of the United States, the high court denied certiorari in October 1940. As a result, Norfolk's African-American teachers entered a series of controversial negotiations with the city government, ultimately agreeing to a three-year salary equalization plan.[22]

Although Thurgood Marshall and the leadership of the NAACP disapproved of Norfolk's three-year salary plan–arguing that the city's black teachers should demand immediate pay parity–they recognized that the *Alston* case established a legal precedent for teachers throughout Virginia and the wider nation. In addition, the NAACP's victory in cases like Alston's set the stage for a direct attack on the "separate but equal" doctrine. Of course, it took Marshall and the NAACP legal team until 1954 to score their major victory in *Brown v. Board of Education*. But that decision brought on the second major educational showdown in Norfolk.[23]

The Second Educational Battle: *Brown* and Massive Resistance in Norfolk

In 1954, when the Supreme Court issued the *Brown* decision, Norfolk was an urban oddity in an otherwise rural and agricultural state. The port city had a burgeoning population of 250,000 and it was home to the U.S. Atlantic Fleet and NATO's Supreme Allied Command. Norfolk was so promising, in fact, that by 1955 it had surpassed Richmond as the largest metropolitan area in Virginia.

The new mayor of Norfolk, W. F. Duckworth, took great pride in the city and was actively involved in planning a redevelopment campaign for the downtown area. The "improvement"–and continued segregation–of Norfolk's school system was also a part of Mayor Duckworth's urban renewal strategy.[24] He and John J. Brewbaker, the superintendent of Norfolk schools, oversaw the largest public education system in the state. With almost forty-five thousand students, the city ran thirty white schools and twenty black schools, and the district built nine new school buildings before the end of the decade.[25]

Since the time of the *Alston* case, Norfolk had made great strides to equalize its white and black schools. By 1950, for instance, the Norfolk city government paid higher salaries to its black teachers, who had more training and more years of experience than their white counterparts. But it was not only teachers who benefitted from the equalization effort. By 1953, Norfolk's School Board could claim–with what now appears to have been a good bit of number crunching–that the cost of educating a black child in the city's public schools was equal to that spent for a white child.[26]

The equalization strategy of the early 1950s was, no doubt, an effort to forestall any further challenge to the city's segregated public school system. Thus, when news of the *Brown* decision arrived, Duckworth, Brewbaker and the other white leaders of the Norfolk community viewed it as an unwelcome surprise. These men had no desire to dismantle the segregated society they helped construct, and the Supreme Court's decision in *Brown II* did little to change their minds. Although the high court ordered localities to desegregate with "all deliberate speed," Duckworth and many of the city's leaders did all they could to delay implementation of *Brown*.

First, the city's leadership promoted the existing residential patterns in Norfolk in an attempt to make desegregation seem practically unnecessary. As School Board Chairman Paul Schweitzer said, "There are only thirty percent Negroes in the Norfolk school system," and they are "geographically located so that they are well-taken-care-of in their present schools." Superintendent Brewbaker agreed with Schweitzer, saying that even if desegregation occurred, "There would be few Negroes in white schools because of existing residential segregation." This did not mean Brewbaker assured the city's white community that integration was a good idea. "We are all in favor of segregation," he said, "It is just a question of what is the best plan ... I'm not in favor of integration. I'm in favor of carrying out the Supreme Court decree with the least harm to the pupils…and the schools."[27]

This sort of obfuscation tactic was used by the Norfolk leadership because they found themselves in a difficult situation. As the largest city with the largest school district in the state, Norfolk was obviously a center of attention. White segregationists throughout Virginia insisted that Norfolk resist the federal mandate to integrate. Even though African-Americans were in the minority in Norfolk, integration of the city's schools would affect other regions of the state, including the Southside, where African-American students would make up a majority of the population in any new integrated schools. African-Americans and civil rights advocates, on the other hand, insisted that Duckworth, Brewbaker and Schweitzer meet their obligations under the *Brown* decree. As black families petitioned the school board to desegregate, and NAACP lawyers threatened lawsuits to enforce the *Brown* decision, the city's white leaders decided on a second course of action.

Rather than take full responsibility for the developing crisis, Norfolk's white leaders left it to the state Department of Education to formulate a policy for integration. The state's policy was directed from afar by U.S. Senator Harry F. Byrd, Virginia's powerful political boss who called for "massive resistance" to integration in February 1956. That winter, the Byrd organization drew on the work of James J. Kilpatrick, editor of the *Richmond News Leader* who claimed to have discovered a legitimate constitutional defense against the *Brown* decision. Kilpatrick was enamored with James Madison's doctrine of interposition, which, although ultimately rejected by Madison himself, held that a state could "interpose" itself between its people and the federal government if the United States attempted to violate the people's fundamental rights. On February 1, 1956, at the behest of Byrd, the Virginia legislature passed a corresponding "Interposition Resolution," pledging that the assembly intended "to resist by every means available the federal government's encroachment upon Virginia's sovereign powers" over state education policy. A month later, Byrd championed a similar document at the national level when he co-sponsored the "Southern Manifesto" in the U.S. Congress. Signed by 101 Southern senators and congressmen, the document declared that the *Brown* decision was a "clear abuse of judicial power," and that the legislators who signed it agreed to "use all lawful means to bring about a reversal of this decision." In the end, however, the most pragmatic legislative tactic that the Byrd machine sponsored in Virginia was the Pupil Placement Act (1956), which established a three-member, governor-appointed Pupil Placement Board. The board successfully delayed integration in Norfolk, as in other Virginia cities, by keeping black students from white public schools because of locale, preparation and other nonracial factors.[28] Through the case, parents hoped that their children might gain access to the most up-to-date and well-funded schools in the city.[29]

In early 1957, U.S. District Judge Walter Hoffmann ruled in favor of the plaintiffs, ordering that the Norfolk School Board must disregard Virginia's Pupil Placement Act.[30] The act, Hoffmann declared, was unconstitutional, since its clear intent was to prevent African-American and white children from attending the same schools. A year of legal appeals delayed the implementation of Hoffmann's decision, however, and in June 1958 the *Beckett* case was back before his court. This time, he ordered the city to begin integrating its schools in September 1958.[31] In response to the decision, Senator Byrd's head man in Norfolk, William Prieur, Jr., wrote to his boss: "Norfolk will be on the front line when the schools open [in the fall of 1958]. Our definite plans are to close the schools if the Negroes attempt enrollment. All of this, of course, within the new laws of Virginia."[32]

Indeed, it was. Earlier in 1958, the Virginia state legislature gave the governor the power to close any of the state's white public schools scheduled to be integrated. On September 27, when seventeen black students sought to enroll at six of Norfolk's white public schools, Governor Almond issued an executive order closing all six of Norfolk's white schools that were to be integrated. Two days later, almost 10,000 white students found that they had no institution to attend. In addition, the seventeen African-American students who sought to transfer into the previously all-white schools were locked out. The "Norfolk 17" – Geraldine Talley, Louis Cousins, Betty Jean Reed, Lolita Portis, Reginald Young, LaVera Forbes, James Turner, Jr., Patricia Turner, Edward Jordan, Claudia Wellington, Andrew Heidelberg, Alvarez Gonsouland, Delores Johnson, Johnnie Rouse, Olivia Driver, Carol Wellington and Patricia Godbolt – attended school at Bute Street Baptist Church where they were tutored by local teachers and supervised by the NAACP.[33]

As the school-closing crisis intensified in the winter of 1958, an effort was launched by James G. Martin IV and W.I. McKendree, the leaders of the segregationist Tidewater Educational Foundation, to divert public money to white private schools in Norfolk. Fittingly, however, the entire effort fell apart on the anniversary of Robert E. Lee's birth, January 19, 1959. It was at that time that the Virginia Supreme Court of Appeals declared in *Harrison v. Day* that the school closings violated Section 129 of Virginia's State Constitution, which required the state to "maintain an efficient system of public free schools." At the same time, the federal district court in Norfolk ruled in *James v. Almond*—a case brought by white parents—that Virginia's school-closing statute violated the Fourteenth Amendment to the U.S. Constitution, and that it was therefore illegal. After a semester of showdown, the

"Norfolk 17" entered six of the previously all-white schools in the city and massive resistance ended.[34]

Although Norfolk's six closed schools reopened in February 1959 on a so-called "integrated" basis, the school closings were important for two reasons. First, the closings in Norfolk affected the largest school district in the state of Virginia, and resulted in the largest school-closing crisis in the nation. And second, when Norfolk's schools were reopened in 1959, it seemed as if a peaceful and legal resolution to the integration crisis might be possible, for massive resistance had been bested in the courts. This proposition would be tested over the next three decades, and would ultimately lead to the third major educational showdown in Norfolk—over busing and desegregation.

The Third Educational Battle: Busing and Desegregation in Norfolk

Although massive resistance failed in 1959, school integration in Norfolk did not proceed with any "deliberate speed." By 1962, there had been little progress. There were still 33 all-white schools in Norfolk and 24 all-black schools. In the 10 so-called integrated schools, with a total population of 12,922 students, there were only 101 black students enrolled. No white students attended a majority black institution.[35]

By 1968, the situation had not significantly improved. At the time, there were 73 public schools in Norfolk, with 55,499 students. Ten schools remained 100 percent white and 19 schools were 100 percent black. In addition, 9 schools were 99 percent white or black. For example, Ruffner Jr. High had 1 white student and 1,023 black students. This meant that 38 of the 73 schools in the city, with a student population of 25,929, were either totally segregated or 99 percent white or black. Of the remaining 35 schools, 10 were over 97 percent white or black, with a student population of 7,968; and 11 were over 90 percent white or black, with a student population of 10,767. In total, then, 59 of 73 schools in Norfolk were more than 90 percent white or black, which meant that more than 45,000 of 55,000 students attended a school that was racially segregated.[36]

In response to these figures, black parents in Norfolk filed *Brewer v. School Board of the City of Norfolk* (1970), a continuation of the old *Beckett* case. When the *Brewer* case appeared in the U.S. District Court for Eastern Virginia, the court ordered that Norfolk must develop a plan to achieve real integration. The proposal to end the crosstown busing of elementary schoolchildren for desegregation purposes had its origins in the demographic transformation taking place in Norfolk. It was soon thereafter that Norfolk, under the court's guidance, began mandatory regional and crosstown busing. In 1971, for the first time in the city's history, public schools moved swiftly toward integration. More than 24,000 students at all levels were bused to meet the directives of the court.[37]

The U.S. District Court for Eastern Virginia, now under the leadership of John MacKenzie, oversaw the integration process in Norfolk. It was terribly short-lived, however. In 1975, Judge MacKenzie found that "the School Board of the City of Norfolk has satisfied its affirmative duty to desegregate," and that "racial discrimination through official action has been eliminated from the system." Norfolk's school system, Judge MacKenzie said, "is now 'unitary.'"[38]

Norfolk did not immediately end its crosstown busing program, however. It took several further years for the city to consider such action, yet when it did, the issue raised a firestorm of controversy. The proposal to end the crosstown busing of elementary schoolchildren for desegregation purposes had its origins in the demographic problems Norfolk faced. A survey of the record presented in the *Riddick* case tells the story. In 1970, the year before busing began, Norfolk's schools enrolled 56,830 students, of which 57 percent (32,586) were white and 43 percent (24,244) were black.[39] By 1983, when the plan to end elementary school busing was debated by the school board, the situation had changed dramatically. Total enrollment in Norfolk's schools had declined by more than 20,000 to 35,540. In addition, the racial composition of the school system had changed. Now, 58 percent of the students (20,681) were black and 42 percent (13,327) were white. The city had witnessed, therefore, a 59 percent decline in white enrollment over 12 years.[40]

The demographic transformation in Norfolk Public Schools troubled the district's school board as early as 1981. That year, the board established an ad hoc committee to examine the issue of crosstown busing. The biracial committee, which included Jean Bruce (white) Hortense Wells (black), Tommy Johnson (white), Robert Hicks (white), and John Foster (black).[41] As part of their consideration, the committee members visited Shreveport, Louisiana and Richmond, Virginia, two cities that had gone through recent struggles with white flight and other desegregation issues. The committee also solicited information from scholars and public policy experts, including Dr. David Armor, Dr. Ron Edwards, Dr. Sarah Lightfoot and Dr. Robert Green. By the end of the study, John Foster was the only member of the ad hoc committee to disagree with the proposal to end the crosstown busing of elementary students.[42]

Once the proposed plan to end busing was before the school board, the body hired Dr. Armor to report on the future problems that crosstown busing might cause the city's school system. Armor's controversial report suggested that if crosstown busing was not halted, white flight would continue and that Norfolk's school system would become predominantly African-American. Specifically, Armor argued that 75 percent of the student body would be black by 1987, thus ending any hope of an integrated education for students in the city's public schools.[43]

Following Armor's report, the school board held 6 public hearings to discuss a new pupil-placement plan entitled, "A Proposal For a Voluntary Stably Desegregated School System." The plan called for a return to "neighborhood schools" at the K-6 level, but left middle and high school busing in place. Supporters of the plan emphasized three points: 1) that crosstown busing was causing white flight, which was fundamentally altering the city's demographic makeup; 2) that crosstown busing reduced parental involvement in city schools and 3) that crosstown busing was difficult for young children, who should not be forced to bear the burden of the society that their parents and grandparents had created. Opponents of the plan countered with three points of their own: 1) that at least 10 and possibly 12 schools would become completely black as a result of ending busing; 2) that their city was witnessing the resegregation of the public schools and 3) that materials would not be equally allocated once white and black schools appeared in Norfolk.[44]

When the public debates ended in 1983, the school board voted 5-to-2 in favor of the proposal to end crosstown busing, which would take effect in September 1984. Or so it seemed. In response to the school board's decision, Paul Riddick and other African-American parents in Norfolk, filed suit in U.S. District

Court to halt the end of elementary school busing. Riddick and the other plaintiffs contended that the school board's plan was "racially motivated and that its implementation would violate the rights of the plaintiffs under the Fourteenth Amendment."[45]

The U.S. District Court for Eastern Virginia disagreed. In an opinion written by Judge John MacKenzie, the court said that the evidence presented by the plaintiffs "falls short of demonstrating the requisite discriminatory intent." There was no proof that the proposed plan of the Norfolk school board was "racially motivated." On the contrary, Judge MacKenzie wrote, there was ample evidence to show that the school board was trying to "meet the threat posed by white flight … [and] to increase the level of parental involvement" in Norfolk Public Schools. The District Court, therefore, found for the City of Norfolk.[46]

Riddick and his fellow plaintiffs then appealed the decision to the Fourth Circuit Court of Appeals, which heard the case in 1985. In the opinion, issued a year later, Circuit Judge Hiram E. Widener, Jr. upheld the decision of the District Court and emphasized many of the points it had made. For instance, Judge Widener rejected the plaintiffs' allegation that the school board's decision to end elementary school busing was "racially motivated." "The school board of Norfolk is racially mixed," Widener wrote, quoting from MacKenzie.

The Superintendent of Schools, Dr. Gene R. Carter, is black. Two of the three regional assistant superintendents are also black. There are 88 principals in the system, 59% are white, 41% are black. The faculty is likewise fully integrated, 56% white, 44% black…. Given that the staff is completely integrated and given that very qualified blacks are at the top of the organization, the fear that white students will stand to reap some benefit over black students is totally lacking in credence.[47]

If the plaintiffs could not show that the school board's decision to discontinue crosstown busing was *intended* to benefit white elementary students at the expense of black elementary students—and thus was "racially motivated"—could it be said that the decision endangered the Fourteenth Amendment rights of the black students? On this question, the Fourth Circuit Court of Appeals again found itself in agreement with the District Court. Judge Widener wrote that the school board's decision to end elementary busing may have a deleterious effect on African-

American students, but if the plaintiffs could not prove intent to discriminate, there was no constitutional violation. "This purpose, or intent to discriminate," Widener said, "marks the difference between *de facto* and *de jure* segregation"[48]–the former being legal, the latter illegal.

With these words, Judge Widener closed *Riddick v. School Board of the City of Norfolk* (1986), the first federal decision to permit a school district to dismantle its desegregation plan. Six months later, in September 1986, the crosstown busing of elementary schoolchildren ended in Norfolk and ten all-black elementary schools appeared on the city's books.[49]

Norfolk's Recent History and *Brown v. Board of Education*

Since 1986, Norfolk's Public School System has continued to evolve. In 2001, the city ended cross-town busing for middle school students, and as recently as November 2003 the school board considered a proposal to end busing for high school students. Yet, it appears that the end of crosstown busing at the elementary and middle school levels has not produced a more integrated district, as was predicted in the mid-1980s. This does not mean, however, that Paul Riddick and his allies were any more correct than Dr. David Armor and the defenders of the Norfolk School Board. The clear problems facing Norfolk Public Schools in 2004 are similar to those that the district has faced throughout the last century: urban poverty, racial strife, and, in the more recent era, white flight.

These pressing issues have fundamentally altered Norfolk Public Schools since the era of *Brown v. Board of Education*. In 1959, when Norfolk's schools were first integrated, total enrollment stood at 47,334. Of these students, 32,163 were white and 15,171 were black. In 2002, when the latest figures were available, total enrollment stood at 36,745. Of these students, 9,995 were white and 24,913 were black.[50] This racial transformation was caused primarily by "white flight," which did not begin in earnest until 1971, when busing was instituted. The tragic irony is that without busing, the schools never would have been truly integrated, and with busing, so many whites left the city that integration became virtually impossible. In fact, the figures from 2002 show that the district is more segregated today than at any time since 1970. A full half of the 8 middle schools are over 70 percent African-American.

In addition, 11 of 34 elementary schools are over 80 percent African-American, and 8 of those are over 95 percent African-American.[51]

There can be no doubt that these figures will lead to continuing debate as members of the Norfolk community seeks to negotiate the difficult terrain left in the wake of *Brown v. Board of Education*. As we have seen, the *Brown* decision was an integral part of a much larger and longer struggle for educational rights in Norfolk. Although the Supreme Court's ruling overturned the doctrine of "separate but equal," *Brown* did not desegregate public schools any more than it made them equal. For we in Norfolk still have a far way to go to achieve the type of equality that Thurgood Marshall envisioned when he said that "Equal means getting the same thing at the same time and in the same place."

Chapter 11

LEVELING THE PLAYING FIELD:
THE CHALLENGE OF PREPARING GLOBALLY COMPETENT
AFRICAN-AMERICAN COLLEGE GRADUATES

Roberta J. Wilburn
Introduction

Although significant strides have been made in the area of education since *Brown v. the Board of Education*, there is still much that needs to be done to bring true educational equality for African-Americans in this country. It is estimated that if we continue at the current rate, African-Americans will not reach college graduation parity with European-Americans until 2075 or 200 years after slavery.[1] In examining the highlights of the Equality Index Findings that were presented in the 2004 *State of Black America* report, out of the issues examined, education was one of the areas with significant gains toward equity. According to the report, "Black students have made substantial progress when it comes to college enrollment and graduation," however, in the area of taking advantage of opportunities to prepare for the global marketplace, African-American students are still significantly lagging behind their European-American counterparts. This chapter will examine the status of African-American student involvement in international studies and "study abroad" experiences, factors that contribute to their nonparticipation, advantages of having such experiences, existing programs that are effective in this area as well as how public and private Historically Black Colleges and Universities (HBCUs) can take a leadership role in preparing globally competent college graduates.

Despite the fact that we are living in a highly advanced technological age that has shortened the distance between nations, many Americans have failed to see the need to embrace global education and the importance of having greater knowledge and awareness of people and cultures outside of this country. This is particularly true of African-Americans, even those who are seeking higher education and desire to increase their knowledge and skills.

As a result, only a small percentage, approximately 5%, of African-American college students take advantage of "study abroad" and other international experiences available to college students. According to a study published by Cornell University Task Force on International Education in December 1995, "Effective international education programs must be an integral part of an overall strategy to develop the teaching, research and service contributions of colleges and universities... "Study abroad" must be seamlessly linked academically and administratively to study on campus." The question is how can we encourage African-American college students to become actively engaged in international studies and global education experiences which are "designed to cultivate a perspective of the world which emphasizes the interconnectedness among cultures, species and the planet"[2] in order for them to become productive contributors and leaders in the larger global community in which they live? To answer the aforementioned question, we must look at the barriers that hinder African-American college students from becoming meaningfully engaged in cross-cultural experiences.

According to Linda Meggett Brown, African-American students are under-represented in international studies and the challenge is to make such experiences attractive and affordable.[3] Historically, collegiate "study abroad" experiences have been "predominated by a narrow spectrum of the population, white females from highly educated professional families majoring in the social sciences and the humanities."[4] However, Dr. Julius Coles says that if African-American students are going to be able to compete in a world marketplace and environment they have to have the proper preparation. Despite the fact that there are serious obstacles that hinder African-American college students from participating in international studies and "study abroad" experiences, they are not insurmountable.

Current Status of African-American Students and "Study Abroad"

To say that African-American students are under-represented in "study abroad" experiences is an understatement. According to the Report on International Educational Exchange during the 2001-2002 academic year, 160,920 students in the United States studied abroad. However, only 3.5% were African-American as compared to Caucasian students who represented 82.9% of this pool. Over the last three years, there has been no increase in the level of African-American students even though overall participation has increased by 4.4 percent in just one year. While the report celebrates the fact that "U.S. students' interest and participation in "study abroad" has grown dramatically since the mid-1990's," nothing is said about the significant absence and lack of growth in participation rates of African-American students in "study abroad" programs.

These statistics clearly demonstrate that a significant disparity still exists in global education for African-American students as compared to their white counterparts. But you only glean the significant disparity by the one sentence in the ninety-six-page report which indicates the majority of U.S. "study abroad" students are Caucasian and by examining the table which presents the statistical data of the profile of U.S. "study abroad" students. One has to wonder why the writers of this report would find it necessary to discuss gaps such as gender or host countries but failed to mention the disparity in the race of the students studying abroad, especially since the gap in this area is greater than the other two areas.

According to the 1990 report, *A National Mandate for Education Abroad*, "Efforts to expand the number of undergraduates who study abroad must address the lack of diversity among them. Traditionally, American "study abroad" students have come from affluent, middle or upper class, white, professional families rather than the broad spectrum of American society."[5] Nonetheless, there has only been a 0.7 percent increase in the level of African-American student participation in "study abroad" experiences since the 1993-94 academic year.[6]

The under-representation of African-American students in "study abroad" experiences are further documented in the opening address of the 43rd International Conference, on Educational Exchange in 1990. At this conference Johnnetta Cole, former president of Spelman College; Holly Carter, associate Dean and Special Assistant to the President for International Education at Northeastern University; and Gus John, Director of Education, Borough of Hackney, London, addressed the issues of under representation of African-Americans and minorities in "study abroad" programs. In her presentation, Cole indicated that it is difficult to adequately determine the level of minority participation in "study aboard" programs because statistics were not being kept. Whether this is just an oversight on the part of researchers, or a deliberate attempt to hide, cover up or gloss over the significant absence of African-Americans and other minorities in "study abroad" experiences is unclear. The Institute on International Education's report, *Open Doors*, is one of few documents with data on this area, and its coverage of the topic is limited. It wasn't until the 1990s that concern for lack of minority representation began to become a concern, but even with the increased interest Carter states "as colleges and universities in the United States continue to seek ways to internationalize their campuses, there is little emphasis placed on who is to benefit from the internationalization or on how to assure that all students have the opportunity for gaining 'international competence' as an integral part of their educational experience."[7]

Gus John discusses the issue of under-representation of African-Americans from a personal perspective as a student in the Caribbean and in Britain, as well as a teacher, lecturer and education administrator. He makes a strong case to take steps to eradicate this problem:

> "I am arguing that we need to have an internal focus on the issue of under-representation in relations to who has access to education and at what levels, the extent to which the curriculum...and student support services take into account under-represented groups, and more generally, the historical contributions of under-represented people and nations to the development of knowledge across all disciplines. I am arguing for a genuine curriculum of inclusion which by its very existence poses a challenge to cultural supremacist values whether or not they originate in racism, ethnocentrism or Eurocentrism, and has within it and its pedagogy the potential for a dynamic education for liberation."[8]

Burris' electronic survey of HBCU Web sites indicates that there are few opportunities for these undergraduate students to become fully engaged in international studies and "study abroad" experiences, and information concerning these limited opportunities were not easily accessible.[9] In a review of earlier surveys of HBCUs in the mid-90s, Burris identified Morehouse College as the only school having an international studies major, she found that at Spelman students could have a concentration in international studies even though they couldn't major in it. Howard University and several other schools offered a major in African-American Studies, but the primary focus of these programs was to gain greater understanding of the plight of African-Americans in this country.

Barriers That Hinder Participation

Since there is without question a significant disparity in the numbers of African-American students who take part in international studies and "study abroad" experiences, it is important to examine why this phenomenon exists. Dr. Johnnetta Cole has identified four major barriers which hinder and prevent African-American students from participating in international educational exchanges and other types of "study abroad" experiences.[10] These barriers that she calls the four F's are as follows: (1) faculty and staff, (2) finances, (3) family and community, and (4) fears. While not listed in order of their importance, each is a critical area which can be a barrier to participation.

First and foremost, if a college's faculty is not convinced that "study abroad" experiences are worthwhile, then they will not encourage their students to participate. Many faculty on HBCU campuses have not traveled outside of this country themselves, therefore, they may not feel that such experiences are necessary. Cole states that HBCUs are "often working with far fewer resources to sustain a "study abroad" program, and carrying out all the work of these programs may be viewed as a 'luxury' that folks who teach four courses a semester feel they 'cannot afford.' At Predominantly White Institutions (PWIs), they seek out the best and brightest students to compete for awards and to participate in special programs such as "study abroad" experiences and they may not feel that their African-American students 'fit the bill.'" Another issue is that there are few African-American faculty members in "study abroad" leadership positions.[11]

There is also a presumption by some faculty and staff at PWIs that African-American students would not be interested in studying abroad because the majority of the "study abroad" experiences take place in the United Kingdom and other European countries.[12] Carter further states that "minority students are often reluctant to explore the validity or feasibility of an international dimension to their academic programs with faculty or administrators whom they perceive might not understand their constraints or be willing to support their efforts. The limited number of professional minority role models in the field creates a limited frame of reference for minority students who might be interested in international affairs but perceive real limitations for professional success in the field."[13]

The second barrier which Dr. Cole addresses is finances. Financing a college education is often a major challenge for many African-American students. The thought of adding an international component to their academic program is often perceived as a non-essential extra that they just can't afford. She emphasizes that "money is clearly an important issue for any student considering "studying abroad"…because our students are disproportionately found among students who simply cannot attend college without substantial financial aid…if we want to substantially increase the number of African-Americans "studying abroad," we must make every possible effort to allow students to use their financial aid during a "study aboard" experience…In addition, the administration of our institutions need to fund-raise specifically for "study aboard" scholarships for black and other minority students."[14] Others have suggested alternative ways to subsidize "study aboard" experiences so students don't have to worry about going into debt.[15]

The third barrier relates to family and community. Many African-American families are struggling to be able to send their students to college and "study abroad" is often considered to be an unnecessary and expensive extracurricular activity. Families are also reluctant to have their college students "study aboard" because they have many negative preconceived ideas about other countries, they don't feel comfortable about them going so far away, and they are concerned about their well-being. According to Cole, African-American parents are less likely to have traveled abroad themselves, and may be concerned about racial attitudes abroad or feel uncomfortable about flying. These views and sentiments are often passed on to their children.

The last barrier that Dr. Cole describes is fear. There are many fears attached to "study abroad." Fear of the unknown, fear of flying, fear of not being able to speak the language, fear of not being able to make friends, fear of not being able to graduate on time, fear of missing out on various social activities that take place on their home campus, fear that their boyfriend or girlfriend might find someone else while they are gone, fear that they won't have enough money to sustain themselves while they are away, fear of taking the required vaccinations, fear that their family at home will suffer without their financial assistance or support while they are away, etc. These fears are real and they need to be addressed in order to help African-American students feel comfortable about participating in "study aboard" experiences. A good way that this can be done is through an intensive orientation, either in the form of a course or a pre-trip workshop before students are scheduled to travel abroad.

According to Dr. Pinder from Dillard College: "The major hindrance for students is information...we have to market the programs and articulate the benefits of studying abroad instead of using broad clichés. We want our kids to be competitive, whether on majority campuses or HBCUs."[16]

Other barriers that have been identified as possible hindrances to African-American students studying abroad include: inability to work while studying abroad, lack of portability of some financial aid, curriculum issues on the student's home campus, difficulty transferring credits, language and admissions requirements, rigidity in program models, restricted programs for honor students, the places promoted for "study aboard" experiences may not be of interest to African-American students, most promotional materials are not targeted toward African-American students, etc.

Importance of Participation for African-American Students

As we reflect on the advances since *Brown v. the Board of Education*, it is time for us to rekindle the fight for excellence in education. In so doing, we must raise the bar of our expectations of African-American students in higher education. Having a college education is not enough, having a quality education that will prepare our students to be competitive on all levels is a must. In order to level the playing field, we must also prepare them to meet the challenges of the broader global community. This is why international "study aboard" experiences should not be considered luxury or optional;

instead, it should be considered a critical necessity. According to April Burris:

> "The obvious and evident relevance of international studies is the growing demand by employers for graduates who are knowledgeable about global affairs. This generation of college students need the skills, knowledge and cross-cultural understanding required for their competitive entry into the global market. Certainly, as educated world citizens, our students also must acquire appreciation for complex human independencies and in-depth knowledge of world systems and perspectives within their own disciplines."[17]

Craig, in an article in *The Black Collegian Online* indicated that preparing African-American college students for global leadership should be a national imperative for the 21st century.[18] He goes on to state that: "The institutionalization of the American economy is driving undergraduate students to acquire an international perspective. African-American collegians who study abroad are enhancing their resumes and acquiring competitive edges for employment opportunities in the global marketplace."

Brown and Kysilka further reiterate the importance of educational experiences in broadening the development and marketability of our students as it relates to HBCUs.[19] They state that "today's most effective managers are those who are able to understand other cultures." If HBCUs do not recognize this fact and begin to provide their students with the tools necessary to effectively work in a global society, they run the risk of becoming an endangered species because African-American students realizing the need for these kinds of experiences will seek out majority institutions who will be able to provide them with the preparation which they need. They further expound on this issue by saying "as the world is brought into the classroom, the students must go out into the world. Teachers have a responsibility to help their students prepare for the world in as many ways as possible. Part of this responsibility is to help students be actors rather than spectators in their world."[20]

"Study aboard" experiences also increase students' ability to think critically from a global perspective, increase interest in world affairs and the larger international community, rather than just focusing on their own immediate environment. It also helps them in redefining themselves, understanding the different cultures and customs and our interconnectedness.

Success Stories: Overcoming Obstacles and Barriers

Despite the many obstacles and barriers, African-American students who participate in "study abroad" find that it is a valuable, life-changing experience. The following case studies describe the experiences of two students that attended LeMoyne-Owen College, a historically black college located in Memphis.

Case 1: James

James is a nontraditional student majoring in humanities with a concentration in religion and music. He is fifty-two-years, old and has returned to school after having a successful career in politics and raising his family. James has had two "study aboard" experiences while attending LeMoyne-Owen College. Due to his family responsibilities, James did not want to go study abroad for a semester, so he opted for short-term "study aboard" experiences during the summer. His first experience was to Paris where he toured and performed with the college concert choir. He recently completed his second short-term program. For this experience, he and two other music students went on a jazz study tour to Senegal where he performed and learned about the music industry from an international perspective.

Although these were not James' first experiences outside of the country, studying abroad has given him another perspective on international issues and has increased his understanding of how to establish and work with international businesses and people from diverse cultures.

James found financing the endeavor to be very difficult. In most cases, nontraditional students have very little extra funds to cover the expense of studying abroad, even for a short-term period. In both cases, James had to seek outside support for his trips. The trip to Senegal was even more difficult to plan for. Even with a partial scholarship, he only had approximately a month and a half to raise the remaining two-thirds of the cost. Along with other students who were going on the trip, James actively solicited donations and participated in several different forms of fund-raising activities. The faculty of the college was extremely supportive of the students and donated their personal resources to enable the students to take the trip, once again demonstrating the nurturing and familial attitude found at HBCUs.

The other difficulty James experienced during his "study aboard" was the living conditions. While traveling to Paris, the choir stayed in hotels which were clean and comfortable. However, the Senegalese sponsors were more concerned with cutting corners and making a profit than ensuring that students and other tour participants had adequate and comfortable lodging and food. James found himself in substandard housing conditions such as a dilapidated and poorly kept building which was supposed to be a hotel, while the sponsors of the trip stayed in comfortable accommodations with all of the traditional amenities. After having been on prior "study aboard" and international trips, James was frustrated by the poor living conditions, and was concerned that the other students who were visiting Africa for the first time, would believe that this experience was typical and would reinforce the many negative attitudes toward Africa.

Despite the problems with the living conditions, James still expressed that his "study aboard" experience in Senegal was a very valuable one. While he was there, he learned to speak some words in Wolof. The people in Senegal treated the students very well and were extremely helpful in showing them places of importance and teaching about their culture and communities. James readily encourages other students to take advantage of "study aboard" experiences because it will expand their knowledge of what's going on in the world and can help them to learn to "think out of the box."

Case 2: Crystal

Crystal was an incoming freshman from Atlanta who received a Presidential Scholarship to attend LeMoyne-Owen College. The summer before she was scheduled to start college, Crystal participated in a special precollege summer-abroad experience sponsored by LeMoyne-Owen in conjunction with the National Caucus of Black State Legislators (NCBSL). Usually, "study aboard" experiences are reserved for upperclassmen at colleges and universities;

however, Crystal was selected to be the first incoming freshman to participate in this precollege program. Crystal wanted to participate in this "study aboard" experience because she enjoys traveling and wanted to experience living in another culture. She had a very supportive family and they were extremely anxious to purchase all the necessities needed to prepare her for her trip. While in the Dominican Republic, Crystal participated in a service-learning experience at the Woman's Bank.

Crystal advocates "study aboard" experiences for other students. She feels that "study aboard" is a valuable learning experience that gives you the opportunity to explore many new things in the world. Crystal believes that there are no boundaries as to the knowledge one would gain having the opportunity to study abroad. Furthermore, she feels that "study aboard" experiences are important for African-American students because many of them lack the knowledge of the world in which they live. She states that there is no better way for African-American students to expand their horizons other than to travel abroad. Crystal feels that there is only so much information you can obtain from a textbook or even from the television; it cannot compare to actually experiencing living and learning from being in another country.

Crystal's advice to other students preparing to study abroad for the first time is to be prepared for unthinkable things that could occur, and they should travel with an open mind. She also feels that it is very helpful for students to research everything there is to know about the country that they will be visiting. Crystal said that she definitely wants to have more "study aboard" experiences and intends to study in different countries every summer of her college career. She would like to travel to China, Africa, Europe, Latin America and many more places across the globe. After staying in the Dominican Republic, Crystal would like to incorporate more service learning and internships in her field of study.

Lessons Learned From Other HBCUs

Although the numbers of HBCUs offering strong international studies and "study aboard" experiences have been limited, we can still learn from the work of those schools who have pioneered the effort to increase African-American student participation in international studies and "study aboard" programs. Some of the HBCUs that have been in the forefront of this endeavor have been

Morehouse, Dillard, Howard University, Florida A & M, Spelman and FAMU.

One way HBCUs can get their institutions and students involved in "study aboard" experiences is by partnering with other colleges who are already involved in such activities. For example, "FAMU is part of a 14-member college consortium which encourages more students and faculty to travel abroad, fostering interest among students at schools without "study aboard" programs... in addition to the 14-college consortium, FAMU also is involved in a program that allows its students to participate in Florida State University's "study aboard" programs. It allows students additional options for scholarships and expands the choices for "study aboard" in Europe, Asian and African countries that are developed."[21]

According to Ernest White, a graduate from Florida A & M, there are many things which colleges and universities can do to get more students involved in "study aboard" experiences if they "promoted programs, broadened the range of courses and provided more financial assistance, more students of color would express an interest in participating."[22]

Dillard is another HBCU that has been able to significantly increase the level of participation of the students and faculty in "study aboard" programs. One important factor that is needed to help increase "study aboard" opportunities for African-Americans is the commitment of the administration to institutionalize international studies and "study aboard" experiences. In 2000 Dillard's president and provost began a campaign to institutionalize international studies and to make Dillard an "international institution" where international studies are integrated throughout all phases of their academic program. Prior to 2000, Dillard had only about ten students participate in "study aboard" experiences. Two years after the initiation of the campaign to internationalize the college, they had between 50-60 students to participate in international/"study aboard" experiences, and they are hoping to expand this number to the point where 50% of their student body will have international experiences.

One way that Morehouse College is increasing student interest in international studies is by increasing the number of international students on campus. In 2001, they estimated that approximately 5% of their student body, or 180 students, represented over twenty countries. Additionally, other HBCUs are establishing articulation agreements and memorandums of understanding with other colleges and universities as a means of fostering international cooperation in educational endeavors and research. Bethune-Cookman College in Florida and LeMoyne-Owen College are two examples of this type of international collaboration. Bethune-Cookman has a partnership with the College of the Bahamas' hospitality and tourism studies program. LeMoyne-Owen has a partnership with the Catholic University in the Dominican Republic and the University of Gaston Berger in Senegal.

Increasing Interest and Access: Methods of Engagement

Several strategies have been identified to help increase the interest of African-American students in "study aboard" experiences, and to develop effective strategies for engaging our students so they will seek active participation in these programs. The Council for International Educational Exchange has identified four major categories to increase the under-representation of minority students in "study aboard" experiences. They are as follows: (1) conducting special outreach campaigns, (2) making "study aboard" more accessible, (3) making adjustments in "study aboard" programs to make minority students feel at home, and (4) focusing on strategies at the national level.[23]

Craig feels that by providing service learning and internships abroad is another good way to get African-American students involved in international studies: "Both "study aboard" and work through volunteer services or international internship programs are effective approaches to prepare college students for leadership and work in a global economy."[24]

There are many strategies that are currently being implemented as a means of increasing African-American student representation and participation in international studies and "study aboard" experiences. A three-tier approach is very effective in helping to engage African-American college students. The first tier of this approach is to increase the cultural awareness of students and faculty. This process should begin on campus with a variety of activities to get each to begin to think globally and begin to exercise social responsibility. For example, at LeMoyne-Owen College, a drive was conducted to collect clipboards to send to Africa for an elementary school that did not have any desks. The second tier of the engagement process should build on the interest of the students. Students who have traveled abroad or have interest in other countries should be encouraged to conduct research and then give presentations to the student body. Guest speakers and international students can share information. Short-term cultural awareness trips can be planned to visit places of interest. The third tier of the engagement process involves institutionalizing international studies and "study aboard" activities which should include making "study abroad" appealing and accessible to all students, not just a selected few.

National Initiatives

In 1995, the United Negro College Fund created the Institute of Public Policy (IPP) to identify, recruit and train students for careers in international affairs. The value of many of these initiatives is that they provide opportunities for networking, collaboration and partnerships, and finding out about best practices and grant opportunities.

Other national initiatives which are designed to increase African-American faculty and students in international affairs and study abroad experiences and exchanges are described below:

National Caucus of Black State Legislators (NCBSL): sponsors the International Technical Assistance Center (ITAC) and the International Education Resource Center (IERC) to support students, faculty and administrators in post-secondary institutions serving minority students to facilitate student participation in "study abroad" and internships in the Dominican Republic.

Charles B. Rangel International Affairs Program (Howard University): program designed to attract outstanding individuals who have an interest in pursuing a career in the U.S. Foreign Service. They provide conferences for international affairs/ "study abroad" advisors from HBCUs, international student leadership retreat, international affairs summer institutes, internships and graduate fellowships.

White Initiative on HBCUs: designed to be a vehicle to ensure that HBCUs are model institutions of teaching, learning, research and service, effectively educating diverse populations of the nation and the world. They sponsor conferences and technical assistance workshops, enhance capacity-building and encourage collaboration and linkages with federal agencies and HBCUs.

United Negro College Fund Special Programs (UNCFSP): holds conferences and technical assistance workshops related to international initiatives. In the past, they had grants opportunities for HBCUs for education, development and democracy, international development partnerships and cross-hemispheric partnerships. They are currently in the process of reassessing their international initiatives.

Conclusion: Leveling the Playing Field

When we examine the issue of international educational experiences for African-American college students, we find that we have made little significant progress, and we still have many hurdles and challenges to overcome if we are going to prepare globally competent African-American college graduates. Despite the bleak picture that currently exists, we should be encouraged because there is an increased awareness of the need for international experiences for African-American students, as well as increased national initiatives which are designed to assist HBCUs in internationalizing their campuses.

As African-Americans we have always had to struggle for equal rights and to get an equal share of the American pie, the fight for appropriate international opportunities and experiences for our African-American students is no different. The dream for equality is ever before us, however, we must take the steps to make the dream a reality. It is up to us to continue the fight until we have leveled the playing field in the international education arena, and every African-American college student has an opportunity to participate in international studies and can graduate from college knowing that they are adequately prepared to compete in the global marketplace.

Part III

ITS IMPACT ON PUBLIC POLICY,

CURRICULUM AND RESOURCES

Chapter 12

SCHOOLING AS A MORAL ENTERPRISE: RETHINKING EDUCATIONAL JUSTICE FIFTY YEARS AFTER *BROWN*

Garrett Albert Duncan

As the United States observes the Fiftieth Anniversary of the *Brown v. Board of Education* decision, we must celebrate the unprecedented improvements the ruling has brought about in the education of black students. At the same time, we must also acknowledge the fact that *Brown* did not and could not completely resolve the struggle that has shaped questions of race and education in the United States for nearly 400 years.[1] For instance, in upholding the Equal Protection Clause of the 14th Amendment the Warren Court largely affirmed civil and political rights or what are also known as First Generation Rights in its rendering of *Brown*. Unlike the Universal Declaration of Human Rights, the U.S. Constitution gives only scant attention to cultural, social and economic rights, or Second Generation Rights.[2] In failing to fully account for these latter rights, *Brown* neither challenged white supremacy, a force that plays out largely throughout the cultural, social and economic realms of society, nor called for an examination of how it shaped and continues to shape our notions of race and education in the country.

In this chapter, I argue that the intransigence of white supremacy in public education informs the contradictory effects that school desegregation policy has had on the education of black students since *Brown*. Specifically, I examine the textured legacy of the landmark decision in the context of my ethnographic analysis of City High School (CHS), a magnet academy located in the Midwestern United States.[3] The conversion of the urban-based CHS into a magnet academy occurred as part of a voluntary desegregation settlement agreement between Monticello School District (MSD), where CHS is located, and surrounding area suburban school districts. As it stands now, CHS represents a paradox of sorts: Although the state has designated MSD as an at-risk system, it consistently ranks the academy as its top public high school. In many ways, CHS exemplifies all that school desegregation policy promises: a first-rate, harmonious, racially integrated educational institution; in short, an exemplar of what other schools in the area and the nation can be. Anyone who visits CHS will readily sense its friendly culture and the high value that students, parents, teachers and administrators place on education. Yet, despite the presence of a student-centered curriculum and in the absence of overt racial hostility, CHS nonetheless has color-coded inequalities that mirror other beleaguered urban schools in the area and across the nation. I argue in this chapter that white supremacy in post-Civil Rights era education, and the way it shapes how we view, educate and evaluate black students, accounts for the racial stratifications, or achievement gaps, that are observable in contemporary public schools.

Schooling is not simply about the project of inclusion implied by the First Generation Rights upheld by the *Brown* decision and extended by subsequent civil rights legislation. Rather, schooling is primarily about changing lives and about the social construction of virtue and vice in accord with unexamined racial norms. It follows that the tacit arrogation of white cultural norms in public schools creates a veiled moral predicament for students and educators alike. It is for this reason I posit that at its most fundamental level schooling is a moral enterprise.[4] Understanding the function of public education in this way helps to explain the ethical issues that frame the schooling of students of color, in general, and of black students, in particular.[5] To clarify how these dynamics play out in public education, the analysis in this chapter proceeds as follows: First, I overview the historical and socio-cultural contexts of the MSD and CHS as a backdrop to presenting an educational dilemma for which school desegregation policy does not adequately address. I then connect this dilemma to deeply embedded assumptions about the role of schools in Western societies and to constitutional constraints around rectifying Second Generation Rights violations. I conclude the chapter by discussing how the lessons learned from CHS may inform our future work as educational researchers, teachers, school administrators and policymakers.

Desegregation in a Midwestern Metropolis

In the 1940s and 1950s, the nationally acclaimed Monticello School District served a mostly white student population of over 110,000. By the 1980s, this city public school district, located in the Midwestern United States, had experienced a significant decline in the number of its students as well as a shift in its racial makeup. Both of these changes were the result of larger population trends over several decades that saw the city losing residents, mostly white citizens, to its suburbs. For example, in the 1980s alone, the city's population declined by over 12 percent and the suburbs population increased by over 7 percent. As was the case in similar settings across the nation, governmental, educational, economic and political institutions in the region were complicit in facilitating these shifts and helping to create patterns of residential segregation in the metropolitan area.[6] *De facto* residential segregation is linked to other forms of social injustice, not the least being the unequal distribution of resources to educate students in city and suburban schools. Therefore, by the early 1980s, the metropolitan region was embroiled in a contentious 10-year battle over how to provide quality education for students in the now-predominantly black Monticello School District.

After a number of truncated attempts, the issue was formally resolved in 1983 with a court-supervised settlement agreement between the city, state, U.S. Department of Education, the plaintiffs who filed the original suit in the early 1970s, the NAACP and over 20 suburban school districts. A major provision of the *Consent Decree* was a voluntary transfer program to reconfigure the student population throughout schools in the region. The provision allowed some 13,000 black students from the city to enroll in predominantly white schools in the suburbs and about 1,400 white students from the suburbs to attend MSD magnet schools with black and white students from the city. In addition to the two-way inter-district student transfer program, the settlement agreement sought to ameliorate the conditions of the vast majority of MSD students who remained in the city public system by including provisions to implement quality education and capital improvement plans in their neighborhood schools.

The *Consent Decree* between the city and suburban districts officially ended in 1999 with confusion and uncertainty. This also left the post-desegregated MSD and its largely black student population of 42,000 at risk for losing state accreditation. It should also be noted that the current demographic configuration of MSD is also greatly influenced by the fact that more than 20 percent of white school-age children and youth who live in Monticello attend private schools and that 80 percent of their black peers attend public schools. Thus, fifty years after *Brown*, twenty-one years after the Monticello-area *Consent Decree* was implemented, and five years after it ended, parents and leaders in the lay, civic and business communities are understandably still disillusioned about the state of the urban school district.

The decision of the lawyers for the plaintiffs to opt for integration to achieve racial justice for black students in MSD must be placed within the contexts of the politics that informed the social, political and economic life of the Monticello metropolitan region and of the broader social agenda of those who provided financial backing for the petitioners. Following the lead of the national office of the NAACP, the architects of the Monticello school desegregation policy defined the problem largely as separation and as the unequal distribution of resources, or skills, information and social capital between black and white students in the metropolitan area. According to this view, the lack of contact between groups engendered racial stereotypes, resentment and conflict. In addition, material imbalances contributed to social inequalities in schools and the larger society by creating differentially skilled classes of individuals. Thus, it was reasoned, integration was the logical strategy to ameliorate the conditions that prevented black students in the MSD from receiving a quality education and from fully participating in the economic and social networks of the broader society.

Rethinking Educational Justice Fifty Years After *Brown*

Contemplating the effects of *Brown* several decades after it was declared the law of the land, William Tate and his colleagues note that a flaw in desegregation policy is that it provides "an essentially mathematical solution to a socio-cultural problem ... and propose[s] that by physically manipulating the students' school placement the problems of inequality would be addressed."[7] Such policy, other critics note, "fails to encompass the complexity of achieving equal educational opportunity for children to whom it so long has been denied."[8] As Derrick Bell further points out that failure to attack "all policies of racial subordination almost guarantees that the basic evils of segregated schools will survive and flourish, even in those systems where racially balanced schools can be achieved."[9] Critics generally agree with this assessment and critique desegregation policy for failing to provide relief for forms of injustice related to decision-making procedures, social division of labor and culture.[10]

Such failure was all but guaranteed in the desegregation of Monticello-area schools by the manner in which the *Consent Decree* was produced and implemented. In this instance, although the court found that Monticello's suburbs were complicit in the segregation of the MSD and threatened to merge the metropolitan region into a single district, it placed the onus of the educational malfeasance that injured black students on the state and survived legal challenges by two attorney generals, one Republican and one Democrat, to force it to pay for most of the costs of desegregating the area schools. In framing the decision in this manner, the court made the prospect of desegregation attractive to suburban districts by compelling the state to pay both state *and local* costs for each transfer student enrolled into their schools. This decision led to an enormous financial windfall for the participating suburban districts, translating into millions of dollars over the past twenty years to be used at the discretion of the respective districts. In contrast, the financial benefits promised to non-magnet city schools by the *Consent Decree* for the enhancement of curriculum and development and for capital improvements never materialized.[11] Such politics, critics argue, are the stuff of the "silent covenants," or brokered deals that benefit white students at the expense of black students and plague desegregation education policy.[12]

Although, the provisions of desegregation policy designed to direct much, needed resources to black students are absolutely necessary to rectify conditions of injustice in public schools, these alone cannot ameliorate circumstances linked to forms of injustice better characterized as domination and oppression.[13] Domination and oppression are injuries that are expressed through socio-cultural processes, as Tate and his associates point out, such as the established conventions, rules and assumptions about rightness, goodness and appropriateness that normalize inequality in school and society.[14] This point is especially relevant for an examination of the case presented in this chapter. Similar to *Brown*, an underlying assumption that guided the Monticello-area settlement was that "black schools, whatever their physical endowments, could not equal white ones [and] ... that integration was a matter of a white benefactor and a black beneficiary."[15] In other words, assumptions of white superiority and black inferiority informed the creation of desegregation education policy in MSD, and, in effect, reinforced, if not altogether institutionalized, forms of domination and oppression in the schooling of black students in both the city and the suburban schools.

In many ways, the obstacles that black students encounter in contemporary U.S. public schools are distinctly post-civil rights era problems, that is, a part of the legacy of education policy that was created as the result of the 1954 ruling. For instance, as the racial demography of schools began to change as a result of integration, black students encountered white educators who had very low expectations for their academic success. Black students who managed to exceed the expectations of their teachers were and are still commonly regarded as "unusual" and as exceptions to racial academic norms.[16] Contemporary ethnographic accounts of race and education show how preferential treatment accorded to these "unusual" black students in schools contributes to an untenable situation where these students either become estranged from or ostracized by their black peers. Included in this body of scholarship are studies that document the dilemmas of "acting white" and that report on oppositional attitudes, forms of academic disengagement and stereotype threats that constitute part of the legacy of race and education in post-civil rights America.[17]

On the other hand, the implementation of desegregation policy often emphasized integration for the sake of integration and not for the sake of education, social justice and cultural democracy. Michelé Foster's critique of Jonathan Kozol's *Savage Inequalities* succinctly captures the general limitations of school desegregation policy in this regard. She describes the burdens black communities often bear in meeting social expectations, often at the expense of the academic achievement of their children and youth while white communities, whose children and youth continue to flourish academically, are rarely challenged to make adjustments to accommodate black students.[18] These involuntary sacrifices include having to endure various forms of second-generation discrimination, from the resegregation of students within desegregated schools to the disproportionate suspensions and expulsion rates of black students. With respect to the former kind of injury, desegregated schools typically sort students into homogeneous subsets by so-called ability groupings. This generally results in the concentration of white students in honors and gifted classes and of students of color in lower tracks, remedial courses and special education programs.[19] A recent study of St. Louis metropolitan area suburban schools calls into question certain aspects of the merits and fairness of ability grouping. In their book *Stepping Over the Color Line*, Amy Stuart Wells and Robert Crain observe, that what some teachers in the suburban schools called "intelligence" was little more than the cultural capital exhibited by their middle-class white students.

The findings in the study conducted by Wells and Crain point to a pattern in schools whereby teachers reward black students for their conformity to white cultural norms and sanction those students for their displays of expressive black culture.[20] Second-generation discrimination is also attributable to these socio-cultural processes. For instance, offenses that implicate black expressive culture comprise the majority of typical violations that contribute to exorbitant black student referral, suspension and expulsion rates in schools. Such offenses are generally related to communicative issues such as defiance of authority, failure to follow instructions in a timely manner, modest displays of recalcitrance, attire, demeanor and gait. Disparities are also attributable to double standards whereby educators typically condemn and punish behaviors exhibited by black students that they often overlook and sometimes praise in white students.[21]

It should be noted that such rates are considerably reduced in schools that are under the leadership of black educators who are apt to interpret the behaviors that black youth exhibit from a cultural frame of reference and a social perspective that differs dramatically from many of their white colleagues.[22] Not only do these black educators readily distinguish between forms of conduct that require disciplinary responses and those that do not, they are also less prone to employ punitive measures in those situations that warrant some sort of administrative action or intervention. This point in particular underscores the significance of affirming the Second Generation Rights of black students in reform efforts to enhance their success in school. In the following section, I take a closer look at how second generation issues play out in the education of black students at City High School.

City High School: A Caring, High-Achieving Magnet Academy[23]

City High School was established in the Monticello School District in the early 1970s as a "school without walls" to provide an alternative educational setting for students who experienced difficulty in the district's traditional high schools. Teachers viewed the students for whom the school was created to be bright, but unable to adjust to the highly structured environments typically found in urban secondary schools. Unlike students who had been expelled from other high schools in the district for violent conduct, CHS students were mainly those who did not engage in day-to-day academic and social activities or perhaps did not comply with educational conventions to the point where they were at risk for "falling through the cracks."

With this in mind, the founding principal, a black woman, established CHS around the premise that marginalized students need both a rigorous curriculum *and love* if education was to play a meaningful role in their lives. Her pedagogical vision was one in which schools not only developed minds but cultivated hearts as well. In addition, the principal embraced an explicit social justice ethics and integrated it into every aspect of her educational plan, from curriculum and instruction to governance and discipline. She instantiated her philosophy through a flexible curriculum that attended to the individual needs of students by allowing them to develop an academic program based on course selections around their personal interests. In addition to providing a curriculum that appealed to teenagers who did not fare well in traditional educational settings, the principal used further measures to address the emotional and social needs of her students.

City High's academic program, social climate and success with students made it a logical choice to become a magnet academy once the Monticello voluntary settlement agreement between the city and suburban school districts went into effect. For instance, the academic program and social climate were amenable to white suburban families who were otherwise reluctant to send their students to city schools. Thus, despite opposition from the principal, in the early 1980s the MSD education board designated CHS as one of the secondary magnet academies it established as part of the *Consent Decree*. The founding principal retired in the mid-1990s with the school continuing to build around the academic program and caring social climate that she had been so central in establishing. Prior to her retirement, the school moved into a single physical plant built and maintained by the district. More recently, the school moved again, this time into a state of the art physical plant located centrally within the city, amid a mixture of working- and middle-class family neighborhoods, shopping and business districts, and cultural, religious and academic institutions.

Post-Desegregated City High

Today, City High School, with its fifty-fifty percent black-white student population, remains among the top secondary schools in the state. In 1999, its tenth-graders were ranked first among sophomores in the state's 400 public high schools in general performance and test scores. Similarly, in both 2000 and 2001, CHS's juniors were first among the state's eleventh-graders in communication arts and social studies. The school's 1999 average ACT score of 25.8 surpassed the national average of 21 and nearly all graduating seniors go on to attend four-year universities. In addition, the school's original emphasis on care and reconciliation resonates today in displays throughout the building that links virtue to academic achievement or race relations: "Twenty-Five Years of Excellence" reads a large banner that overlooks the cafeteria; "We are a nation of many cultures but only one species: so let's make respect part of our cultural heritage" announces a poster that hangs above a water fountain.

The school's amiable culture is also evident in its virtual absence of violence and racial conflict. For instance, only one student was either expelled or suspended during the 1998-1999 academic year. This number stands in stark contrast to the suspension and expulsion rates of other secondary schools in the metropolitan area with significant numbers of black students. For example, a high school in a nearby suburban school district with a student population of just more than 150 students reported over 33 suspensions and expulsions; in another neighboring district, a middle school with a student enrollment of less than 900 reported over 700 suspensions and expulsions during the 1998-1999 year.

City High appears to contradict popular images of urban high schools throughout the U.S. As one student put it in 1999, "we feel as if we're a separate community at times, and I guess we take a certain pride in that." However, like the "good" high schools captured in Sarah Lawrence Lightfoot's portraitures, CHS also has its shares of "imperfections, uncertainties and vulnerabilities."[24] Probably the most glaring of its imperfections is that the benefits of attending CHS do not extend to its entire student body. As opposed to the random expressions of student "failure" that may be explained away in terms of individual differences that normally occur within any population, academic disparities at CHS occurs along systematic gender and racial lines. Although the school has an equal number of black and white students, girls regularly outnumber boys, sometimes by as much as a two to one ratio. This discrepancy is the result of the unequal number of black female and black male students who normally enroll at CHS, with black girls typically outnumbering black boys. This discrepancy was especially apparent during a recent academic year when there were three times as many black girls as there were black boys at CHS.

The (Dys)Education of Black Males at City High

Educational studies in the U.S., Canada and the United Kingdom consistently reports on the plight of black male students in public schools and details their disproportionately high placement in special education programs, suspensions and expulsions, both in urban and suburban settings.[25] Such findings tend to give credence to conventional wisdom that makes the plight of black male students at CHS all the more unremarkable because it is perceived to be par for the course. Perhaps the greatest obstacle that black male students face at CHS is conventional wisdom that this plight is a normal, albeit problematic, fact of life in secondary schools. This holds especially true in schools like CHS with high-powered academic programs and codes of conduct that rely on student compliance for their enforcement. This is implicit in the remarks of a recent CHS principal, as reported in an article for a local magazine: "The students that come here are self-motivated and just very disciplined," says their current principal. "They take on that responsibility. We haven't had a problem." It is reasonable to surmise that the principal's conception of self-motivated and disciplined students does not include black males. For instance, later in the article, the writer declares, "black males don't attend City" and also that "sometimes boys spell trouble."

Despite its acceptance by many within the school and the district, the exclusion of black males at CHS is indeed troubling. For instance, all CHS students, including black males, have histories of high academic performance and records of exemplary behavior in elementary and middle school and have passed an examination to qualify for entrance to the school. This means that, on paper, black male students are no different from the rest of their City High peers: they have adhered to all the rules and have met all criteria for admission to the school. However, once these students enter City High, they encounter problems that are characteristic of black male students in other educational settings. Further, the exclusion of these students occurs within a setting in which overt racial hostility is generally absent.

Data from my ethnographic research at CHS suggest that exclusion and marginalization of black males occurs as they are tacitly framed in opposition to the high-status curriculum and amenable social environment that are valued at the school: black males are viewed by peers and adults alike as prone to jeopardizing the school's academic reputation and as inimical to its social climate.[26] Interview data with black male students indicate that they believe their peers typically ignore them, staff members consistently police them, and their teachers regularly mistreat them. The general complaint of these students is that they are subject to double standards at the school, in and out of the classroom. Perhaps nowhere do they perceive a double standard more than in the "zero-tolerance" policy that CHS and the district implemented with respect to school violence. During my initial visit to speak with members of the school's black male mentoring group, students contemplated this double standard in the context of an example of one of their white male peers who recently had given a classmate a haircut during a lunch period:

Kevin: "I mean he was right there in the middle of the cafeteria cutting that dude's hair! Everybody saw him, even [a teacher and an administrator]"

Bruce: "And, ain't nobody said nothing to him. I mean, you know if it was a brother, we would have been kicked out of the school…"

Lyle: "Shoot, out of the district. And handcuffed...."
Kevin: "And, it wasn't like he had the electric clippers like we use. He had those–what do you call those big scissors?"
Bruce: "*Yeah*, he had shears!"
Kevin: "Yeah, shears! Now, you know they ain't even trying to let a brother up in here with some toenail clippers, let alone some big scissors like that!"

The views that these young men have concerning double standards and their general treatment at CHS echoes other studies and are supported by data from interviews with and participant observations of their peers and teachers. Students and teachers may accord black male students little respect because of their perceived dependency on others, a purported trait that runs contrary to the value placed on the individualism implicit in competition and in the assumption of meritocracy that generally underlies explanations for academic achievement in U.S. schools. During a "focus group" interview, black and white female students complained that the school gave preferential treatment to black male students and argued that, if these students couldn't compete with others at the school, no special effort should be made to either attract them to or keep them at CHS.

The view that black males are overly dependent on others at CHS is pervasive at the school. This rather demeaning assumption is sometimes expressed rather openly, as in unsolicited comments made to me by Rick, a white male junior at CHS, after observing an interview session that I conducted with one of his black male peers in the school's library: "I hear you're doing a project on why there are no black guys at the school. My response when it first came to my attention was, 'So what?' I mean, if they can't cut it here, why should we care? I would say the same thing if it was any other group." Sometimes the notion of dependency is implicit in words intended to be supportive of black male students, such as the following remarks that a CHS staff person, a black woman, who was generally sympathetic to the circumstances of black male students at the school: "You know, our black males here need a lot of help. They don't always take care of business and end up getting into a lot of trouble. It's good that you're coming out to help them." Implicit in the language that students, faculty and staff members employ to describe the circumstances of black men is that they are naturally academically and socially deficient and are largely (if not solely) to blame for their marginalization and exclusion from the school. The characterization of black male students as dependent is so pervasive at the school that, with the exception of a few of their allies, the average person at CHS and, indeed, the district, simply do not find their exclusion and marginalization to be all that remarkable. As a consequence, black male students have little chance of appealing to those who hold these intuitive views of them.

The administration has indeed attempted to address the school's marginalization of black males. However, the data suggests that, given the lack of respect accorded to black male students, some of these responses may be informed by false empathy. Regardless of their good intentions, these responses may very well be at odds with the students' interests because the former fail to consider how the latter might interpret and would respond to their circumstances.[27] In fact, ill-informed social policy may actually perpetuate the conditions that it intends to ameliorate.[28] Along these lines, well-intentioned responses to the marginalization of black males at CHS, such as professional development workshops and the creation of the black male mentoring program by adults may actually reinforce the marginalization of black males at the school.

In the fall of 1998, the principal invited a nationally known black educational consultant to CHS to address the school on issues related to the education of black males. According to the principal, the all-day workshop was met with resistance from teachers, students and parents. Although such resistance is to be anticipated, interviews and informal conversations with students suggests that even those who agreed with the consultant's views were concerned about not being able to respond to him or to have a meaningful and ongoing dialogue about the larger issue of the experiences of black male students. Further, the lack of input by black male students regarding their experiences, coupled with a failure to follow up on the workshop only made students question the school's sincerity and willingness to grapple with real race and gender issues at CHS.

Even the black male mentoring program at the school functions in some ways to marginalize the very individuals it seeks to serve. For instance, during an all-school assembly on the first day of the 2000-2001 academic year, I scanned the audience for the faces and expressions of black male students during an announcement regarding the mentoring program. I experienced that "peculiar sensation," described by W.E.B. DuBois. This sensation was brought on by "a world that looks on in amused contempt and pity."[29] For the most part, the young men I observed either looked down or straight ahead, suggesting that they were shutting out the announcement. Their behavior was cause for me to wonder what the program meant to them. Although all the young men I interviewed stated that they found the mentoring sessions to be helpful, their low and inconsistent attendance suggested that the program represented something more complicated in their lives at school. Indeed, some of the peers of these students openly deride the program and point to it as evidence that black male students are unqualified to be at the school.[30] In addition, during sessions, mentors sometimes conveyed contradictory messages to the mentees: they encouraged them to do well academically but also blamed the young men for the stereotypical attitudes that their teachers had of them.[31]

Schooling as a Moral Enterprise: Implications for Education in Post-Civil Rights America

The experiences of black males described in this chapter suggests that their plight cannot be ameliorated by the redistributive or mathematical formulae that underpins desegregation policy. Certainly, the competitive nature of CHS complicates their situation. Unbridled competition gives rise to values that reinforce individualism, not only making it difficult to sustain caring relationships but also reinforcing what the ethicist Victor Anderson calls "ontological blackness" or "the blackness that whiteness created."[32] Thus, the competitive culture at CHS reinforces the notion that black male students are strange and do not belong at the school. However, the data presented in this article indicates that the competitive culture of CHS alone fails to adequately account for the exclusion and marginalization of black male students at the school.

In addition, one might argue that a contrived caring community at CHS blinds it and others to its exclusionary practices. The school's caring reputation, as is the case with other codified, normalized and normalizing discourses, ensures maximum conformity to a particular view of CHS and builds resistance to an examination of how such a model institution, a paragon of equity and excellence, contributes to the oppression of any of its students. As the evidence presented in this chapter suggests, mere access to schools like CHS does little to address relationships and structures that are more fundamental to the ways that we organize institutions and to how we shape human lives within them. Therefore, attempts to transform the academic and social experiences of black students at competitive schools must go further than compensatory programs and professional development workshops and examine the moral dimension of schools.

The notion that schooling is primarily a moral project that cultivates virtue and assigns vice is embedded in the very foundation of education in Western societies. For example, such a view is plainly evident in Plato's *The Republic*, a book that is widely regarded as one of the most influential writings on Western education. *The Republic* takes up the issue of schooling around the question of "what is justice," or "what is morality," depending on the translation of the book. After rejecting or sidestepping a number of arguments presented by his companions in response to the question, Socrates shifts the argument from an emphasis on virtue as a possession of the individual to an analysis of it as a social value and concludes that individual virtue is whatever it takes to maintain justice at the societal level. For Socrates, a just state is a "healthy" or harmonious state, because such it is good, as opposed to "diseased" or tumultuous. Further, a harmonious state, or society, is one in which each person works according to *his* end to fulfill a specific occupation to keep the social body functioning smoothly. The body, in Socrates' analysis, is comprised of three parts: (1) rulers or leaders; (2) guardians or military and police; (3) everyone else who form the civic and economic majority of society. In this line of thinking, just individuals are those who demonstrate the intestinal fortitude to defer their various wants and desires to the rational decisions and sacrifices that we must make to maintain the status quo, that is, the "just society."

Although a number of progressive thinkers such as Rousseau, Dewey and Freire, have influenced our conceptions of children and education in the U.S., the ideas presented in *The Republic* clearly have had the greatest purchase on the way we organize public schools in contemporary American society. These ideas also help to explain the problems that black students have historically encountered in U.S. public schools as well as the dilemma faced by black male students in settings such as CHS. However, color-coded forms of oppression and inequality, such as those that are observable at CHS are symptomatic of the racial injustice that is particular to the organization of U.S. society. Critical race theorists posit that, for the most part, though many aspects of racial injustice are shorn of the more explicit and formal manifestations of power that we typically associate with oppression, they nonetheless inform relations of social dominance that we attribute to random expressions of inequality in contemporary American society.[33] And, to reiterate a point made elsewhere in this chapter, the intransigent nature of white supremacy in the U.S. is further ensconced in a society that is hard-pressed to affirm the cultural, social and economic rights of people of color and that is given to sanctioning them when they are asserted.[34]

The post-civil rights educational narrative construes the problems that black males encounter in schools as resulting from dispositions that make these students too different from their peers, and oppositionally so. Moreover, it comes as no surprise that they have difficulty in schools, especially in those with high-powered academic programs and codes of conduct that rely on student consent and compliance for their enforcement. Given the taken-for-granted nature of these racial norms, it is no wonder that much of the research, literature and conventional wisdom constructs black males as a strange population, thereby contributing to the widespread perception that their plight in schools is unremarkable. However, in my view, black students, males in particular, suffer a more fundamental condition of estrangement that is owed in part to historical educational narratives that rationalize social inequality, in part to the tacit arrogation of white cultural norms in contemporary education. Such a condition normalizes the marginalization and exclusion of these students in schools and society. Rather than a *strange* population, then, black students, especially males, are often *estranged* from the social and academic networks in schools. Further, the failure of education policy to address what are essentially Second Generation problems in post-civil rights-era education, problems that are moral at their core, places not only black students at risk but jeopardizes all who are engaged in the enterprise of public schooling as well.

Conclusion

What, then, are the sources of a new ethical orientation which may have roots in Negro tradition and yet also reaches into the heroic striving for a new identity within the universal ethics emanating from worldwide technology and communication?

—Erik H. Erikson[35]

I speak to the black experience, but I am always talking about the human condition–about what we can endure, dream, fail at, and still survive.

—Maya Angelou[36]

When asked for his definition of "equal," Thurgood Marshall once answered, "Equal means getting the same thing at the same time and in the same place." However, some fifty years after he made his prescient remarks on behalf of the plaintiffs in the landmark *Brown v. Board of Education* case, black students are still denied access to "the same thing," even when they exist "at the same time and in the same place" with resources that often benefit their white peers. As the discussion in this chapter illustrates, such inequality has little to do with the native academic abilities of black students or with their attitudes toward schooling and may have more to do with educators' attitudes toward black students and with their unwillingness to educate them to their highest potential.

In closing, it should also be noted that the denial of access to material resources takes on particular meanings in the post-industrial U.S. The prominence of communicative technologies in organizing economic and social life in contemporary American society alters the imperatives of public schools as institutions that, in addition to technical functions, promote citizenship and social justice. This means that black student access to resources is not only a means for them to obtain control over the material forces needed to mitigate economic disparities but also over the flow of images and information that shape how others perceive and relate to them. Finally, as I suggested in the previous section, the treatment of black youth in schools may very well be symptomatic of a more generalized repression of students. It bears to reason then that an education that affirms the social, cultural and economic rights, or Second Generation Rights, of black students may yield sources of a new ethical orientation in educational reform that does much more than just loosen the stranglehold of unexamined racial norms on their lives. Indeed, a new ethical orientation that emerges from their liberation has far-reaching implications for not only how we treat them, but also for how we may go about organizing schools and other social institutions in the larger society to serve the common interest.

Chapter 13

THE FORGOTTEN ONES:
AFRICAN-AMERICAN STUDENTS WITH DISABILITIES
IN THE WAKE OF *BROWN*

Wanda J. Blanchett & Monika W. Shealey

The *Brown v. the Board of Education* decision transformed American public education, not just for African-American students, as some would have us believe. In addition to prohibiting racial segregation in public education, the *Brown* decision was especially important in securing appropriate educational services and opportunities for students with disabilities. Prior to the *Brown* litigation and subsequent decision, African-American students and students with disabilities had similar experiences in the American educational system. Both were treated as second-class citizens. Moreover, African-American students with disabilities have experienced double jeopardy in the American educational system. Although few would have predicted that the *Brown v. the Board of Education* case would have any implications for special education and students with disabilities in particular, this decision laid the foundation for challenging the constitutionality of excluding children with disabilities from public schooling opportunities.[1]

Prior to the *Brown* decision and even in the 16 years after the decision, public schools were not *obligated to* educate students with disabilities. Consequently, excluding them from public education and/or educating them in segregated settings with little or no exposure to their non-disabled peers was perfectly legal. Losen & Orfield estimates that nearly 2 of the nation's 4 million children with disabilities were not served at all or were inadequately served in public schools during this time period.[2] When students with disabilities were served, they were often educated in "ghetto-like" isolated and "run-down" classrooms within buildings that housed students without disabilities or in separate facilities altogether.[3] Such terms as "ghetto-like" and "run-down" have often been utilized to describe the physical environments of some of the segregated schools African-American students attended prior to

Brown regardless of the presence or absence of a disability.[4] The *Brown* decision provided advocates and parents of students with disabilities a legal precedent for challenging the educational inequities that children with disabilities experienced.

The legal challenge to segregated schooling and exclusion of children with disabilities came on the heels of the *Brown* decision in the form of two very significant court cases, *PARC v. Commonwealth of Pennsylvania* and *Mills v. the District of Columbia. PARC v. the Commonwealth of Pennsylvania* (1972) guaranteed special education services to children and youth with mental retardation.[5] However, the decision in this case did not address educational provisions for children with disabilities other than mental retardation. In 1973, *Mills v. the District of Columbia* extended the provisions of *PARC* to all children with disabilities.[6] The victories in these cases set the stage for the principle of normalization for individuals with disabilities, now known as the disability rights movement. The concept of normalization was based on the idea that individuals with disabilities have the right to participate in all aspects and facets of life, including the right to be educated in public schools, to have access to their peers without disabilities, to live in their communities versus institutions, and to develop the skills needed to work and engage in recreational activities. The disability rights movement, using much of the language and many of the tactics of the civil rights movement, was able to spin this philosophy of normalization into legislation that protected the rights of individuals with disabilities with regard to education, participation in public and private entities, and prohibited discrimination on the basis of disabilities.

Three legislative actions have been credited with significantly changing the way American society views, treats and responds to the needs of individuals with disabilities. These include: Section 504 of The Vocational Rehabilitation Act of 1973, the Education for All Handicapped Children Act of 1975, currently known as the Individuals with Disabilities Education Act (IDEA), and the Americans with Disabilities Act of 1990 (ADA).[7] Section 504 has been hailed as the first major legislative step toward securing and protecting the rights of individuals with disabilities because it was the first piece of legislation to define a disability, to prohibit discrimination on the basis of disability in the public sector, and to provide educational services to students with disabilities. The ADA has been credited with extending civil rights protection to individuals with disabilities and mandating appropriate accommodations and modifications in both the private and public sectors. While all of these legislations have brought about great positive changes for individuals with disabilities, IDEA is acknowledged as the single most important education legislation for students with disabilities because it guarantees students' right to: (a) a free and appropriate public education; (b) the least restrictive environment or placement; (c) individualized education program; (d) appropriate and nondiscriminatory evaluations; (e) parental and student participation in decision-making; and (f) procedural safeguards.[8]

Currently, more than 6 million children enjoy a free and appropriate public education with the protections and safeguards mentioned above. Although we have not fully arrived in being responsive to the educational needs of students with disabilities, today, more are educated in general education classrooms with their non-disabled peers and attend post-secondary schools than at any other point in American history. In addition, they are living in communities and participating in competitive employment at much higher rates. Despite the remarkable benefits and opportunities afforded students with disabilities, the benefits of special education have not been equitably distributed.[9] African-American children with disabilities have not received schooling opportunities comparable to their white peers. Segregation on the basis of race, disability and the intersection of race with disability is still a pervasive problem in the educational system as a whole and in special education programs in particular.[10]

Original Intent of Special Education in Theory and Practice

Although the field of special education has undergone several philosophical changes over the last couple of decades, it is a fairly new field and is still evolving. In theory, special education was conceived to provide support and training for students who were perceived as a challenge for the general education system, including African-American students, students with disabilities, and African-American students with disabilities. Students who were eligible received specialized services such as individualized instruction, tutoring and other forms of intervention to assist them in reaching their potential. Once students' needs were either met and/or appropriate strategies or modifications implemented, they would return to general education settings.

As special education theory evolved, it became very clear that many students with disabilities were being educated in segregated self-contained settings with little to no exposure or access to their non-disabled peers. More importantly, these students did not have access to the same curricula content as their non-disabled peers. As a result, many were not living up to their potential and often exited public schools with insufficient skills to gain meaningful employment and to participate in all aspects of adult life. These revelations lead to the initiation of several longitudinal studies to examine the post-school outcomes of students with disabilities and to compare their post-school outcomes to their in-school experiences and learning opportunities.[11] The findings of these studies suggested that special education theory and practice was not robust enough to prepare individuals with disabilities for life after school. Specifically, these studies revealed that students with disabilities often lack the social skills, life skills, basic academic skills and employment training to participate in all aspects of adult life.[12] To prevent students with disabilities from continuing to experience such dismal post-school outcomes, disability rights advocates called for the reform of special education to address these shortcomings.

Although the 1980s gave birth to many special education reform ideas, the most radical of the special education reform ideas was the theory of inclusion. Full inclusion called for providing all special education services to students with disabilities in the general education context without removing students from the classroom. Advocates of inclusion have been very successful in arguing that incorporating these students is consistent with the concept of normalization, the disability rights movement, the major tenets of the civil rights movement, and the promise of *Brown*. Moreover, research suggests that the benefits of inclusion are significant for all students. Students with disabilities who are included in general education classrooms have higher levels of social skills, are more accepted by their nondisabled peers, and have greater exposure to the general education curriculum. According to the 24th Annual Report to Congress in 2004, the majority of students with disabilities are included in general education classrooms for some portion of their school day. This represents a significant increase in their access to general education and integrated classrooms and is a radical shift from early special education theory and practice.

The field of special education has evolved considerably since its inception. For the past fifty years, the field has been in the midst of change, most of which is directed at humanizing educational interventions, practices and obtaining better results. The calls for accountability in general education have been amplified due in part to the assertion in the report from the President's Commission on Excellence in Special Education that, "children placed in special education were general education students first."[13] This represents a shift from simply advocating for and providing access to physical facilities to including such students in state and district assessments, and working to ensure access to the general education curriculum. The field is currently entrenched in a debate over the legitimacy of placing students with disabilities in self-contained settings, the level of access to the general education curriculum afforded to students in those settings and what constitutes a highly qualified special education teacher.

Special Education in Practice for African-American Students

In its original and subsequent conceptualization, special education was not conceived as a place or location, but rather, a service delivery structure. However, for many African-American students, "special education has too often been a place—a place to segregate minorities and students with disabilities."[14] African-American students with disabilities have had a number of experiences in the American special education system that raises concerns. Among the concerns most frequently cited by researchers are: (a) the persistent problem of disproportionate representation of African-American students in special education, (b) the trend of placing African-American students with disabilities segregated instead of inclusive or general education settings, (c) the lack of culturally responsive interventions and instructional practices in both general and special education classrooms, and (d) the significant shortage of fully credentialed special education teachers, including teachers of color. Disproportionality exists when a specific group's representation in special education as a whole and/or in specific disability categories exceeds their representation in the general school population or in the special education program.[15] During the 2000-01 school year, African-American students accounted for

14.8% of all school-aged children between the ages of 6 to 21, however, they represented 19.8% of those receiving special education services.[16] Although students served under IDEA are representative of all racial/ethnic, cultural and linguistic backgrounds, African-American students are disproportionately represented in the high-incidence disability categories of mild mental retardation, specific learning disabilities and emotional/ behavioral disabilities categories.

Persistence of Disproportionality

In the years shortly after the inception of special education, it became apparent that some schools and teachers were likely utilizing special education referral and placement to avoid desegregation efforts. In 1968, Lloyd Dunn first called attention to the fact that African-American students in New York were being labeled as having mild mental retardation and were being placed in segregated classrooms. In his work with poor inner-city students, Dunn noted that African-American students' representation in programs for those with mild mental retardation exceeded rates that would be expected given their relative size in the general population of school-aged children. The work of Dunn and other concerned researchers helped to end the use of intelligence tests as the sole basis for determining special education eligibility and played a role in securing some of the safeguards guaranteed by IDEA.[17] While this issue has been studied by a number of researchers in education, law and sociology including the Harvard Civil Rights Project, disproportionality has persisted for more than thirty years and seems resistant to change.

Although a number of factors have been identified as contributing to the disproportionate referral and placement of African-American students with the shortage of teachers from ethnically diverse groups, faculty referral and placement procedures, and the lack of appropriate early-reading instruction and intervention are among the most frequently cited.[18] Researchers have cited the shortage of teachers from under-represented groups as a contributing factor to the disproportionate representation of students of color in special education.[19] The lack of diversity in the teaching force negatively impacts students of color's achievement, prevents students with disabilities from exposure to adults with disabilities, limits white students' exposure to teachers from diverse backgrounds and perspectives, and results in few opportunities for students of color to experience members of their communities in instructional leadership positions. Teachers from under-represented groups must be available to minimize cultural conflict between professionals and families, to serve as role models, and to help the educational setting reflect the ethnic diversity of the U.S.[20]

Significant Teacher Shortages and Lack of Preparation for Cultural Diversity

The increasing supply for high-quality special educators and the high attrition rate of special education teachers presents a daunting challenge for teacher-preparation programs seeking to meet the demand while providing programming consistent with an established knowledge base on teacher practices and beliefs. The magnitude of the shortage is also felt by school districts forced to fill vacancies for special education teachers with uncertified teachers. According to *Brownell et al.,* the number of special education students has grown to 20.3 percent from 1992 to 1999.[21] Consequently, the most recent data available from the U.S. Department of Education reveals that approximately 11.4 percent of all teachers filling special education positions during the 2000-2001 school year lacked appropriate special education certification.[22] For urban schools and schools with a large percentage of students of color, the shortages of qualified special education professionals and the attrition rate is exacerbated.[23]

Despite the acknowledged value of having a diverse teaching force for both students of color as well as their white peers, there is a significant shortage of teachers from traditionally under-represented groups to serve students with high-incidence disabilities. Using data compiled by the National Clearinghouse for Professions in Special Education (NCPSE), Crutchfield reported that 86% of special education teachers are white, 10% African-American, 2% Hispanic and 2% other.[24] What is even more disturbing than these percentages is that research suggests that the percentage of teachers from ethnically diverse backgrounds is declining.[25] As a result, the racial/ethnic composition of special education teachers to serve culturally and linguistically diverse students has grown increasingly disproportionate in recent years to the number of students attending urban schools. In many large urban school districts, students from ethnically, culturally and linguistically diverse backgrounds comprise 60-80% of the student population while the teaching force remains almost completely the opposite.

When comparing the racial and ethnic backgrounds of educators and students in America's public schools, it is evident that there is a cultural mismatch between the backgrounds and experiences of teachers and their students. This mismatch is manifested in the school policies and procedures which have been found to be more punitive towards students of color[26] and the growing number of students of color referred for special education services due to lowered teacher expectations, faulty assumptions and mis-diagnoses.[27] Students of color make up approximately 37.7% of the nation's special education students and 38% of all public school students.[28] However, only 14% of individuals currently teaching in special education and 14% of those currently in teacher-education programs are from traditionally under-represented groups.[29] According to Olson, the percentage of teachers of color will decrease by the year 2009.[30] This prediction is particularly troublesome given the fact that the percentage of students of color in public schools across the country is steadily increasing and recent trends in special education suggest that the population of students with disabilities will continue to rise.

Resegregation of African-American Students with Disabilities

IDEA addresses the need to provide services to students with disabilities in the least restrictive environment (LRE), however, many African-American students with disabilities are still being educated in self-contained segregated settings. The least restrictive environment refers to the extent to which students with disabilities are educated with their non-disabled peers. The mandate on least restrictive environment emphasizes that students should have this opportunity "to the maximum extent appropriate."[31] However, what remains unclear for many practitioners actively involved in the referral and placement process is how to mediate issues associated with race, culture and poverty and the influence of these variables on placement decisions. The disconcerting reality for African-American students placed in the high-incidence disabilities categories of mild mental retardation, learning disabilities and emotional disturbance is that they will most likely be served in the most segregated and isolated settings.

National and state placement data suggests that African-American students with disabilities are still spending the majority of their time in segregated settings. During the 2000-2001 school year, 52.0% of white students compared to only 35.3% of African-American students spent 21% or less of the day outside of regular or general education classes.[32] In addition, African-Americans spend twice as much time outside of the general education classroom than their white peers. According to the 24th Annual Report to Congress, 31% of African-American students compared to only 15.3% of white students with disabilities spend 60% or greater of their school day outside of the regular classroom. A recent state study in four Delaware school districts on placement decisions for African-American students and their European counterparts found major discrepancies. Hosp and Reschly found that decisions regarding the restrictiveness of a student's placement resulted from several factors including: (a) the severity of the student's academic difficulties; (b) the presence of behavior problems; and (c) the level of involvement of the student's family.[33] Though placement decisions in these schools did appear to be linked to some larger construct or data, these researchers still noted that there remained differential outcomes for African-American students based on these factors.

Similarly, Ladner and Hammons found that when examining statistical data in order to determine the impact of a student's race on receiving a special education label, seven out of the nine states involved in the study revealed a statistically significant relationship between race and special education rates, even after controlling for variables such as poverty and spending per pupil.[34] Despite sufficient data that points to the prevalence and influence of racism and discrimination in the special education referral, placement, service delivery and exiting process, the above researchers as well as others in the field of special education have been reluctant to acknowledge that these are systematic issues that need to be addressed. Instead, many of these researchers would have us continue to debate whether or not inequities exist in the treatment of African-American students with disabilities and to provide empirical evidence to substantiate the inequities that have already been documented for more than thirty years.

Ensuring Equal Access to High-Quality Services, Resources and Integrated Classrooms

The need to provide equitable access to high-quality services, resources and integrated classrooms is a mandate that unfortunately has failed to yield systemic benefits for students of color, particularly those with disabilities. However, the recent interest in the types of intervention offered to students with disabilities as well as the emphasis on providing access to general education curriculum has created a rich dialogue, particularly among teacher educators and policymakers, on what constitutes research-based or evidence-based practices. One area of instruction essential to ensuring students of color experience greater access to the general education curriculum is effective literacy instruction. Poor reading performance and perceived behavior problems are primary indicators for referral and placement of students of color in special education.[35] According to recent data, approximately 80 percent of students with mild disabilities experience significant problems with language and reading.[36] *Lyon et al.,* reports the largest number of students referred and placed in special education are labeled as learning disabled (LD) and most of the placements in this category involved reading problems.[37] Recent debate in the area of reading has focused on the nature of reading, elements of reading that must be addressed in instruction, and the identification of research-based reading approaches.

The controversy surrounding reading instruction has primarily focused on the nature and use of phonics instruction in beginning reading instruction, specifically with students of color and those with disabilities. The term direct instruction stems from the federally funded project called Follow Through, which evaluated major approaches to educating primary grade students from low incomes. Rosenshine used the term direct instruction to describe the set of instructional variables that are highly correlated with high levels of academic growth for students in elementary grades.[38] The components of direct instruction, which emphasize skill mastery over meaning construction, teacher control and the use of workbooks has been viewed antithetical to a philosophy which should be extended when working with students of color and students with disabilities. Instead, the use of an eclectic approach, grounded in the principles of multi-cultural education which acknowledges and builds upon the strengths and experiences of student have been recommended by many researchers.[39]

Culturally responsive and relevant teaching represents the application of the principles of multi-cultural education and has been found to be an effective method of effectively teaching culturally and linguistically diverse students. Culturally responsive and relevant literacy instruction must first include a greater understanding of the role of teachers' prior experiences and attitudes about diverse learners and its impact on the type of literacy approaches teachers relied upon in their instruction. Researchers have found that teachers are willing to improve their pedagogical skills, yet they are often unaware of how their beliefs and attitudes toward teaching affect changes they might make.[40] In addition, the instructional approaches utilized by culturally responsive and relevant literacy teachers are grounded in providing skills found to be effective in the development of reading in meaningful and relevant ways. The approaches range from direct instruction, which can be provided in a variety of formats to cooperative learning strategies which capitalize on the social nature of learning and the learning styles of many students of color. Finally, assessment in literacy instruction is viewed as dynamic and ongoing. Traditional assessment measures have proven to be ineffective and insufficient in evaluating students of color.[41] For example, students who speak African-American Vernacular English (AAVE), or Black English, are at a greater risk of being labeled as low-performing readers due to a failure of educators to recognize the structures of their language patterns and utilize this information in making appropriate decisions about their reading capabilities. Thus, curriculum-based assessment and performance-based assessment are prominent features of an effective literacy program. These assessment approaches promote an emphasis on the learning processes rather than simply focusing on products.[42] In light of a growing body of literature supporting culturally responsive and relevant literacy instruction,[43] there remains a great deal of work in preparing educators to provide high-quality literacy instruction inclusive of a multi-cultural emphasis. This is especially critical in light of the growing diversity of America's public schools and the consequent increase of students referred and placed in special education programs.

The instructional practices used by African-American teachers in a pre-*Brown* era is rooted in an Afrocentric philosophy which places "African-American students within the context of their traditions and experiences so that they are better able to relate to other cultural perspectives."[44] Desegregation not only changed African-American students and their schooling experiences, it also impacted the extent to which African-American teachers were able to provide the services they believed promoted academic excellence and general student empowerment.[45] In recent years, Afrocentricity's major features such as culturally responsive and relevant teaching[46] have been advanced as effective ways of teaching students of color. Culturally responsive and relevant teaching seeks to relate learning experiences by utilizing the culture of students without requiring them to sacrifice their cultural identities.[47] With growing evidence supporting the infusion of multi-cultural education in school-reform initiatives, which ultimately drives decisions made about curriculum, pedagogy and school-wide polices and procedures, the key to ensuring access to the services and resources for African-American students lies in how these instructional practices, which for years preceding the *Brown* decision promoted academic and social success for students of color, can be used in today's schools to reach the very same goals.

It is imperative that school-reform initiatives recognize and mediate the political nature of schooling and its impact on students of color. Mandates such as high-stakes testing, although rooted in a need for greater accountability, have failed to enhance the quality of educational experiences for students of color, particularly those in urban settings. One of the unintended consequences of such misguided mandates has resulted in diminished opportunities for students to engage in authentic and meaningful tasks. In fact, efforts to provide more inclusive practices and curriculum reflective of the growing changes in our global society are thwarted by the influx of test preparation and basic skills workbooks.[48] Even during segregation, African-American teachers recognized the political nature of teaching, however, they actively engaged in activities that fostered emancipatory thinking in their students. Despite the state of affairs in the country during that time, African-American students believed they could succeed because their teachers believed and expected them to do so. Thus, there is a need to continue and expand efforts to recruit and retain teachers of color as well as those committed to ensuring equitable educational experiences for all students.

Albeit, teachers and students of color may experience commonalities based on lived experiences and shared cultural traditions. Culturally responsive and relevant teachers may not always be from culturally and linguistically diverse backgrounds. However, it is important to continue to target individuals of color to enter the teaching force. There are a number of benefits inherent in having culturally and linguistically diverse teachers represented in America's public schools. The impact of a diverse teaching force may influence the comfort level of students of color and may provide them with role models.[49] Additionally, teachers from diverse backgrounds also may serve as liaisons between the school and the community and may serve as translators for students and professionals from the majority culture.[50] Finally, teachers of color utilize their understanding of the cultural patterns and learning styles of students of color in providing educational experiences that are culturally compatible and promote success.[51]

The prerequisite for building cultural competency lies with the ability of educators to understand the culture and experiences of their students and use this information in teaching and in interactions with students and their families. This level of competency requires one to move beyond the cultural awareness stage of understanding to the social action stage. Teachers at the social action stage of cultural competency engage in and promote activities that incorporate the knowledge students bring to school in a manner that translates into positive student outcomes. It also involves working actively to counteract racism and injustice within the school context.

Therefore, professional development for teachers should move beyond the traditional "sit and pray" formats which offer one-day workshops on a particular topic and facilitators later pray that teachers will utilize the information in their classrooms. Professional development initiatives should include an emphasis on self-examination and critical reflection. Critical reflection refers to a level of processing which examines moral, political and ethical contexts of teaching such as equity, access and social justice.[52] Additionally, educators must be provided with the supports and resources necessary to develop their cultural competency. Professional development and resources that will build teachers' capacity to meet the needs of African-American students with disabilities include: (a) time for reflection and dialogue regarding their assumptions regarding race, gender, culture and the intersection of these variables with disability, (b) an opportunity to utilize curriculum which reflects the growing demands of our global and technological society but also builds upon students' prior knowledge and experiences, and (c) developing shared decision-making and leadership skills, and (d) a willingness to be coached and/or mentored to enhance their practice.

In the fifty years since the *Brown* decision, remarkable progress has been made in the field of special education and in serving students with disabilities. The most notable of this progress has been the passage of legislation to prohibit discrimination against students with disabilities and to secure appropriate educational services. Despite these significant gains in legislative protections and access to general education settings, few African-American students with disabilities have benefitted from this progress. To bring about more positive educational experiences and post-school outcomes for African-American students with disabilities would require both general and special education to take responsibility for all students and to acknowledge the fact that the racism and discrimination that exists in the larger society is also prevalent in the dual-track school system. Moreover, affecting change would entail developing and implementing strategies to counter such institutionalized racism and discrimination so that some of the suggestions for reform offered above would actually have a chance of succeeding.

Chapter 14

UNEQUAL ACCESS TO COLLEGE PREPARATORY CLASSES: A CRITICAL CIVIL RIGHTS ISSUE

Karen Miksch

Access to college preparatory courses is a seminal civil rights issue. The promise of *Brown* will never be actualized without rectifying the disparity in access to quality college preparatory courses in U.S. public high schools.

Academic rigor of high school curricula is especially important for African-American and Latino students.[1] "Answers in the Toolbox," a report published by the U.S. Department of Education, determined that rigor of high school curricula is a more important predictor of the probability that a student will graduate college than test scores or class rank.[2] Advanced Placement (AP) courses are among the most rigorous courses offered in high school. Administered by the College Board, AP courses are also the most common college preparatory programs in public high schools. Recognizing their assumed value, many select colleges and universities assign additional weight to AP courses in the admission process. After completing an AP course, students also have the opportunity to take an AP examination in that particular subject. If a student receives a passing grade on an AP examination, 90 percent of the colleges and universities in the U.S. will provide free college credit and allow the student to opt out of related introductory classes.[3]

This seemingly neutral process in university admissions actually reinforces inequality. Close to fifty percent of U.S. high schools do not offer AP classes and students in urban and rural communities are the least likely to have access to AP courses.[4] In addition, the availability of college preparatory programs and other advanced course work decreases as the percentage of students of color and low-income students increases. Thus, access to AP is a critical civil rights issue.

U.S. courts have tangentially addressed the lack of AP classes in a number of desegregation lawsuits. Two cases filed in California were the first to challenge the lack of AP classes directly. In the case *Daniel v. State of California*, the American Civil Liberties Union (ACLU) represented a group of high school students residing in Los Angeles County. The complaint alleged that the state of California was denying students equal and adequate access to AP courses. The complaint asserted that low-income African-American, and Latino students in particular, were disproportionately disadvantaged. In *Castaneda v. Regents of the University of California*, the NAACP Legal Defense Fund represented students who were denied admission to UC-Berkeley. The African-American, Latino, and Filipino-American applicants to UC-Berkeley alleged that the university's admission procedures unfairly disadvantaged applicants of color in violation of their federal civil rights by not taking into account the full range of indicators of academic "merit."

This chapter addresses unequal access to rigorous high school curriculum, specifically AP course work, and the impact on African-American students' access to higher education. First, previous research on the educational and economic benefits of Advanced Placement will be briefly discussed. Next, national data obtained from the College Board will be utilized to describe the unequal distribution of AP classes. Admission policies and AP data from the six states[5] where race-based affirmative action in college admissions was challenged, will also be analyzed to show how AP acts as a gatekeeper for African-American students. Finally, the potential of civil rights challenges to unequal access to AP will be explored.

This study combines legal research and analysis with in-person interviews conducted with the parties, attorneys and expert witnesses involved in the *Daniel* and *Castaneda* cases. The research is guided by Legal Mobilization Theory and uses "case study" techniques.[6] During qualitative interviews, I asked each subject to design an admission policy. It became clear that there is a tension between individual and societal definitions of academic merit. Similar contradictions arose within the affirmative-action debate. As such, I suggest fairer and more equitable ways to define academic merit in higher education, drawing on perspectives offered by attorneys, experts and students involved in recent AP litigation.

Educational and Economic Benefits of Advanced Placement

The College Board is responsible for the Advanced Placement Program and currently has 34 AP courses available for high schools to adopt. The subjects range from Art History, Music Theory, English and Spanish Literature, World History, Biology, Calculus, Chemistry and Physics. Few schools offer all 34 courses. However, in higher-income schools it is not uncommon for a school to offer 20 AP courses. In 2003, 14,353 high schools, 57% of U.S. high schools, participated in AP.[7] States with the lowest participation in public schools were: Alaska (13.2%), Kansas (26.6%), Louisiana (22.2%) and Nebraska (17.8%). States with the highest participation were Connecticut, Delaware and Massachusetts with 100% public school participation.

Each AP course is developed by a committee composed of college faculty and AP teachers, and is designed to cover the same content and breadth of the corresponding introductory college course. Once a student has completed an AP course, he or she is eligible (and in some schools required) to take the corresponding AP examination.[8] If a student receives a passing grade on the AP examination (a score of 3, 4 or 5 is considered passing), 90 percent of colleges and universities will provide the AP student with college credit for the introductory course and waive the course as a prerequisite. The student is thus allowed to continue in that field of study, for example, physics, without taking the introductory course.

There are direct economic benefits for students who pass the AP examination. AP students who pass the AP examination receive free college credit and preference in registering for classes. Students also get higher grades and graduate faster than students who have not had access to AP. For example, a recent study by the College Board analyzed college grades of over 72,000 college students at 20 different colleges from the fall of 1996 to the summer of 2001. According to the College Board, students who receive a score of 3, 4 or 5 on the AP examination, and thus bypass introductory college courses, are more likely to receive an A or B in a higher-level class than their non-AP peers.[9] Students who pass AP examinations are also able to graduate in less time and more likely to double major because of the "free" college credits.[10] This is particularly unfair because tracking and unequal distribution keeps African-American,

Latino and low-income students from taking AP classes and reaping these economic benefits.[11]

There are substantial educational benefits for students who have access to AP courses. The academic rigor of a students' high school curriculum is strongly associated with post-secondary GPA and rates of persistence in college.[12] Several of the advocates I interviewed were "blown away" by *Answers in the Toolbox* when it was released by the Department of Education. The study found that African-American and Latino students' success in AP classes was a better predictor of college success than high school grade point average, class rank or SAT scores. Parents' level of education continues to be a significant factor in retention and graduation, but first-generation college students who take AP are more likely to stay in college and graduate than those without access to AP.[13] All the research agrees: students are more likely to graduate from college if they have taken AP classes in high school.[14]

Math, according to several studies, is the cornerstone of a rigorous high school curriculum and students who take AP calculus are more likely to go to a 4-year institution.[15] According to *Answers in the Toolbox*, "of all precollege curricula, the highest level of mathematics one studies in secondary schools has the strongest continuing influence on bachelor degree completion."[16]

The challenging content of an AP course not only prepares a student for college work, students also get better information about how to apply successfully for college admission.[17] According to *Betraying the College Dream*, AP and honors students receive better information than their peers from school counselors, university representatives and AP teachers, who are often more knowledgeable about college-level standards than non-AP instructors. In addition, AP teachers have been found to be better teachers than those who do not teach AP classes. That is, AP teachers are better prepared academically, more enthusiastic about teaching, and have higher expectations for their students.[18] Students who are in the same schools, but not in AP classes, rarely get the same attention from university recruiters or college counselors. First-generation college students (including many low-income African-American, Latino and immigrant students) often do not receive information from their parents about college. Outreach from a college or university is essential, yet often denied to students without access to AP courses.

There is a major benefit in the college admission process for students who take AP classes. A high school transcript with AP courses is often weighed more favorably by an admission officer than a transcript without AP.[19] In 2003, 3,435 colleges accepted AP examination results as part of the admission process. In addition to admission officers rewarding students for taking rigorous course work, some colleges and universities value an AP course more when calculating the student's GPA. For example, a student will receive five points for an "A" in an AP course, four points for a "B," etc. Thus, students who take AP classes often have high school GPAs above 4.00. Several of my interview subjects were particularly concerned about this "double-dipping" in the college and university admission process.

There are a number of criticisms of AP classes. There is a common concern that the classes are content-driven instead of emphasizing critical thinking and inquiry-based learning.[20] Some students find that AP instructors teach to the test, rather than engage students in the subject matter.[21] There is also a concern about quality. For example, some schools offer AP classes, but do not provide any training for the teachers. Although many schools encourage students to take the AP examination, other schools have no expectations that students will take the examination. Furthermore, just because a student takes the examination does not mean she or he will pass. In addition, researchers have questioned the College Board's assertion that two-thirds of students taking AP exams score high enough to qualify for college credit.[22]

The most serious critiques of AP classes concern ability grouping, tracking based on race, class, gender and inequitable access. The College Board frowns on the practice of using standardized tests for determining access to AP classes, yet many schools still employ that practice. It is an especially problematic form of ability grouping because of the inherent racial and class biases in tests and test scores. Tracking based on race and ethnicity continues to make it more difficult for students of color to take the most rigorous classes when they are offered.[23] The school within a school—where poor African-American, Latino and immigrant students are placed in low tracks, and upper-income European American students are more likely to be tracked into AP classes—is an ongoing problem.[24]

Unequal Distribution of Advanced Placement

The student groups traditionally underrepresented in AP classes include African-American, Native American, Native Alaskan, Mexican-American and Puerto Rican students. Most research reports on inequitable access to AP focuses on African-American and Mexican-American students, largely because they provide the greatest sample size. All of the studies concur: African-American and Mexican-American students do not have equitable access to rigorous high school classes.[25]

The National Research Council determined that access to advanced study in high school is uneven, especially in the sciences.[26] The availability of AP and other advanced course work decreases as the percentage of students of color and low-income students increases. This is especially true in mathematics and science. This is particularly troubling given the importance of rigorous math courses to college access and success. Even where AP math and science courses are offered, students from under-represented populations are disproportionately tracked out of college preparatory classes. Thus, just providing more AP is not the answer. As long as tracking based on race and class continues, low-income students and students of color will disproportionately miss out on the education and economic benefits afforded by rigorous secondary course work, including AP.

Advanced Placement as a Gatekeeper for African-American Students

This study focuses on six states and their public flagship institutions to demonstrate how AP acts as a gatekeeper for African-American students. The six states were chosen because they either have done away with race-based affirmative action in college admissions (California, Florida and Washington) or were the subject of legal challenges to the use of race as an admission criterion (Georgia, Michigan and Texas).

The University of California at Berkeley

Berkeley no longer admits half of its first-year class based on academic factors and the other half based on a comprehensive review of the application. Rather, Berkeley currently conducts individualized review of all 30,000 or more applications. In reviewing applications, Berkeley continues to consider both weighted and unweighted GPAs in evaluating applicants as well as the opportunities applicants have had to take AP classes. Currently, there is less emphasis on standardized test scores than in the past. Students who receive a score of 3, 4 or 5 on an AP examination receive college credit at Berkeley for the corresponding introductory course.

The University of Florida

The state of Florida has implemented the "Talented 20 Program," a percentage plan that admits the top 20 percent of high school graduates to a state university. Unlike the Texas 10 percent plan, students are not guaranteed enrollment in a state flagship institution. The University of Florida (UF) considers grades, rigor of curriculum and standardized test scores as measures of academic merit. UF weighs the grade point averages of students who take AP courses and provides college credit to students who receive a score of 3, 4 or 5 on an AP examination. A score of 3 generally lowers the amount of college credit the student receives.

The University of Georgia

The University of Georgia (UGA) uses grades, rigor of the curriculum and standardized test scores to determine if a student has "demonstrated academic achievement." GPA and rigor of curriculum weigh roughly two-to-one in relation to standardized tests. UGA gives extra weight to the GPA of students who have taken AP classes. Each AP grade is raised by one-half letter grade. According to UGA, 98 percent of first-year students admitted to UGA pursued either an honors or advanced-level curricular track.[27] Students who pass an AP examination with a score of three or higher receive college credit at UGA.

The University of Michigan

An individualized review of each application includes evaluation of academic achievement, quality and potential at the University of Michigan (UM). To assess academic achievement, UM combines grades, strength and quality of curriculum, test scores and class rank. The UM evaluation guidelines make it clear that AP enrollment must be considered within the context of the high school.[28] That is, are AP classes offered at the school, and if so, are there strict prerequisites for entrance? Students must receive a score of 4 or 5 on an AP examination to receive college credit at UM. A score of 3 may exempt a student from taking a course, but will not count for college credit.

The University of Texas at Austin

In addition to admitting the top 10 percent of high school graduates to the University of Texas at Austin (UT), UT conducts individualized reviews for students who do not get admitted under the percent plan. In the individualized review process, UT considers rigorous course work and views students who have chosen a rigorous curriculum "in a more positive light." Students must receive a score of 4 or 5 on an AP examination to receive college credit at UT. A score of 3 may exempt a student from taking a course, but will not count for college credit. Unlike the other institutions in this study, UT will also assign a grade to the AP examination so that a score of 5 on an AP test will equal an "A" grade in the corresponding college course.

The University of Washington

Curriculum, grades and test scores are of primary importance in the admission process at the University of Washington (UW). Although the UW does not weigh the GPA, they do consider enrollment in AP, the relative competitiveness of an applicant's high school and completion of academic courses beyond the required minimum as admission factors. Students who receive a 3, 4 or 5 on an AP examination receives college credit at the University of Washington for introductory course work.

Each of the flagship institutions provides educational and economic benefits to students who have access to AP. If AP access was equitable, we would expect African-American students to be enrolled and take AP examinations at approximately the same percentage rate as African-American students enrolled in K-12. However, as Table I illustrates, African-American students in each state do not have equitable access to AP courses. AP courses are especially important in defining "academic merit" at the Universities of Florida and Georgia where they give extra weight to the

GPA's of applicants with AP classes. Yet, African-American students are woefully under-represented in AP in those states.

	TABLE I			
	African-American Students in AP Classes			
Area in U.S.	Percentage of African-American Students in Public K-12	Percentage of African-American Calculus AB Test Takers	Percentage of African-American English Language & Composition Test Takers	Percentage of African-American Biology Test Takers
NATIONAL	17	5	6	6
CALIFORNIA	8	3	4	3
FLORIDA	25	8	10	10
GEORGIA	38	17	14	18
MICHIGAN	20	3	5	3
TEXAS	14	6	7	6
WASHINGTON	6	1	3	3
Source: *Education Trust (2004) and College Board (2004).*				

When the plaintiffs filed their cases against the University of Texas at Austin, University of Washington, University of Georgia and finally, the University of Michigan, they did not challenge the use of so-called "academic factors" in the schools' admission policies. Rather, the plaintiffs focused on the use of race as a plus factor in the admission process and claimed that it was unconstitutional discrimination. For example, although the challenged University of Michigan admission policy was based on a 150-point scale with up to 110 points awarded based on "academic factors," the Supreme Court challenge focused on the 20 points awarded to under-represented minorities. The 110 points for academic factors included points for grades, standardized test scores, quality of high school and strength of high school curriculum. The majority in *Gratz v. Bollinger* failed to address the biases built into the academic criteria in Michigan's undergraduate admission process. Test scores, quality of high school and rigor of high school curriculum favors students in the highest socioeconomic statuses and dispropor-tionately disadvantaged lower-income African-American applicants.[29] Tracking based on race and ethnicity also makes it more difficult for students of color to take the most rigorous classes when they are offered.[30] Furthermore, stereotype threats also negatively impacts standardized test scores of under-represented minorities.[31] It is these inequities that Michigan's admission policy attempted to ameliorate. Yet, other than Justice Ginsberg's dissent, there was little mention regarding the unequal nature of secondary schools in the U.S., nor of the racial barriers built into many college and university admissions systems.

African-American students are also not getting access to the economic benefits of AP at the same rate as their peers. All of the institutions provide free college credit to students who receive a passing score on an AP examination. As Table II illustrates, the pass rates on AP examinations for African-American students lag behind the statewide averages. White students' scores are on the whole above the statewide averages listed in Table II. This disparity in test scores is at least partly attributable to segregation.

| | TABLE II | | | |
| | Comparison of AP Scores | | | |
Area in U.S.	Percentage of test takers receiving a 3, 4 or 5 in Calculus AB	Percentage of test takers receiving a 3, 4 or 5 in English & Composition	Percentage of test takers receiving a 3, 4 or 5 in Biology	Mean Score for all AP tests taken
National All test takers African-American	6534	5829	5736	2.95 2.11
California State-wide African-American	6547	5228	5628	2.91 2.16
Florida Statewide African-American	6032	5328	4223	2.69 2.02
Georgia State-wide African-American	5826	6031	4822	2.86 1.98
Michigan State-wide African-American	7145	7238	6428	3.05 2.31
Texas Statewide African-American	5338	4825	4422	2.69 1.97
Washington Statewide African-American	7161	6634	5924	2.98 2.18
Source: *Education Trust (2004) and College Board (2004).*				

Disparities in educational opportunities has continued to contribute to, and reproduce, social inequality in the U.S.[32] A recent study by the Civil Rights Project determined that access to college is strongly related to residential segregation, even after income and other factors are taken into account.[33] Urban areas, which educate many African-Americans and the largest amounts of Latinos, have very different access patterns than suburban areas. Students in urban settings are less likely to take the SAT, have lower SAT scores, and apply to fewer colleges than their suburban counterparts. Urban students are also more likely to attend community colleges and less likely to get a college degree than suburban students. According to the study, African-American and Latino students continue to face barriers to post-secondary access including lack of information, lack of a rigorous high school curriculum, access to qualified teachers, and cost. According to a Harvard Civil Rights Project report,[34] there is a trend away from need-based aid and toward so-called merit-based programs. Merit-based aid programs, like college admissions, define academic merit based on incorrect notions that standardized test scores and AP classes are neutral measures of merit. According to the report, merit awards disproportionately go to students who are wealthier and in the racial majority. Florida, Georgia and Michigan all have state scholarships based on these same reified views of merit. These merit-award scholarships act as additional gatekeepers to low-income African-American students.

Civil Rights Challenges to Unequal Access

College and university policies that reward AP courses in the admissions process or provide college credits may be at risk of being sued unless AP is equitably available to all applicants. U.S. courts have addressed the unequal distribution of AP classes in public high schools as an issue related to desegregation of the public schools. Two cases filed in California were the first to challenge the lack of AP classes directly. In the case *Daniel v. State of California*,[35] the American Civil Liberties Union (ACLU) represented a group of high school students residing in Los Angeles County. The complaint alleged that the state of California was denying students equal and adequate access to AP courses. The complaint asserted that low-income African-American, and Latino students in particular, were disproportionately disadvantaged and raised a state equal protection cause of action due to unequal allocation of AP courses in California.

The ACLU attorneys responsible for filing the *Daniel* case, Rocio Cordoba and Mark Rosenbaum, met with Professor Jeannie Oakes at UCLA and asked her to assemble a research team to study AP access in California. The research team, using data and analysis provided by the Tomas Rivera Policy Institute, proved that distribution of AP courses is extremely skewed in California. The research recognized the link between race, place and class and documented the low number of AP courses in low-income, predominantly Latino and African-American public high schools by geographic area in the state of California. For example, at Inglewood High School, where 99.5 percent of the students are

African-American and Latino, only 3 AP subjects are offered. Conversely, University High School in Irvine, California offers 17 AP subjects. Only 8.8 percent of the students at University High School are African-American or Latino. University High School offers 19 AP Math and Science class sections, whereas Inglewood High School does not offer any.

According to the plaintiffs' attorneys, race and class combine in California when it comes to who has access to AP classes. The attorneys argued that this disparity violated the students' rights because AP classes would provide the academic benefits of a rigorous high school curriculum, a level of rigor lacking in their schools. They further argued that AP classes had become a *de facto* admission requirement at the University of California, and thus were required as part of an equal education. The lack of equitable access to AP classes, according to the *Daniel* complaint, violated the fundamental right to education in the California Constitution. The complaint also alleged a state equal protection violation due to discrimination against a suspect class, that is, African-American and Latino students denied equal access to AP classes.

The case did not go to trial and was recently dismissed. Legislation promoting increased access to AP classes was introduced in the California legislature. The resulting AP Challenge Grants in many ways are a result of *Daniel* incorporating many of the recommendations made by scholars from the University of California at Los Angeles (UCLA) Graduate School of Education.[36] In 2003, over 80 percent of public high schools in California offered at least one AP class. Expansion in access to AP in California has been largely due to the AP Challenge Grants. Unfortunately, the Challenge Grant Program ended after only three years and no grant money is currently available to schools.

An enormous discrepancy in AP access remains. For example, over 20 percent of high schools in California have no AP or offer just one course. Ten percent of the state's public high schools offer 19 or more AP classes, and some offer 30 or more. The case recognized a link between race, place and class and documented the low number of AP courses in low-income, predominantly Latino and African-American public high schools. Unfortunately, this disparity continues in California and nationally. States with unequal distribution of AP classes could be challenged if their constitutions, like California, contain provisions recognizing a fundamental right to education.[37]

The second case to challenge inequitable access to AP in California directly went after the use of AP in the University of California admission process. In *Castaneda v. Regents of the University of California*,[38] the NAACP Legal Defense Fund and other nonprofit legal organizations represented students who were denied admission to UC-Berkeley. The *Castaneda* case claimed Berkeley was violating the equal protection clause.[39] The African-American, Latino and Filipino American applicants to UC-Berkeley alleged that the university's admission procedures unfairly disadvantaged applicants of color in violation of their federal civil rights by not taking into account the full range of indicators of academic "merit."

The plaintiffs alleged that the University of California admission policy, adopted after race-based affirmative action was made illegal in California, discriminated on the basis of race. In 1998, after the policy was adopted, the number of applications from under-represented students of color increased, but the number of non-Asian students of color admitted decreased by 55 percent. Central to the Legal Defense Fund's argument was the University's policy of admitting half of its first-year class based on standardized test scores and uncapped grade point averages (GPA).

The *Castaneda* (2003) case challenged the biases built into the academic criteria in Berkeley's undergraduate admission process. Berkeley admitted half of its first-year class based on an "academic score." The academic score was based on weighted and unweighted GPAs standardized test scores, strength of curriculum, class rank, etc. Weighted GPAs give an automatic 1-point increase for each AP class taken (For example, a B for an AP class is calculated as 4.0, and an A is calculated as 5.0). According to the *Castaneda* plaintiffs, this negatively impacts 40 to 50 percent of the high school students in California who go to schools with three or fewer AP classes.

Counsel for the *Castaneda* plaintiffs asked Professor Walter Allen in the UCLA Department of Sociology and director of the CHOICES Project, to provide research on the discriminatory impact of AP in college admissions. Professor Allen prefers collaborative research, especially when working on a legal challenge, and thus he assembled a team of professors and graduate students to conduct the research.[40] Utilizing the team's research, plaintiffs were able to introduce evidence of inequality of AP opportunity in California public schools. The team used an "Opportunity Index" comparing the number of students enrolled in AP courses in a particular school to that school's total enrollment. The analysis calculated the AP Opportunity Index for each public school in California by dividing the number of students enrolled in AP classes by the total number of students enrolled in the school and multiplying the result by 100. The Opportunity Index is thus the number of AP opportunities available per 100 students at a given school.

According to the Opportunity Index analysis, white students have 30 percent greater AP opportunity than African-American students. The AP Opportunity Index increased as the concentration of white students became larger and decreased in schools with a higher concentration of African-American or Latino students.

The plaintiffs also provided evidence of bias in standardized test scores based on socioeconomic status, race and gender.[41] They argued that stereotype threats negatively impacts standardized test scores of under-represented students of color. Quality of high school and rigor of high school curriculum favor students in the highest socioeconomic statuses.[42] Tracking based on race and ethnicity also makes it more difficult for students of color to take the most rigorous classes when they are offered.[43]

The case settled in June 2003, and the University of California agreed to provide plaintiffs' counsel with data regarding admission outcomes. According to the plaintiff attorneys and experts, at the heart of the AP debate is the need to redefine academic merit in higher education. The plaintiffs thus recognize that not all students have access to a rigorous high school curriculum and that there are other indicators of merit that exist beyond standardized test scores and AP credit. The case appears mindful of Gary Orfield's assertion that policies must raise standards in schools serving poor youth and remove barriers that stratify educational opportunity on the basis of race and class.

Although there were gains in African-American, Latino and Filipino enrollment at UC-Berkeley for several years, as of late spring 2004, only 98 African-American students had registered for fall enrollment out of an expected class of 3,821.[44] According to Gary Orfield, co-director of The Civil Rights Project at Harvard University, "possible explanations include higher tuitions across the nation as well as publicity over a U.S. Supreme Court ruling that struck down Michigan's system for giving admission preference based on race."[45] Campus officials point to poor recruitment because of new restrictions on their practice of flying students from predominantly minority high schools to campus for pre-application visits. Apparently, UC lawyers advised that targeting minority schools could violate Proposition 209, the 1996 voter-approved law banning the use of race in California college admissions.

Redefining Academic Merit

To more fully understand inequity in the AP program, I conducted in-depth interviews with experts involved in the *Daniel* and *Castaneda* cases, as well as the lead attorneys, plaintiffs, advocates and state officials involved in the AP debate in California. I was particularly interested in determining the types of admission policies each of the actors involved hoped to bring about through their participation in these cases. Over the course of the interviews, it became clear that all informants felt it was critical to redefine the concept of "academic merit" in order to make meaningful change in institutional policies.

In order to get at the informant's vision for admissions and, specifically, their conceptions of "academic merit," I conducted a simulation exercise. I asked each of my informants to design an admissions policy. They were to imagine that they were an admissions officer at a selective public university. They have received roughly 15, 000 applications for only 4,000 seats, similar to the University of Michigan undergraduate program. The mission of the admissions officer was to admit a diverse class of the "best and brightest" students. The results of the simulation exercise were instructive.[46]

All of my 20 interview subjects in one way or another focused on the necessity to redefine academic merit. As Professor Jeannie Oakes succinctly stated in her interview, "We are not going to crack the admission question until we rethink our notions of merit in a diverse society." Oakes advocates a dynamic and collaborative admission process to redefine academic merit:

I am very concerned about how our definition of merit is so conditioned by dominant culture and power and the amazing consequences this has for students of color ...maybe it's not predetermining what merit is, but I would set up a process for constructing socially relevant and culturally fair conceptions and operational definitions of merit.

Several of the interviews argued against reifying AP and test scores as measures of academic merit, claiming that the current testing system leads to feelings of entitlement among many privileged applicants for college admissions. Peter Eliasberg, one of the ACLU attorneys who worked on the *Daniel* case, explains:

The people who pretend that, "I'm 10 points better on my SAT or I have more AP classes than you, therefore I *deserve* to go to this school," when these other kids don't have the opportunity to take the AP classes is kind of laughable to me. But it is said with a totally straight face. In their opinion it is merit.

Christopher Patti, the lead counsel for the University of California in the *Castaneda* case, offered his opinion:

I don't particularly like the word "merit" because it encourages the notion that there are students out there who have earned a place at the university and it's a matter of selecting who has earned it and who hasn't. And I think the reality is that college admissions are really doing something else, which is attempting to build a class that will create the best academic atmosphere that the college can.

In addition to Patti, all of the researchers, attorneys and plaintiffs noted that admission officers must build a class of learners but applicants often have feelings of individualized entitlement to a seat at the public flagship university. Kimberley West-Faulcon pointed out that some of the feelings of entitlement come from misplaced emphasis on standardized test scores: "Starting with kids taking SAT prep courses in the 5th grade is teaching the kids that if I get a good score I deserve a seat. I am entitled."

Many of the interview subjects were concerned about feelings of entitlement and the problematic nature of selective institutions. Again, Jeannie Oakes summed up many of these comments when she said, "The reason why Americans tend to act on our worst instincts rather than our best instincts is because of the scarcity of seats." An aide to one of California's senators involved in the passage of the AP Challenge Grant Program echoed Oakes:

> I think people are looking for colleges to be fair, and so everyone who is the same should be admitted... Do you have a right to be admitted to a college if your GPA is the same as someone else's GPA who got admitted? I would say, "no," the school has a right to format its student body the way it sees fit. Unfortunately, there are always going to be more applicants for a selective university, so you're going to have a lot of upset people.

The students' reasons for getting involved in the court cases also underscores the tension between individual entitlement and group rights. For example, students became involved in the *Castaneda* case because they wanted to change the university's policy. They did not expect a seat at Berkeley, but rather participated in order to change the policy on others' behalf. As Kimberley West-Faulcon said, "Our clients were never coming in and saying, I know for a fact I should have gotten a seat.'" Conversely, in reported interviews with plaintiffs challenging race-based affirmative action at Michigan, those students said they felt personally entitled to a seat at the University of Michigan. This difference between using the courts to gain individual admission versus changing a policy for future applicants is significant and goes to the fundamental definition of merit.

All subjects agreed that academic merit must be more broadly defined than just standard measures of GPA, test scores and curricular rigor in high school. Rocio Cordoba, a lead attorney on the *Daniel* case, echoed many of the other interview subjects when she said:

> I think academic merit should be not just a demonstration of what a student has done in terms of how they competed on standardized exams or GPA, but also a demonstration of their potential.

How to measure potential, creativity and leadership was a recurrent theme in the interviews. All of the interview subjects discussed how difficult it was to come up with measures. Rasheda Daniel, the named plaintiff in the *Daniel* case, said she would look at volunteering and community activism, as well as grades, to delve into "how much they are willing to give to their community and society." The researchers advocated a variety of measures to assess academic potential. Walter Allen argued for multiple measures in admissions:

I'd use a multistage process. I would look at the standard indicators. But those would not be my sole and determining factors... I would want to have letters of reference and recommendation as one screening device. I would want to use personal interviews as another screening device. And then I would want to use a whole set of noncognitive indicators of the sort developed at the University of MD. For example, what are your leadership qualities? How tough are you? ...How determined are you? How quick a study are you? What is your learning curve? ...Are students willing to burn that midnight oil, are they tough enough to weather that period when everything is new and they're behind and they're not doing as well as they'd like to do? . . . I'm actually looking at an instrument for admission where people are assembled into problem-solving teams. I was very struck by that. See who leads the efforts, see who makes the contributions and take that kind of measure. What are your interpersonal skills? How creative are you? How innovative are you? I would have a whole set of those kinds of measures.

Professor Daniel Solorzano, the chair of the UCLA Graduate School of Education, was specific in the types of methods he would use to select a diverse student body:

I would do admissions like we do [at the UCLA Graduate School of Education where standardized test scores are no longer used]. It is a much smaller group here, only 600 students, and we interview every student who applies. ... Every student gets an interview. We interview them around certain issues that are important to us ... One is commitment to teaching. The second is a commitment to teaching in urban schools. And the third: commitment to social justice. I would have a set of goals that I would want my incoming class to have, and interview everyone on the goals that are important for our institution.

Although many of the interview subjects discussed the need to use a variety of measures of academic potential, as well as creative ways for students to demonstrate potential, there were also concerns that wealthier students would have advantages based on privilege under new admission systems. For example, John Rogers, co-director of IDEA at UCLA, noted:

> Here's the challenge. My first response was trying to think of a portfolio-based model of assessment that allows students to demonstrate a broad set of experiences that could enliven the undergraduate life at the college. The challenge that I see is that any time you formalize these processes, it's going to send signals to the most affluent parents and private counselors, and they are going to be able to direct students to take steps that will allow them to be more successful. I'm not sure that you can out-clever the market, either the market of cultural capital or the market of private counselors, which is becoming increasingly powerful...

Many of the interview subjects also wanted to consider race and ethnicity as part of the admission process. Liz Guillen, who worked on the AP Challenge Grant in Sacramento as a policy advocate for the Mexican-American Legal Defense and Educational Fund (MALDEF) explained: "I'm supportive of race-conscious decision- making because I know that the opportunities to succeed along the way are limited based on race." Several subjects focused on recruitment efforts to attract a diverse group of students. Professor Mitchell Chang, a member of the *Castaneda* research team, advocated "a big recruitment effort." He explains:

> First, you need to develop connections in the local community. I would focus on recruitment ...building a reputation in those communities so you can draw students from them ... that would be one start. I really believe that diversity by race, from my own experience and research, makes a big difference and it can also be an engine for change at an institution.

When asked about what they hoped would happen in California, now that the *Daniel* and *Castaneda* cases were over, several subjects noted that tracking based on race needs to be challenged in California. For example, Professor Solorzano said:

> What *Daniel* didn't spell out, and this was my concern about the case, is that there are in-school differences,

what we call a school within a school, and *Daniel* never talked about that.

Professor Walter Allen offered an important reminder of what the issue of access means in human and institutional terms:

The reason I came here was that this was a high-quality institution. I went into the classroom and it was a rainbow. The rainbow has dimmed considerably. Black students are few and far between now. Chicano and Latino students are fewer and further between . . . Those numbers have dropped. And the presence of males of Latin extraction and African-American males, those numbers have dropped precipitously. For example, this department that I am a part of now, over the last few years had many classes where there were no black students coming in, or one black student every other year; and this was so different when I first got here [in 1989] . . . I was excited when I came here from Michigan, [but] around the time of [Proposition] 209, you had a 50% drop in the enrollment of black students, and about a 40% drop in Latino students, and the school's population has not recouped yet. I mean there have been quote-on-quote gains, but they have been relative gains. Not to where we were before. That's what I would like to see changed. And that's been my greatest disappointment recently is just to be in a situation where those numbers of students of color, black students and Latino students, have fallen so precipitously.

Conclusion

The attorneys, plaintiffs and experts in *Daniel* and *Castaneda* all recognized the need to challenge the purported neutrality of academic "merit" factors.[47] As universities revamp admission procedures to comply with the University of Michigan's affirmative-action cases,[48] it is imperative that policymakers understand how AP classes work against low-income students, first-generation college students, and students of color. Admission policies should not provide a plus factor for rigorous high school classes unless all students in a given school have access to them. Even then, students who go to high schools without access to AP or other rigorous curriculum should not be disadvantaged in the admission process. There are other, more equitable ways for colleges and universities to assess a student's academic potential.

Redefining academic merit in college admissions is one step toward living up to our national rhetoric of access and equity.

Chapter 15

RACIAL INTEGRATION IN HIGHER EDUCATION AND STUDENTS' EDUCATIONAL SATISFACTION 50 YEARS BEYOND *BROWN*

Darnell G. Cole & Jerlando F. L. Jackson

Fifty years after *Brown*, the educational system continues to struggle with racial desegregation and fulfilling the intent of this historical legal precedent.[1] As the major legal precedent for education reform in the twentieth century, *Brown* is credited with inspiring significant periods of increased enrollment for students of color.[2] Teddlie and Freeman reported that the period immediately following *Brown* and the Civil Rights Act of 1964, from 1964-1973, revealed the largest increase for the participation of students of color in higher education. For instance, the college attendance for African-American students increased approximately 200%. The second period, from 1974–to 1984, which was linked to subsequent legal rulings in the *Adams*[3] and *Bakke*[4] cases, reflected a decrease in total percentages of students of color enrolled in college.[5] From 1985-1997, the last period described by Teddlie and Freeman, revealed a 61.3 % increase in college participation for students of color, which meant almost a 50% increase in enrollments for African-Americans, 83.8% for Asian-Americans, and 86.4% for Latinos. In 2003, enrollments for students of color reached 28.2% of all undergraduate students attending in higher-education institutions a percentage projected to increase over the next twenty years.[6] Currently, African-Americans and Latinos are still under-represented in higher-education institutions while Asian- Americans are over-represented in comparison to their United States population by 2.1%.

As a result of these changing demographics, a watershed of research literature examining students of color college experiences emerged and took shape during the mid-1980s.[7] Most of this research delimited students of color experiences by only comparing African-American and white college students. Relatively little attention was given to other ethnic and racial groups and the developing multi-cultural context of college,[8] which becomes more or less significant depending on whether the inquiry focuses on racial integration or desegregation, respectively. With research emphasis shifting from desegregation to integration, often without distinction, an emerging body of scholarship has found significant student outcomes as a result of campus diversity such as increased openness to diversity,[9] enhanced critical thinking,[10] higher levels of academic development, and increased intellectual engagement.[11] Cole, for instance, reported growth in intellectual development for those students attending diversity functions;[12] whereas interracial socialization was reported to increase discussions and understandings of racial issues.[13] In sum, students' intellectual development seems improved as a result of participating in diversity-related activities and interracial interactions, but do these measures of racial integration enhance the overall quality of students' education?

Conceptualizing Racial Integration in Higher Education

Three theories appear to show promise in framing the empirical and conceptually-grounded literature of students' integration in higher education: (a) Tinto's theory of integration; (b) 4-dimensional model of campus climate; and (c) Allport's social contact theory. First developed as an outgrowth of Durkhiem's theory of social integration and supported by research on college student persistence, Tinto's theory[14] of integration has conceptually framed much of the research examining students' integration into the campus environment.[15] Within this theory, students' academic and social experiences are conceptualized as mechanisms of institutional engagement and subsequent integration. Although variables measuring these students' experiences and interactions vary across research studies, they generally include college experiences with faculty, staff and peers in various on-campus or near-campus environments (e.g., library, class, residence halls).[16] Students' interactions across race/ethnicity are typically subsumed within the larger grouping of peer-to-peer interactions. These college experiences reportedly affect students' personal and social development, progression and persistence.[17] As such, it is often concluded that the more students engage in these college-related activities, the more likely they are to be integrated in the campus community, thus becoming committed to the institution. However, recent challenges to this interpretation of integration have questioned its applicability across racial/ethnic groups.[18]

For example, students actively participating in ethnic-focused organizations may or may not become integrated into the institution or develop profound levels of institutional commitment. In fact, the nature and frequency of experiences for students of color may simply reflect social participation and not institutional integration.[19] To assume such a direct correlation between social participation, a conceptually distinct concept,[20] and integration, two issues are likely ignored: (a) the extent certain racial/ethnic groups are expected to assimilate, or at least accommodate, norms established by the dominant racial/ethnic group on campus; and (b) the incongruence between certain ethnic-related student activities and the institution's objective(s) and mission. While some researchers[21] have suggested that this interpretation of integration raises methodological inadequacies in research studies, others[22] have equated this interpretation of integration as a theoretical framework reinforcing the cultural assimilation for students of color. As suggested by the latter, students of color bi-cultural and multi-cultural development goes overlooked and unexamined within this interpretation of integration.

Another theoretical model, which has informed research on institutional integration, is Hurtado, Milem, Clayton-Pedersen and Allen's 4-dimensional model of campus climate.[23] The 4-dimensional model consists of: (a) historical legacy of inclusion or exclusion, which includes resistance to desegregation, mission, policies, and rituals and traditions; (b) structural diversity, which includes the representation of students of color enrollment, faculty, and staff of color; (c) psychological dimensions of climate and its impact on students, which includes attitudes and prejudice reduction, and perceptions of racial/ethnic tension and discrimination; and (d) behavioral dimensions of climate and its impact on students, which includes positive or negative social interactions with others, peer involvement and classroom diversity. In general, this model provides a sociohistorical and socio-cultural context for evaluating individual and institutional levels of campus climate, and considers student interactions with racially/ethnically different peers as central to the behavioral dimension. It was this individual/student level of analysis that proved critical to this chapter's purpose; in that, students' interracial interactions and attendance at diversity functions were used to measure racial integration.

Embedded in these measures of racial integration is the assumption that through interacting and participating in events with students different than oneself, they will become more understanding and sensitive to race-related issues. Allport asserted that racial desegregation alone will not produce prejudice reduction.[24] Although such interracial contact is undoubtedly necessary and does have the potential to imbue attitudes of racial/ethnic acceptance, racial desegregation is just as likely to cement racial/ethnic prejudice. Higher education literature has not frequently cited Allport's social contact theory in discussing the assumptions and interpretations of students' interracial contact. But Allport's social contact theory, published in 1954, the same year as *Brown*, proposed six aspects of social contact important when examining interracial interaction: (a) quantity; (b) status; (c) role; (d) social atmosphere (e) personality; and (f) areas of contact. In this chapter, racial integration considers the following combination of Allport's aspects of social contact: (a) frequency of interracial contact; (b) equal status of individuals in contact; (c) cooperative relationships; (d) and a relatively egalitarian college campus where students have opportunities to develop a variety of relationships with racially/ ethnically different peers.

The difference between racial desegregation and integration, of course, is fundamental and lies in the distinction between "mere contact and actual interaction between students of different racial backgrounds."[25] While racial desegregation, especially those steeped in legal interpretation, focus on the racially diverse presence and representation of students, staff and faculty; a racially integrated campus environment extends beyond physical representation and addresses, among other issues, the quality and nature of interracial contact. Without argument, a racially/ethnically diverse campus has greater capacity to encourage racial integration, but it is not sufficient. Even as educational institutions achieve marginal levels of racial diversification, racial integration cannot be assumed without direct intervention and purpose in creating opportunities that foster interracial contact.[26] The *Brown* decision and other policies established as an outgrowth of its precedent have increased the enrollment rates of students of color attending Predominantly

White Institutions (PWIs). Yet, how has such legal decisions affected students' educational experience?

Methods

The purpose of this chapter is to examine the impact of racial integration, specifically interracial interactions and attending diversity functions on students' educational satisfaction. Unlike previous research exploring student satisfaction, this research differs in three distinct areas: (a) the conceptual framework; (b) variables and analysis; and (c) longitudinal data. As one of four clusters of student experiences, racial integration is conceptualized as theoretically integral to students' educational satisfaction. Student experiences and interactions (i.e., student-faculty interactions, peer involvement and classroom experiences), common in research, grounded on Tinto's theory are also important to these analyses, as these variables are empirically supported and remain important in determining students' educational satisfaction.[27]

Second, few studies have included each of these variables together in separate analyses of African-American (n=231), American Indian (n=109), Asian-American (n=430), Latino/a (n=285), and white (n=9434) students' educational satisfaction *(see Table 1, p. 261)*. And finally, where most studies examining similar issues are cross-sectional in design, this study used longitudinal survey data collected from Cooperative Institutional Research Program (CIRP) on 10,398 students attending 163 PWIs during their first year of college in 1994 and follow-up survey data in 1998. In line with national estimates of college-student enrollment,[28] most of the students in the sample were female, representing more than 60% of each racial/ethnic group; 72.7% for African-American, 61.5% for American Indian, 65.6% for Asian, 66.3% for Latino, and 65.3% white students. While Latinos reported that 27.1% of their parents had no more than a high school education, 41.4% of Asian-American students indicated their parents had attended graduate school. Despite these variations in parental education, most students reported high school grades of 'B' or better.

Variables

Background characteristics (e.g., gender, intended college major) and pretest variables for student-faculty interactions (e.g., asked teacher for advice) were the independent variables collected in 1994 during the students' first year of college. Four clusters of college experiences collected in 1998 during the students' four years of college included classroom experiences, peer involvement, racial integration and student-faculty interactions. Classroom experiences consisted of four variables and peer involvement included three variables. Racial integration consisted of two factors *(see Table 2, p. 262)*: (a) interracial interaction, which included five variables with fairly good reliabilities (5-items: std. α=.7314, African-American; std. α=.7854, American Indian; std. α=.8010, Asian-American; std. α=.7827, Latino/a; std. α=.7655, white); and (b) participated in diversity functions, which included three variables reliable only half of the time (3-items: std. α=.5859, African-American; std. α=.6031, American Indian; std. α=.5859, Asian-American; std. α=.6256, Latino/a; std. α=.4297, white). And finally, student-faculty interactions included three factors, as derived from Cole's (1999) examination of these interactions: (a) general faculty support, which consisted of six variables with high reliabilities (6-items: std. α=.8371, African-American; std. α=.8018, American Indian; std. α=.8258, Asian-American; std. α=.7893, Latino/a; std. α=.7865, white); (b) faculty critique of students' work, which included three variables with moderate reliabilities (3-items: std. α=.5285, African-American; std. α=.4548, American Indian; std. α=.6578, Asian-American; std. α=.6589, Latino/a; std. α=.5880, white); and (c) developing personal-professional relationships with faculty, which included six variables with reliabilities ranging from very low to very good (6-items: std. α=.5262, African-American; std. α=.3761, American Indian; std. α=.5961, Asian-American; std. α=.5206, Latino/a; std. α=.7865, white). The dependent variable, educational satisfaction, was also collected in 1998 and provides a measure of students' overall educational satisfaction (i.e., Likert-scale from 1 = dissatisfied to 3 = satisfied).

Analysis

Descriptive statistics, factor analyses and regression analyses were conducted for this research. Principal Component Factor Analyses were conducted and Cronbach's Alphas were calculated to reduce the number of variables in the equation and develop conceptually supported factors *(see Table 2, p. 262)*. Regression analyses for each racial/ethnic group was conducted and each set of variables were entered in the regression in blocks: (a) Block 1 consisted of students' personal attributes and pre-test variables for student-faculty interaction; and (b) Block 2 consisted of classroom experiences, racial integration, peer involvement and student-faculty interactions. Betas/beta-ins (i.e., beta if included in the model), generated as a result of the regression analysis, were examined using the Causal Analytical Modeling via Blocked Regression Analysis (CAMBRA; Astin, 1991). CAMBRA is a comprehensive analysis of beta and beta-ins as each variable enters the regression equation. Suppressor effects and multi-collinearity are discernible when using this method.

Students' College Experiences

Similar to other research findings,[29] most students in this analysis reported being actively involved in the college environment. Yet, despite their high levels of involvement, large percentages of students of color reported being neutral or dissatisfied with the quality of their education *(see Table 3, see p. 263-264)*. For African-American students, this seems especially problematic. Of all ethnic and racial groups, African-Americans were particularly critical to the racial integration of their institutions, in both the frequency and nature of their diversity-related activities and interracial interactions. For instance, every African-American student in the sample reported that they participated in at least one type of diversity-related function and over half indicated that they were involved in each of the three types of diversity activities: (a) ethnic study course; (b) cultural awareness workshop; and (c) racial/ ethnic student organization. No other racial/ethnic group reported such high percentages in activities related to the racial integration of their college campus. When considering students' interracial contact, only 35% of white students indicated that they frequently interacted across racial/ethnic lines while the other groups reported frequent interracial contact of more than 50% and some groups as high as 83.5% (i.e., Asian-Americans).

The racial integration of PWIs assumes direct involvement from each racial/ethnic group. Yet, students of color, through their extensive interracial contact and participation in diversity-related activities, seem to bare the brunt of racially integrating their institutions. This enormous responsibility is further magnified by the small numbers of students of color attending PWIs, who as a result have little choice as to whether or not to interact across racial/ethnic groups. Asking these students how many different racial/ethnic groups they have interacted with, would perhaps, offer supplementary information about the diversity of their cross-racial interactions. Additionally, given the historical development of institutional support systems for students of color such as cultural centers,[30] these student groups are also more likely to participate in diversity-related activities specifically designed for and by them. Nevertheless, college students from all racial and ethnic backgrounds have opportunities to participate in diversity-related functions in at least one form or another during their college years.

More equitable patterns of college experiences occurred when students indicated that they frequently discussed their classes (between 77.9% and 83.5%), studied with (between 43.7% and 48.6%), and tutored other students (between 44.4% and 55%). In the classroom, students reported that they often worked in groups, occasionally felt bored in class, occasionally felt that faculty did not take their comments seriously, and would more often than not challenge a professor's ideas in class *(see Table 3, p. 263-264)*. Some differences across racial/ethnic groups were observable. For example, American Indian students reported the lowest percentages of feeling bored in class and the highest percentages for challenging a professor's ideas. Perhaps as a result of these challenges, they reported the highest percentages for feeling as though faculty did not take their in-class comments seriously.

A closer examination of student-faculty contact outside of class, however, revealed that all student groups reported frequently receiving general faculty support, an average of over 60%. This type of faculty support included a variety of academic and personal experiences between students and faculty, and has been described in previous research as a collage of faculty contact, more superficial in nature than faculty critique of students' work and personal-professional faculty relationships.[31] The second type of faculty contact, faculty critique of students' work, included direct feedback on students' assignments and other class-related projects. Students are more likely to pursue these interactions to improve their grades and seek clarity regarding the academic content and assignment(s). American Indian (40%) and African-American (35.7%) students reported the most faculty interactions concerning the critiques received on their work; other student groups indicated moderate levels of this type of faculty contact. Surprisingly, African-American students also reported the highest frequencies of personal-professional faculty relationships (13.9%). These student-faculty relationships have been characterized as the most in-depth interactions, where working with faculty on research projects or being a guest in a faculty's home is usually initiated by faculty. Perhaps through seeking faculty assistance about the quality of their work, African-American students were able to establish and develop more salient faculty relationships.

Students' Educational Satisfaction

The regression model explained as much as 25.7% (adjusted $r^2 =$ .242) and as little as 12.4% (adjusted $r^2 = .104$) of the variance for Asian-American and African-American students' educational satisfaction, respectively. This model also explained 21.7% (adjusted $r^2 = .191$) for American Indian, 22.3% (adjusted $r^2 = .206$) for Latinos, and 18% (adjusted $r^2 = .178$) for white students' educational satisfaction. In other words, the regression model, at best, explained about one-fourth of students' educational satisfaction.

Interestingly, none of the measures for racial integration impacted the educational satisfaction for students of color. This was not the case for white students. 'Participating in diversity functions' (â = .034, p < .001) had a positive affect on white students' satisfaction, which is particularly noteworthy given that only 24.2% indicated that they had been involved in more than one diversity-related activity. 'Working on group projects in class' (â = .038, p < .001), 'discussing the course with other students' (â = .058, p < .001), 'studying with other students' (â = .078, p < .001), and receiving general faculty support (â = .248, p < .001) were other college-experience variables positively affecting these students' educational satisfaction. However, 'feeling bored in class' (â = -.103, p < .001) and reporting that 'faculty didn't take my comments seriously' (â = -.149, p < .001) negatively impacted their satisfaction. Student characteristics in predicting white students' satisfaction were receiving good 'high school grades' (â = .049, p < .001), having parents who have high levels of education (â = .062, p < .001), living on campus (â = .051, p < .001), and feeling that the size of their college matters (â = .036, p < .001).

The only variables affecting African-American students' satisfaction was gender (i.e., being a female student; â = -.198, p < .001), having good 'high school grades' (â = .222, p < .001), 'feeling bored in class' (â = -.169, p < .001), and 'challenging professor's ideas in class' (â = .187, p < .001). In other words, African-American males with good high school grades, who were excited about their classes and frequently challenged the professors' ideas, were more likely to be satisfied with the quality of their education. Surprisingly, racial integration was not significant to this groups' educational satisfaction in the final step of the regression, although interracial interactions were significant after the student characteristics were controlled (beta-in = .142, p < .05; see Table 4, p. 265-266). Beta-in coefficients for interracial interactions dropped from .142 to .106 when 'challenging a professor's ideas in classes was controlled.' This suggests that African-American students challenged the ideas of professors racially and ethnically different from themselves, which positively affected their educational satisfaction.

Interracial interactions for Asian-American students were also significant in the regression through the first step (beta-in = .115, p < .01; see Table 5, p. 267-268). In fact, the beta-in coefficients increased from .115 to .140 when 'faculty didn't take my comments seriously' entered the equation, suggesting a suppressor effect. In other words, 'faculty didn't take my comments seriously' was suppressing the observed relationship between interracial interactions and educational satisfaction. Interracial interactions included these less-than-accommodating experiences with faculty, hence constraining the influence of interracial contact on their satisfaction. When general faculty support entered the equation, the beta-in dropped for interracial interactions from .140 to .082, suggesting that Asian-American students whose interracial contact with faculty is supportive, will more likely report greater educational satisfaction. The only variables significant in Asian-American students' satisfaction was having parents with high levels of education (â = .106, p < .001), reporting that 'faculty didn't take my comments seriously' (â = -.275, p < .001), and general faculty support (â = .268, p < .001).

American Indian and Latino students were the only two groups where racial integration was not significant at any step in the regression equation. For American Indian students, general faculty support (â = .502, p < .001) and faculty critique of students' work (â = .307, p < .001) were variables significant in explaining their educational satisfaction. None of the measures for classroom experiences, racial integration or peer involvement, affected their satisfaction. For Latinos, however, classroom experiences such as 'feeling bored in class' (â = -.147, p < .001) and general faculty support (â = .332, p < .001) were variables important in explaining their educational satisfaction.

Limitations of Analyses

A few important limitations must be considered when interpreting the results presented in this chapter. For instance, the data collected does not completely capture the full extent of racial integration in which individuals and university campuses have evolved in order to become racially integrated as suggested in the campus climate framework. In other words, a comprehensive analysis of an institution's racial integration would have to consider a broader array of the environmental measures, including both individual (e.g., psychological dimension and behavioral dimension) and institutional variables (e.g., structural diversity and historical legacy). Additionally, the variables composing each of the factors and their reliability coefficients were other limitations because factors unique to each racial/ ethnic group were not developed. A common set of factors were used across groups, which may mask experiences characteristic only to those specific groups.

Conclusion and Implications

Several conclusions can be derived from these findings. For example, African-American students occasionally reported challenging professors' ideas in class, which had a positive impact on their educational satisfaction. Asian-American and white students occasionally reported feeling as though faculty didn't take their in-class comments seriously, which negatively affected their educational satisfaction. Yet, all students still reported fairly supportive relationships with faculty outside of class. Even when considering that American Indian students reported the most contact with faculty regarding the critique of their work, these interactions had a positive affect on their educational satisfaction. The interactions students have with faculty across racial and ethnic groups cannot be taken for granted for they have proven critical to students' educational satisfaction.

Interestingly, African-American and white students seem to represent opposite endpoints on the continuum of interracial interactions, diversity functions and educational satisfaction. African-American students reported having the most interracial interactions (78.5%) participating in the most diversity-related activities (51.1%), and being the most dissatisfied with their education (22.5%); whereas, white students reported having the least interracial interactions (65.3%) participating in 'no' diversity-related activities (40.7%), and being the most satisfied (42.6%) with their education.

Despite high levels of racial integration, these interactions were not significant in explaining the educational satisfaction for students of color. White students were the only group influenced by racial integration. It can be assumed that the quality of white students' education was enhanced by the opportunities forged by racial desegregation and their subsequent participation in diversity-related activities. This is especially important given that only 59.3% of all white students indicated that they had participated in diversity-related activities. The disproportionate responsibility of racial integration, however, still rests with students of color.

The legal precedent set by *Brown* has been vital in the dismantling of racially segregated educational institutions. In advancing the agenda of this landmark decision, several policy implications seem apparent. First, support for activities sponsored by students of color should be increased because they are the groups most often interacting across race/ethnicities and the majority of white students benefit as a result. Consequently, white students should be encouraged to participate and attend diversity-related functions. Second, academic programs can extend across racial experiences by increasing group work, integrating diversity-related functions, and other innovations for students to learn from each other in a formal educational setting. Third, an evaluation of the curriculum at institutions of higher education may be warranted. Evidence for this examination is supported by the students of color dissatisfaction with their educational experiences and the frequency of challenges to ideas presented by the professors in the class. Clearly, the findings in this research raise questions about curriculum design. While efforts have been made to integrate the individuals who share space at colleges and universities, consideration must be given to whether the same level of commitment has been focused on the racial integration of curriculum content.

Fourth, institutions should continue developing incentives for faculty to incorporate students of color into structured contact experiences. Lastly, the institutional shift from diversity-oriented to integration-focused initiatives is the most critical implication for higher education institutions. Developing programs that create dynamic interaction between and within racial/ethnic groups is central to integration-focused initiatives, such as multi-cultural living or learning communities. Thought should be given by institutions as to how they might be able to adjust diversity-related functions to benefit all students, thus embracing the concept of "integration beyond the individual level." Findings from this research suggest that institutions should begin to move beyond just the integration of individuals on campus to think about how the structural elements of campus can be integrated. While institutions have initiatives in place for individual integration, steps should be taken to examine how the curriculum addresses a broad array of cultural and ethnic environments. In addition, the overall campus experience should be integrative to ensure that all students benefit.

TABLE 1
Descriptive Data for Students' Background
Characteristics by Racial/Ethnic Group

BACKGROUND CHARACTERISTICS	African-American (N=231)	American Indian (N=109)	Asian-American (N=430)	Latinos (N=285)	White (N=9434)
Gender of Student					
Men	27.3	38.5	34.4	33.7	34.7
Women	72.7	61.5	65.6	66.3	65.3
Level of Parental Edu.					
At Least Some Graduate School	23.8	31.2	41.4	23.5	36.5
Undergraduate or Some College	54.2	53.2	39.0	46.0	51.8
High School or Less	13.0	12.0	16.3	27.1	10.6
Average H.S. Grades					
A	20.8	36.7	36.5	27.7	32.8
A-, B+	47.6	38.5	47.4	43.9	45.8
B	20.8	15.6	11.2	18.2	15.2
B-, C+	9.9	8.2	3.5	7.4	5.4
C, C- or lower	.4	0.0	.2	.7	.5
Live Off or On Campus					
Off Campus	13.9	6.4	12.6	15.8	6.3
On Campus	86.1	93.6	87.4	84.2	93.6

Note: Some of the variables may have missing data.

TABLE 2
Composite Measures with Factor Loadings and Reliabilities

COMPOSITE VARIABLES	RELIABILITIES (α)				
Racial Integration	African-American	American Indian	Asian-American	Latino/a	White
Interracial Interactions Socialized with someone of different ethnic group Activities with other ethnic groups: studied Activities with other ethnic groups: interacted Activities with other ethnic groups: dined Activities with other ethnic groups: dated	0.731	0.785	0.801	0.783	0.766
Diversity-Related Function Enrolled in ethnic studies course Attended racial/cultural awareness workshop In racial/ethnic student organization	0.586	0.603	0.586	0.626	0.43
Student-Faculty Interactions					
General Faculty Support Prof. provided advice about educational program Prof. provided respect Prof. provided emotional support/ development Prof. provided letter of recommendation Prof. provided intellectual challenge/ stimulation Prof. provided opportunity to discuss homework	0.837	0.802	0.826	0.789	0.787
Faculty Critique of Students' Work Prof. provided assistant with study skills Prof. provided honest feedback about ability Prof. provided negative feedback about ability	0.529	0.455	0.658	0.659	0.588
Developing Personal-Professional Relationships Prof. provided opportunity to publish Prof. provided opportunity to work on research Prof. provided encouragement for Grad. School Talking with faculty outside of class Was guest in professor's home Worked on independent study project	0.526	0.376	0.596	0.521	0.787

TABLE 3
Descriptive Data for Students' College Experiences and Educational Satisfaction by Racial Group

VARIABLES	African-American (N=231)	American Indian (N=109)	Asian-American (N=430)	Latinos (N=285)	White (N=9434)
Classroom Experiences					
Felt bored in class					
Not at All	2.6	.9	3.5	7.4	3.3
Occasionally	72.3	75.2	70.5	69.5	74.7
Frequently	23.8	23.9	25.3	22.1	21.3
Challenged professor's ideas in class					
Not at All	21.2	12.8	34.2	26.3	22.7
Occasionally	59.3	63.3	56.3	59.6	61.9
Frequently	18.6	23.9	9.3	13.7	14.9
Didn't take my comments seriously					
Not at All	40.3	35.8	50.5	46.3	42.1
Occasionally	49.4	56.0	44.0	46.0	49.4
Frequently	9.5	8.3	5.1	7.7	8.2
Worked on group project in class					
Not at All	3.0	3.7	3.0	1.4	2.0
Occasionally	42.0	52.3	45.1	50.9	45.6
Frequently	54.5	44.0	51.9	47.4	52.1
Racial Integration					
Interracial Interactions					
Not at All	0.0	0.0	.5	0.0	1.3
Occasionally	21.5	47.6	16.1	21.4	64.0
Frequently	78.5	52.5	83.5	78.5	34.8
Participated in Diversity Function					
None	7.8	35.8	21.9	25.3	40.7
At least in one type of activity	19.0	31.2	25.3	26.3	35.1
In at least two types of activities	22.1	17.4	26.0	22.1	19.1
In each type of activity	51.1	15.6	26.7	26.3	5.1

TABLE 3   **(Continued)**
Descriptive Data for Students' College Experiences and Educational Satisfaction by Racial Group

VARIABLES	African-American (N=231)	American Indian (N=109)	Asian-American (N=430)	Latinos (N=285)	White (N=9434)
Peer Involvement					
Discussed Course with Other Students					
Not at All	0.0	0.0	1.2	0.0	.4
Occasionally	21.2	16.5	24.2	28.1	21.9
Frequently	77.9	83.5	74.7	71.9	77.4
Studied with Other Students					
Not at All	3.9	3.7	2.8	2.8	3.5
Occasionally	51.5	47.7	51.9	50.0	21.9
Very Often	43.7	48.6	44.2	47.2	77.4
Tutored Another Student					
No	51.1	45.0	52.3	49.8	55.6
Yes	48.9	55.0	47.7	50.2	44.4
Student-Faculty Interactions					
General Faculty Support	3.9	1.9	2.3	.8	1.0
Not at All	29.2	17.5	30.7	25.3	21.5
Occasionally	66.8	80.6	67.1	73.9	77.4
Frequently					
Faculty Critique of Students' Work	3.5	1.9	7.3	4.3	3.1
Not at All	60.9	58.1	65.7	68.9	66.9
Occasionally	35.7	40.0	27.0	26.8	30.1
Very Often					
Personal-Professional Relationship	0.0	0.0	1.0	.4	.4
Not at All	38.2	31.1	43.3	37.2	37.9
Occasionally	56.9	60.2	47.3	51.1	53.7
Often	13.9	8.7	8.3	11.3	7.9
Very Often					
Overall Satisfaction with Education					
Dissatisfied	22.5	10.1	16.3	12.0	8.9
Neutral	58.4	53.2	53.0	50.4	48.5
Satisfied	18.2	35.7	30.7	37.6	42.6

TABLE 4
Betas and Beta-ins After Student and Pretest Characteristics (Block 1) were entered into the Regression Analysis for Students' Educational Satisfaction

INDEPENDENT VARIABLES	Betas After Inputs				
	African-American (N=231)	American Indian (N=109)	Asian-American (N=430)	Latinos (N=285)	White (N=9434)
Student Characteristics					
Gender of student	-.202**	-0.05	-0.01	0.066	.038*
Pretest for Student-Faculty Interactions					
Reason for Choosing College:					
Advice of Teacher	-.095	-.046	-.021	.027	.018
Activities before Freshman Year:					
Guest in a Teacher's Home	.069	.103	.125*	.000	.016
Asked Teacher Advice after Class	-.009	.160	.058	.050	.071***
Talked with Teacher	.038	-.065	-.005	.073	.018 *
Student Factors					
Major Field of Study:					
Agricultural	---	---	---	---	.003
Biological Sciences	-.105	.111	-.013	-.097	-.015
Business	-.002	.044	-.013	-.002	.011
Education	.014	.016	.013	.060	.054*
Engineering	.016	-.129	.027	.057	.010
English	-.002	-.096	.038	-.082	-.007
Health Profession	.016	-.051	.011	.007	.003
History/ Political Science	.036	-.139	-.008	.132*	.015
Humanities	.013	.111	.010	.022	.017
Fine Arts	.044	-.017	.013	.120	.002
Mathematical/ Statistics	-.083	.149	.041	.100	-.001
Physical Sciences	-.085	.007	-.055	-.008	.102*
Social Sciences	.052	-.084	.022	-.056	-.012
Other Technical	-.045	.007	-.080	-.032	-.141**
Other Nontechnical	.097	.050	.052	.127	-.011
Undecided	-.009	.059	-.006	-.025	-.003
Average High School GPA	.199**	.106	.120*	.054	.049***
Level of Parental Education	.105	-.014	.132**	.028	.014***
Live Off or On Campus	.003	.090	-.010	-.027	.164***
Importance of College Size	.005	.041	.050	.034	.067***
R^2	.064	---	.050	.017	.037
Sign.	.008	---	.021	.045	.023

TABLE 4   **(Continued)**
Betas and Beta-ins After Student and Pretest Characteristics
(Block 1) were entered into the Regression Analysis
for Students' Educational Satisfaction

INDEPENDENT VARIABLES	Betas After Inputs				
	African-American (N=231)	American Indian (N=109)	Asian-American (N=430)	Latinos (N=285)	White (N=9434)
Classroom Experiences					
Felt bored in class	-.161*	-.260**	---	---	---
			.178***	.239***	.182***
Challenged professor's Ideas in class	.180**	-.101	-.017	.074	.018
Didn't take my comments seriously	-.102	-.156	---	---	---
Worked on group project in class	.174*	.012	.336***	.227***	.201***
			.021	.092	.084***
Racial Integration					
Interracial Interactions	.142*	.047	.115**	-.009	.039***
Participated in Diversity Functions	.032	.128	.020	.007	.071***
Peer Involvement					
Discussed course with other students	.145*	-.023	.097	.073	.128***
Studied with other students	.145*	.112	.091	.160	.123***
Tutored another student	.061	.150	.013	.042	.035**
Student-Faculty Interactions					
General Faculty Support	.194**	.318**	.359***	.406***	.319***
Faculty Critique of Students' Work	.027	-.054	.181***	.162**	.146***
Personal-Professional Relationships	.126	.102	.192***	.176**	.156***

*Note: Standardized coefficients are reported. * $p < .05$, ** $p < .01$, *** $p < .001$*

TABLE 5
Educational Satisfaction Regressed onto Student and Pretest Characteristics,
Classroom Experiences, Peer Involvement, Racial Integration,
and Student-Faculty Interactions

	Final Betas				
INDEPENDENT VARIABLES	African-American (N=231)	American-Indian (N=109)	Asian-American (N=430)	Latinos (N=285)	White (N=9434)
Student Characteristics					
Gender of student	--- .198***	-0.06	-0.06	-0.03	-0.013
Pre-Test for Student-Faculty Interactions					
Reason for Choosing College:					
Advice of Teacher	-.030	-.104	-.012	-.034	.002
Activities before Freshman Year:					
Guest in a Teacher's Home	.054	.059	.070	-.023	.001
Asked Teacher Advice after Class	.077	-.055	.016	-.035	.020
Talked with Teacher	-.136	.016	-.024	-.030	-.010
Student Factors					
Major Field of Study:					
Agricultural	---	---	---	---	.004
Biological Sciences	-.098	.099	.006	-.102	-.022
Business	.015	.030	.013	.059	.031
Education	.027	.026	.015	.071	.025*
Engineering	.006	-.123	.042	.019	.011
English	.020	-.075	.043	-.062	-.015
Health Profession	.043	-.083	-.037	-.012	-.006
History/ Political Science	.029	-.101	.017	.080	.004
Humanities	.024	.100	-.014	.014	.018
Fine Arts	.021	-.039	.009	.111	.003
Mathematical/ Statistics	-.088	.169	.032	.073	.001
Physical Sciences	-.114	-.008	-.017	-.004	.007
Social Sciences	.029	-.060	-.042	-.071	-.017
Other Technical	-.071	-.055	-.048	-.037	-.019
Other Nontechnical	.100	.081	.050	.092	-.002
Undecided	-.004	.083	-.026	.007	-.001
Average High School GPA	.222***	.013	.087	.014	.049***
Level of Parental Education	.098	.004	.106*	-.019	.062***
Live Off or On Campus	.012	.120	.007	-.019	.051***
Importance of College Size	-.005	.031	.039	.051	.036***
R^2	.064	---	.050	.017	.037
Sign.	.008	---	.021	.045	.023

	TABLE 5		(Continued)		
	Educational Satisfaction Regressed onto Student and Pretest Characteristics, Classroom Experiences, Peer Involvement, Racial Integration, and Student-Faculty Interactions				

	Final Betas				
INDEPENDENT VARIABLES	African-American (N=231)	American-Indian (N=109)	Asian-American (N=430)	Latinos (N=285)	White (N=9434)
Classroom Experiences					
Felt bored in class	-.169*	-0.09	-0.08	-.147*	--- .103***
Challenged professor's Ideas in class	.187***	-.153	-.075	.017	-.035
Didn't take my comments seriously	-.113	-.045	--- .275***	-.097	--- .149***
Worked on group project in class	.139	-.098	-.046	-.002	.038***
Racial Integration					
Interracial Interactions	.106	.027	.082	-.056	-.017
Participated in Diversity Functions	.000	.081	-.041	-.057	.034***
Peer Involvement					
Discussed course with other students	.104	-.149	.008	-.039	.058***
Studied with other students	.102	.062	.041	.095	.078***
Tutored another student	.044	.032	-.031	-.053	-.019
Student-Faculty Interactions					
General Faculty Support	.137	.502***	.268***	.332***	.248***
Faculty Critique of Students' Work	-.013	.307***	.035	-.052	-.012
Personal-Professional Relationships	.047	-.060	.003	-.116	-.023
Multiple R	.352	.466	.507	.473	.424
R^2	.124	.217	.257	.223	.180
Adjusted R^2	.104	.191	.242	.206	.178

Note: Standardized coefficients are reported. * $p < .05$, ** $p < .01$, *** $p < .001$

Chapter 16

REVISITING THE OPEN LETTER TO JUSTICE CLARENCE THOMAS FROM A. LEON HIGGINBOTHAM, JR.: LOOKING TO THE FUTURE

Joseph F. Johnson

On November 29, 1991, Judge A. Leon Higginbotham, Jr.[1] was moved to write a letter of congratulations to the Honorable Justice Clarence Thomas as the newly appointed 106th Associate Justice of the United States Supreme Court. He initially considered writing the letter to Justice Thomas privately, from one colleague to another, but even in the midst of his ambivalence, he believed that making the letter public was the right thing to do. He stated, "Your appointment is profoundly important to this country and the world, and because all Americans need to understand the issues you face on the Supreme Court."[2] The primary purpose of Higginbotham's letter was to put it into a public record so that the current generation and subsequent generations could understand and evaluate the choices made by Thomas.[3] Judge Higginbotham was also apprehensive about whether Justice Thomas would be a worthy successor to Justice Thurgood Marshall; he wanted Thomas to establish a Supreme Court record that would make his apprehension unfounded.

Judge Higginbotham's open letter deserves revisiting as we commemorate the 50th Anniversary of the *Brown v. Board of Education* decision and as we reflect on *Brown*'s impact on public education. Mirroring Higginbotham's form and style, this chapter serves as my open letter to Clarence Thomas, thirteen years after his Supreme Court appointment. It is from the perspective of an academic dean and professor of educational leadership. This letter advances the debate on how close society is to achieving equality, how improvements can be made, and what history will say about Justice Thomas.

Dear Mr. Justice Thomas:

It has been nearly thirteen years since President George Herbert Walker Bush signed your commission on October 21, 1991 as the 106th Associate Justice of the United States Supreme Court. It has also been nearly thirteen years since you received that well-documented open letter from A. Leon Higginbotham, Jr., who at the time was a federal judge and a professional colleague of yours. As you are aware, Judge Higginbotham died in 1998, and as ambivalent as he was about writing such a letter for all of America to see, he was more compelled to "put into public record the pivotal importance of your commission as an Associate Justice to the Supreme Court and reminded you of what James Baldwin called the 'force of history' within you."[4] You are also aware that Higginbotham distinguished himself as Chief Justice Emeritus of the United States Court of Appeals for the Third Circuit and after twenty-nine years on the federal bench he continued to distinguish himself as one of the best legal minds of our time.[5] His distinguished career, respected perspectives and writings on the rule of law sets him apart from many and commands your listening ear.

More than 17,000 reprints of his open letter to you were sold by the University of Pennsylvania Law Review, not to mention the many photocopies that were made by individuals.[6] I am very confident that if Judge Higginbotham were alive, he would want to know how you have developed in more than a decade, especially as we pause to reflect on the enormous significance of Brown v. Board of Education at this fifty-year juncture. He would also want to know how you have served the greater good of this country and how your performance on the highest court has honored the courageous people who preceded you, especially Charles Hamilton Houston, Thurgood Marshall, Martin Luther King, Jr., Earl Warren, Fannie Lou Hamer and Malcolm X, to name a few.

Higginbotham reminded you, that you have no right to forget our history, and it was his sense that you do not want to be "burdened by the memory of history and the sacrifices made by those who preceded you."[7] The Book of Romans (8:18) reminds us that the struggles of these present times shall not be worthy of the glory that will be revealed in us. In essence, those who suffer without succeeding do so such that others may succeed after them. It also means that those who succeed without suffering do so because others suffered before them. No reasonable individual can truly believe that all he or she is and has become is the result of going it alone and getting there all by oneself—not even you, with all the determination you are known to have when confronted with challenges *and obstacles, as evidenced by the public spectacle of your confirmation hearings. You continue to demonstrate a dogmatic determination of self-reliance that has served you well. However, you must remember that you are indebted to so many individuals, especially people of color, for the lifetime appointment of becoming one of nine Supreme Court Justices. The crossroad to this reality did not start with former President Bush's decision to appoint you. That is a simple truth, not an exaggeration.*

Anyone who has had the privilege to work with Judge Higginbotham knew that he taught by his words and his deeds. His legacy has been summed up in the philosophy, "each one, teach one," and he expected everybody to incorporate this into their lives in order to make America a better place in which to live for generations to come.[8] Frankly, you have the responsibility to do no less, if not more.

I was introduced to you on two separate occasions. The first was through the well-publicized and painstaking confirmation hearings. I, like most Americans at that time, had a curious and intense interest in the proceedings. Frankly, it was the best of times and the worst of times for America. It was the best of times as I witnessed with exhilaration and humility a large number of well-prepared, educated and informed African-Americans who literally dominated prime-time television, regardless of which side of the issues they were on. On the other hand, it was the worst of times when the Senate hearings became a forum to advance perceived and real stereotypes about African-Americans under the guise of a so-called confirmation hearing.

The second occasion was actually in person during one of my many trips to Capitol Hill relative to my work in influencing federal legislation on public education. It was on one of those rare occasions that our paths crossed and we spoke politely to each other. I was struck by the duality of your formal intensity, yet the familiarity of two "baby boomers" who happened to be "brothers" speaking to each other. In a fleeting moment, I felt a sense of who you were, and quickly recognized that I did not know you at all. You tend to give a good rendition of manifesting a self-imposed contradiction, when in fact you may simply be an emerging paradox rout with unexplainable enigmas.

Your ascent to the highest court positions you among only eight peers and one chief justice in a country of more than 250 million citizens. This fact underscores the reality that it is lonely at the top and the added fact of being the only black justice and second to be appointed to the court makes that reality more complex, if not exacerbating. Cornel West is right: race matters. Anita Hill in an interview with Barbara Palmer expands this point asserting that what we really need to understand is that race, gender and power matter, because they all stem from the reality that certain people live with power and authority and want to maintain them.⁹ Like it or not, you are a very powerful man and with it is a responsibility to honor the great Supreme Court Justices who preceded you, especially the Honorable Justice Thurgood Marshall.

As I reflect on the nearly thirteen years since your appointment to the Supreme Court, I am struck by the tremendous zeal in which you continue to maintain a fidelity to your staunch conservative views. There is a thin line between zeal and narrow-mindedness, especially when the zeal you display is static at best and not open to any change.

Measures of Greatness
or Failure of Supreme Court Justices

Higginbotham's letter provided a more than an ample discussion of the importance of the greatness and failures of Supreme Court Justices. He elevated the likes of John Marshall, Joseph Story, Hugo Black, Oliver Wendell Holmes and Earl Warren as being among the greatest jurists. Comiskey updated this discussion from the results of a 2000 survey of the overall quality of Supreme Court Justices and presented his findings at the 2003 Annual Meeting of the Midwestern Political Science Association in Chicago. The survey was administered to 128 legal scholars and the justices were rated from 0 to 4, with 0 equaling failure and 4 equaling excellent. Each scholar was instructed to rate the justices on "their overall performance as Supreme Court Justices, using such criteria as the quality of their legal reasoning, their 'learnedness' in law, their ability to communicate their decisions clearly and their leadership within the Court."¹⁰ The scholars were also asked to rate the justices "in terms of their qualifications for the Supreme Court as they appeared at the time of their initial selection and confirmation."¹¹ I encourage you to read this survey as you are ranked fifth from the bottom fifty-two. Your overall rating was 1.57, and in terms of qualifications you received a score of 1.14.

It is more than possible that you were underrated. Perhaps, what will characterize you as a Supreme Court Justice is yet to be determined. Given that you are the youngest on the Court, you have the envious opportunity to carve out your place in history. So what will it be? Will you choose to be the black Republican justice appointed to think and decide as a predictably ultra-conservative? Or will you grow into a reality that other great justices came to realize. That is, there is an appropriate balance between the Law of Nature and the conventional Law of the Constitution[12] in all decisions you must make. It is not always an either/or approach to jurisprudence.

I submit to you that if this reality has not become more evident to you by now, it will if you are honored during your time on the bench to become the chief justice. If not, you will merely grow old on the Court and never grow up– which will be at the expense of too many.

Our Major Similarities

I must admit that I am very hesitant to suggest that we have major similarities worth noting. Just think. We are black males raised in the South during our formative years and only 316 miles apart. Your experiences in Pin Point, Georgia were very similar to my experiences growing up in Wilmington, North Carolina in the 40s, 50s and 60s. We are both "baby boomers," and I am only one year older. You have a passion for language, learning and books, and so do I. I literally grew up in the "colored" public library after school and was fortunate to secure a job assessing books for the three years I attended high school. Prior to technology, someone had to assess each book in the library by hand-printing in white ink the catalog numbers on them. With a steady hand, good penmanship and a hot needlepoint instrument, I was thrust into an incredible environment of learning that has sustained me to this very day. I, too, remember the day we were able to finally use what you call the "Big Library" after public facilities were desegregated in 1963. My continued passion and interest in libraries has led to serving on our local library board of trustees for six years and chair for two of those years. I truly understand the excitement in your voice when you recall your library experiences as a child.

My understanding is that you were a devout Catholic as a child, but now worship at an Episcopalian church. I, too, am an Episcopalian. That means we both believe in the Apostles' Creed and practice the sacrament of the Holy Eucharist. We understand the ceremony of our religious beliefs and enjoy the comfort associated with passing the peace in the midst of morning worship. With that in mind, may the Peace of the Lord be always with you.

The two of us came face-to-face with the perils of racism early in our developmental years and got actively involved to do something about this–You at Conception Seminary and Holy Cross College where you co-founded the Black Student Union;[13] and me during the Civil Rights

Movement by trying to desegregate the local movies and restaurants in Wilmington.

I am so struck by our similarities, or at least by the parallels. I am also challenged to understand how two black men with such familiar backgrounds and values can be so different. I am moved to capture the essence of who you really are in the midst of the many inconsistencies of your behavior as a person and as a justice. The answer may be that you have been stereotyped out of existence and are controlling a violent anger relevant in your roots. By your own acknowledgment, the book, Native Son *by* Richard Wright, *woke you up and captured "a lot of feelings" you had inside which you learned "how to repress."*[14]

I, like so many, recognize your intellect and your will to succeed. However, I hope that as you continue to sit on the bench that the tension between the Bigger Thomas character in Native Son *will come to terms with the real Clarence Thomas, known only to the people of Pin Point and too few others.*

Critiques of Civil Rights Organizations and the Supreme Court During the Last Ten Years

Higginbotham admonished you in a carefully worded, yet stern, way about your criticisms of civil rights organizations, Chief Justice Warren, and especially your characterization of Justice Thurgood Marshall's 'sensitive understanding' of the Constitution as an "exasperating and incomprehensible assault of the Constitution itself."[15] *You have definitely received your share of fair and unfair criticisms from others on your strict approach to the Constitution, especially in matters of civil rights. Wermiel asserts that you would likely be more comfortable as a justice in 1781 or 1891 than in these present times.*[16] *Of course, the irony here is that because of your color, or for having "chosen" the wrong parents, you would not have been qualified. You espouse a belief in defending liberty at all cost without what appears to be any consideration of what all legal scholars understand as the jurisprudence of race, justice, equity and equality within the rule of law. This "Legal Land of Oz" you have manifested for yourself dismisses the reality of what Higginbotham describes as governing the behaviors of early American law and still lingers in the collective unconsciousness of contemporary America.*[17]

Justice Thomas, I believe that continuing to immerse yourself in the intricate details of absolute constitutional law in an effort to maintain the original intent of its framers is flawed and only lends itself more to conservative judicial theory, to which the majority of your colleagues on the Court are also committed. This is not to question your judgment, rather it is to offer into debate the importance of setting a proper social context that continues to drive the jurisprudence of this land–les' we forget that you and I are no longer slaves.

I have read numerous articles you have published, reviewed speeches you have made, and reviewed many of the opinions you have either written, concurred or dissented on since your appointment. I continue to see examples of that tension between Bigger Thomas and the real Clarence Thomas from Pin Point, Georgia. I have also resigned myself to be challenged by what really undergirds your "mind," especially as you continue to demonstrate your dogma and deference to the Constitution.

I shall not venture to recall for discussion all the cases that provide us with some clear notion of the "mind" of Justice Thomas, but several are most prominent in my mind and I still wonder in amazement and am prompted to ask a series of "why" questions!

Why did you issue a dissenting opinion in 1992's Hudson v. McMillan? *Your argument was that the beating of the Louisiana inmate by three prison guards was not cruel and unusual punishment, even though it may have been immoral, criminal and tortuous. Bell, Jones and Johnson observed in a similar discussion on fairness and inequity that this kind of thinking is akin to the analogy put forth by Malcolm X in 1964: "You don't stick a knife in a man's back nine inches and then put it out six inches and claim that you are making progress."[18] Progress to you may be that you did acknowledge its immorality and that it could be considered tortuous or criminal, but if only he had experienced more "significant" harm. I could not discern if you were referring to his physical person or his spirit.*

Why do you continue to be closed-minded about affirmative action as in Adarand Constructors v. Pena[19] *and* Grutter v. Bollinger et al.?[20] *Your one hundred and eighty degree conversion since benefitting from it now has you believing that it's tantamount to racial paternalism and a pernicious form of discrimination.*

Why did you advance your opinion in Missouri v. Jenkins[21] *by attacking the tenets of* Brown v. Board of Education? *You could have argued your point just as effectively without doing so. Americans, including you, have benefitted from* Brown. *To characterize it as a decision that relied more on feelings rather than reason and moral political principles, is inexcusable. Even as a Supreme Court Justice, you are not bound to present your opinions by any means necessary. You have more than enough discretion as a justice and should use it. A frightening thought just occurred to me, you truly might have thought you were doing just that.*

The Impact of the Work of Civil Rights Lawyers and Civil Rights Organizations

The impact of the tireless work of civil rights lawyers and civil rights organizations on your life can never be overstated, if for no other reason than appreciating that their struggles were moral, physically draining, and never easy nor sudden.[22] Higginbotham made a determined and concerted effort to shake your consciousness by calling your attention to how dismayed he was by some of the comments you made denigrating the work of civil rights lawyers and civil rights organizations. Higginbotham reminded you of pioneers like Charles Hamilton Houston, Thurgood Marshall, William Henry Hastie, Benjamin Hooks, Roy Wilkins, Vernon Jordan, Whitney Young and many others who laid the foundation for the current racial mores of America. I would also add Julius Chambers, Julian Bond, Lani Guinier and Floyd McKissick.

I recall a conversation I had with Roger Wilkins, nephew of Roy Wilkins, in 1992 during one of my visits to Washington, D.C. I was an associate professor at the University of North Carolina at Wilmington and was experiencing what the psychologists would describe as a "pity party." My so-called "pity party" was fueled by my impatience and eagerness to make a difference at the university in the context of my personal and professional assessment that things were moving too slowly or not at all. Roger told me something "Uncle Roy" shared with him when Roy Wilkins was the executive director of the National Association for the Advancement of Colored People (NAACP). He said, "Uncle Roy would always remind me to never underestimate the power of small successes." Ever since that day, I have been able to sustain my optimism about the future.

*I do not know how far you have come since 1991 in your stance on civil rights, but I am confident that there have been some small successes in the manner in which you communicate publicly on what we can all consider a post-*Brown *era. I also remain cautiously optimistic that, as the youngest justice on the Court, there will be increasing evidences of small successes and a change in the opinions you write.*

What Have the Conservatives
Ever Contributed to African-Americans?

First, I am personally insulted by the labels we conveniently give each other in an effort to understand why we think and behave the way we do. In my judgment, labels such as Democrat, Republican, conservative, and liberal are nothing more than lazy shallow tags that don't get at the essence of our minds, bodies and spirits. Gerzon encourages us to move beyond such polarizing views and embrace six belief systems that are struggling for America's soul toward a new patriotism.[23]

I also find it unfortunate that in some iconic way, you are being postured as the poster child for black conservatives for all to emulate. If you are not insulted by this, I am insulted for you. If you simply choose to wear it as a "badge of honor," I shall pray for you.

I have examined you, your writings and speeches and am convinced that you are far more complex than that. The enigmas that truly characterize your basic shyness and social clumsiness at one end and a misunderstood sense of ostentatious arrogance on the other makes you a worthy opponent when you are right, and yet very frightening when you are narrow-mindedly confused by your zeal to be a Republican, a conservative, and a black conservative justice, intermittently and sometimes, all at once.

I agree with Higginbotham and his account of how those who label themselves conservatives in the 50s and 60s tried by tacit approbation or active complicity to derail the struggles for civil rights even with the absurdity that the 1964 Civil Rights Act was unconstitutional. I really don't think that the relevant question is what the conservatives ever have done for African-Americans, but rather what will African-Americans do for each other?

The Impact of Eradicating Racial Barriers to Voting

You have spoken out eloquently about the unfairness and pain you feel when people, especially African-Americans, believe that you would set out to do harm to your race.[24] Nonetheless, you continue to be criticized for your approaches to the Voting Rights Act and to affirmative action. I have made repeated efforts to come up with some profound explanation of why you are so vehemently averse to factoring race or ethnic identity into your personal beliefs and opinions on the Court wherever appropriate. I have even tried to apply some complex theory of organizational development and behavior to explain your dogma and determination to be "*your own man,*" *regardless of the cost. It then occurred to me that the very character trait that was instilled in your early years may very well prove to be your Achilles' heel. The character trait, of course, is self-reliance. Just as I cautioned you about the thin line between zeal and narrow-mindedness, I must also caution you that self-reliance is merely a survival tool.*[25]

I have always discussed with my graduate students and faculty the importance of understanding the frames through which behaviors manifest themselves. I have also discussed my belief that behavior is a function of one's most predominant thought. Clearly, self-reliance is your most predominant thought and it constitutes the frame through which you assess everything. This explains: 1) why you have chosen the color-blindness approach to law, achievement and success; 2) why you believe that your appointment to the Court involved no consideration of race; 3) why you argue that your admission to Yale Law was on the merits of your academic credentials alone; and 4) why you refuse to consider race appropriately to draw voting district lines, yet see no problem in using political identity and affiliation.

If you are truly committed to eradicating racial identity and racial barriers to voting, please consider embracing the concept of cumulative voting as an alternative to the single-member districts.[26] *You may wish to read Lani Guinier's book,* Lift Every Voice: Turning A Civil Rights Setback Into A New Vision of Social Justice, *as it is about America's racial history and its commitment to equality, equity, liberty and the freedom to be a viable participant.*

Housing and Privacy

Higginbotham stated that one could write volumes on the housing and privacy issues, and I agree.[27] *You will continue to be challenged to lend an empathetic ear to the issues of privacy and housing violations. Cheshire encourages you to remember that you are in the best position to promote a more positive point of view, one that is reflective of your current lifestyle.*[28] *That is, we all should have the right to live where we choose to live, marry whom we choose to marry and have private lives, free from invasive or pervasive intrusion.*

Conclusion

In this letter to you, I have made a concerted and respectful effort not to denigrate you in anyway, but must admit that I may have come close. Please know it was not out of malice, but resulted from trying to be clear and true to my beliefs, which is no different from how you tend to present yourself to others.

I am currently reading The End of Blackness *by Debra Dickerson, which presents a debate on whether 'race' is still a valid social construct.[29] In fact, she argues that African-Americans must be fiercely self-reliant and not become stuck on presuppositions and fruitless ways of thinking that no longer predict nor explain their social behavior. I am sure this sounds very familiar to you. Dickerson, in a* Washington Post *article, characterized you as a "lonely guy."[30] She also asserted that you would love for your relationship with the black community to be different, concluding that it must hurt, when you are considered to be outside the fold, given your unpredictable black voice.*

Interestingly, while Dickerson espouses some of your very beliefs, I am not as troubled by her discourse as I am by yours. It may simply reside in the fact that I consider controversial, thought-provoking discourse an expected and expectable part of academia and have placed a higher standard on you as one who ought to uphold 'justice.'

In your 1998 speech before the National Bar Association, you asserted that the greatest offense to you is that most African-Americans feel that you should not have the right to think as you do, because you are black. You also asserted that you are a man, free to think for yourself and do as you please. I respectfully disagree. Your role as a Supreme Court Justice is inextricably intertwined with who you are as an individual. That is why everything you say and do matters. What an awesome privilege and responsibility.

I believe in the power of small successes. The small successes that reveal your true essence are evident when you are talking with children. They are evident when you become emotional in public. They are also evident when you give speeches that advance hope. I submit that if the way you are able to express your love, care and concern for your son Jamal, and grandnephew Mark is authentic; if the manner in which you are willing to be vulnerable in public is authentic; and if the manner in which you speak wistfully about the future is authentic–these sentiments are portable and will find their way over time into your thinking and written opinions.

With all the pause and apprehension I feel about your future on the Court, I share the same sentiments Judge Higginbotham expressed in 1991:

> *"No one would be happier than I if the record you will establish on the Supreme Court in the years to come demonstrates that my apprehensions were unfounded. You were born into injustice, tempered by the hard reality of what it means to be poor and black in America, and especially to be poor because you are black. You have found a door newly open and you have escaped. I trust that you will not forget that many who preceded you and many who will follow you, will find the door of equal opportunity slammed in their faces through no fault of their own. And I also know that the time and tides of history often call out men and women qualities that they even did not know lay within them. And so to balance my apprehensions, I wish you well as thoughtful and worthy successor to Justice Marshall in the ever-ongoing struggle to assure equal justice under the law for all persons."[31]*

AFTER WORD

RHETORIC V. REALITY: EQUALITY OF OPPORTUNITY

N. Joyce Payne

In reading this series of dynamic analyses of the enormity and complexity of challenges and opportunities African-Americans face in public education, one is vividly reminded that the nation continues to sanction inequality in both our policies and practices. In spite of the rhetoric of equality of opportunity and the value of diversity in America, we find ourselves in the midst of an ultraconservative set of federal policies that is shifting resources from the "have-nots" to the "have-mores." Samuel Bowles reminds us that "equality is a political issue, and the only route to a more equal society lies through political struggle...egalitarian reforms in education must seek to disable the myths which make inequality appear beneficial, just or unavoidable."

In *Closing the Achievement Gap*, the National Black Caucus of State Legislators puts the challenge to the nation: "The right to a comprehensive, quality education is a civil right. Yet, almost four decades after *Brown v. Board of Education* declared school segregation to be unconstitutional, quality education is still beyond the reach of too many African-American children." Although the nation has made enormous achievements in creating a world-class educational system for the rich and the famous, it has failed miserably in educating poor children, building state-of-the-art public schools and harnessing the talent of millions of young black men locked in the vicious cycle of crime and poverty. While public schools crumble under the weight of arcane school finance policies, shifting resources from public schools to segregated private academies and religious schools, private and state prisons and mass transportation systems exacerbate the crisis. The Center on Budget and Policy Priorities reports that the Bush Administration's 2002 budget proposed 40 times more money for tax cuts ($1.6 trillion) for upper- and middle-income families than for public education and this administration's 2003 budget proposed the smallest increase for education in the last seven years.

While public schools crumble, "the wealthiest school districts in the nation spend 56 percent more per student than the poorest school districts," as noted by Linda Darling-Hammond. In the midst of the president's crusade to "leave no child behind," black, brown and poor children are being denied school lunches, denied quality teachers, denied advanced placement courses, denied high school diplomas and denied an opportunity to grow intellectually and thrive socially in an America that supports corporate welfare to the tune of $125 billion in the midst of profits exceeding $4.5 trillion. According to *Time* magazine, this amount "is equal to the cumulative paychecks of 50 million working Americans who earn less than $25,000 a year over an eight-year period." The same article notes, "that makes the federal government America's biggest sugar daddy." Clearly, the children of the poor and disenfranchised need a federal "sugar daddy" to transform their schools, their lives and their futures.

The quality, power and class of our public schools must be radically transformed to meet the demands of the nation's accelerating scientific and technological revolution. While we face unprecedented opportunities in science and technology, we are entering a new era of conservativism that is undermining the ability of our children to dream, to hope, to aspire. In the absence of a progressive national agenda, welfare reform will continue to push more than a million preschoolers into barren daycare facilities and home-based day-care services. Welfare reform will continue to force mothers of dependent children into dead-end, minimum-wage jobs. Especially disturbing is the fact these children are already showing evidence of developmental disabilities, as found in a study conducted at Yale University and the University of California. Welfare reform will continue to force fathers out of the homes and daily lives of their children. In many cases, the fathers of these children are incarcerated. In *Lost Behind Prison Bars*, David Evans says, "Though the U.S. population is only 13 percent black, 49 percent of the inmates in state and federal prisons are African-American."

Clearly, the educational development of our children is undermined by our social and economic condition. Today, more than 13.5 million American children live in poverty, a greater share than in the 1970s and 44 million Americans have no health insurance, including 25 percent minorities. We need a radical change in domestic policies that address the human condition of black Americans at every level of the economy and a sustained and substantial investment in the transformation of educational opportunities. How can we tolerate the rhetoric when this nation built a $32 billion space station, obligated more than $8 million a month to warehouse the Hubbell space telescope and supported a $50 billion bailout for savings and loan enterprises? How can we tolerate the rhetoric when the Congress appropriated more than $18 billion in "pork" in FY2001 and over $119 billion over the last 10 years? How can we tolerate the rhetoric when one million new millionaires were created between 1995 and 1998? In the midst of this affluence, we are unwilling to invest in books, computer equipment, smart classrooms, automated libraries, recreational facilities and safe school buses.

The condition of young black men in the public schools of America is particularly alarming. They are disproportionately:
* placed in special education
* diagnosed as emotionally and socially dysfunctional. tracked in general education courses
* pushed out of school
* underachievers in reading, writing and computational skills

While wealth and power converge, the Children's Defense Fund reports that a black young man has a one in:
* 3,700 chance of getting a Ph.D. in mathematics, engineering or the physical sciences
* 2,546 chance of becoming a dentist
* 786 chance of becoming a lawyer
* 395 chance of becoming a physician

It is even more difficult for African-American children to achieve professionally in a knowledge-based society, when less than 35,000 African-Americans, out of more than 1.5 million students, took the advance placement test in 1999. Nor can they achieve when less than one percent enrolls in classical and foreign languages. As Jonathan Kozol says, we are still "teaching the rich and training the poor."

As it is in the nation's public schools, equality of opportunity for African-Americans in higher education is profoundly illusory. For half a century or more, higher education with all its contractions has been viewed as the great social equalizer. It is a place where social consciousness and equal opportunity are built into the cultural fabric; where strong precedents exist for the advancement of progressive ideology and liberal thought. Yet today, white Americans make up over 80 percent of associate, bachelor's and professional-degree recipients and more than 86 percent of all doctorates. In the field of engineering and life and physical sciences, blacks and Hispanics constitute 1.3 to 3.1 percent of all doctorates. Even more revealing is the large number of scientific fields with not a single U.S.-produced African-American doctorate. In 1995, there were no U.S. minorities in applied mathematics, atomic and molecular physics, systems engineering, biophysics, microbiology and other high-demand disciplines. Although the production of minority Ph.D.s increased by 72.2 percent over the last 10 years, they constitute only 16.1 percent of the 40,744 doctorates awarded by American universities in 2000-01. In 2001, American universities produced more than 6,000 non-U.S. doctorates, with the largest number (2,670) originating from the People's Republic of China, followed by South Korea, India, Taiwan and Canada. Further, higher education has been highly successful in dramatically increasing the number of women with Ph.D.s and especially in the life sciences. It is noteworthy that the 30-year upward trend of Ph.D. awards to women continued in 2001, with universities producing a record number of 49.5 percent.

The growing need for a racially/ethnically diverse and scientifically knowledgeable workforce, coupled with shifting sociodemographic trends, demands that the higher education community create new and innovative programs designed to significantly increase the production of minority Ph.D.s and particularly in the sciences. Yet we continue to preach competition, innovation and the importance of a scientifically and technically competitive labor force while cutting student financial assistance, the lifeblood of black higher education. Given the correlation between family income and the college going rate, federal student aid is critical for black and poor students. As noted in *Black Wealth Inequality 10-to-1* by Askia Muhammed, "The typical African-American family has a dime of wealth for every dollar of wealth that the typical white family has in the U.S. It's about $8,000 to $80,000." We generate new trade investment policies and challenge the multinational corporations to produce world managers who can market American ingenuity while dismantling affirmative action and 50 years of liberal policies. We create a White House Initiative on Black Colleges and celebrate Black College Week while concentrating wealth and power among a narrow set of major research universities.

Despite the national rhetoric and firmly established legal imperative to redress inequities in the nation's public schools, higher education and the larger society, persistent patterns of inequity are systemic and embedded in a scientifically mature and socially immature education system. Exploring the underpinnings of inequality requires moral leadership at every level of education, government and industry. It requires reasoned discourse at the highest level of the nation and the inclusion of equal educational opportunity as an economic imperative.

We must challenge the rhetoric of inclusion and reaffirm our commitment to fight for justice, equality and the liberal ideals rooted in the framework of *Brown v. Board of Education*. The rhetoric versus reality of equality of opportunity remains a glaring yet unresolved dilemma for African-Americans. Yet, as Cornel West notes in *Race Matters*, we must remain firmly grounded in the belief that, "The most valuable source for help, hope and power consists of ourselves and our common history. The vitality of any public square ultimately depends on how much we care about the quality of our lives together. Our ideals of freedom, democracy and equality must be invoked to invigorate all of us."

NOTES

Introduction

1. *The Ruling that Changed America* by Juan Williams was first published in *American School Board Journal* in April 2004, Vol. 191 Issue 4, pp. 18-22. The version that appears here is with courtesy from the *American School Board Journal.*

Chapter 1

1. *Brown v. Board of Education*, 347 U.S. 483 (1954).
2. Constance Baker Motley, *Equal Justice Under Law* (New York: Farrar, Straus and Giroux, 1998) at pp. 240-241 (discussing how affirmative action reaches complex discrimination).
3. Professor Derek Bell, Visiting Professor at New York University School of Law and author of the forthcoming book *Silent Covenants: Brown v. Board of Education and the Unfulfilled Hopes of Racial Reform.* Quotation taken from an article written for *The Urban League Opportunity Magazine*, Winter 2004.
4. Sociolegal research acts as a bridge between law and sociology. A sociolegal perspective provides a doctrinal analysis of law and its effect on society as well as societal effects on the interpretation and/or creation of particular laws.
5. A. Leon Higginbotham, *In the Matter of Color* (New York: Oxford University Press, (1978) (Africans captured from Spanish slave ships were brought to Virginia by the Dutch in 1619) at 20, 58.
6. Giddings, Paula. *When and Where I Enter: The Impact of Black Women on Race and Sex in America.* (New York Bantam Press, 1984) at 34.
7. Higginbotham, A. Leon, *In the Matter of Color* (New York: Oxford University Press, 1978) (discussing Irish and Scottish immigrants as well as indentured servants) at 33, 159-160.
8. *Black Survival, 1776-1976: The Urban League Perspective* (Philadelphia: The Philadelphia Urban League, 1977) at 2.
9. Higginbotham, *In the Matter of Color* (New York: Oxford University Press, 1978) (the legal status was indefinite, for example, Virginia legislation of 1859 is the first reference to Africans as slaves) at 33, 58.
10. Higginbotham, *In the Matter of Color*, at 58-59, 75-78, 120-122, 161-163, 261-263 (discussing the colonial legal restrictions on Africans in Virginia, Massachusetts, New York, South Carolina and Georgia).
11. Higginbotham, *In the Matter of Color*, at p. 34.
12. Higginbotham, *In the Matter of Color*, at 161 (discussing the enslaving and in some cases exporting of American Indians to the West Indies).
13. Higginbotham, *In the Matter of Color*, at p. 37.
14. Higginbotham, *In the Matter of Color*, at pp. 34, 38, 53-55.
15. Higginbotham, *In the Matter of Color*, at p. 25.

16. Higginbotham, *In the Matter of Color*, at p. 50.
17. Higginbotham, *In the Matter of Color*, at p. 10.
18. Frederick Douglass, *Narrative of the Life of Frederick Douglass, an American Slave*. Written by himself (Boston: The Anti-Slavery Office, 1845) reprinted (Chapel Hill: University of North Carolina, 1999) at p. 33.
19. Higginbotham, *In the Matter of Color*, at p. 258 (in Georgia, the financial penalty for teaching a slave to read was 50 percent higher than for willfully castrating or cutting off the limb of a slave).
20. *See generally*, The Declaration of Independence, July 4, 1776.
21. The Declaration of Independence, July 4, 1776 at 1.
22. United States Constitution, ratified March 4, 1789.
23. Preamble of United States Constitution.
24. Art. 1, Sec. 2.
25. Population:
26. Ms. Coppin graduated from Oberlin College in Ohio in 1836.
27. *Scott v. Sandford*, 60 U.S. 393, 413 (1856).
28. Justice Taney states the conditions under which Africans in America existed prior and up to the *Dred Scott* decision of 1856: "Their statute books are full of provisions in relation to this class, in the same spirit with the Maryland law which we have before quoted. They have continued to treat them as an inferior class, and to subject them to strict police regulations, drawing a broad line of distinction between the citizen and the slave races, and legislating in relation to them upon the same principle which prevailed at the time of the Declaration of Independence. As it relates to these States, it is too plain for argument that they have never been regarded as a part of the people or citizens of the State, nor supposed to possess any political rights which the dominant race might not withhold or grant at their pleasure." *Scott v. Sandford*, 60 U.S. 393, 413 (1856).
29. *Scott v. Sandford*, 60 U.S. 393, 395-396 (1956).
30. And upon a full and careful consideration of the subject, the court is of opinion, that, upon the facts stated in the plea in abatement, Dred Scott was not a citizen of Missouri within the meaning of the Constitution of the United States, and not entitled as such to sue in its courts; and, consequently, that the Circuit Court had no jurisdiction of the case, and that the judgment on the plea in abatement is erroneous. *Scott v. Sandford*, 60 U.S. 393 at 427.
31. *Scott v. Sandford*, 60 U.S. 393 at 426-427.
32. *Scott v. Sandford*, 60 U.S. at 413, 427, 454.
33. *Scott v. Sandford*, 60 U.S. at 401.
34. Lewis, David Levering, *W.E.B. DuBois: Portrait of a Race, 1869-1919* (New York: Henry Holt, 1993) (discussing the Black migration North of the 1800s) at 117-118.
35. Am. 13, Sec. 1.

36. Am. 14, Sec. 1.
37. Am. 15, Sec. 2.
38. See also Giddings, *When and Where I Enter: The Impact of Black Women on Race and Sex in America* at 95-97; see also author's forthcoming article "Statutory Rape Laws: Early Social Policies, Discrimination and the Moral Reform Movement."
39. Lewis, David Levering, *W.E.B. DuBois: Portrait of a Race, 1869-1919* (New York: Henry Holt, 1993) at 123. (For example, Hampton Normal and Agricultural Institute, now Hampton University, was founded in 1868 by an ex-Confederate general and railroad magnate Thomas Muldrop Logan; Howard University in Washington, D.C. was founded in 1867 by Otis Howard, Caucasian, was a member of the Freedmen's Bureau.)
40. Lewis, David Levering, *W.E.B. DuBois: Portrait of a Race, 1869-1919* (New York: Henry Holt, 1993) at 112-114.
41. Lewis, David Levering, *W.E.B. DuBois: Portrait of a Race, 1869-1919* (New York: Henry Holt, 1993) at 114 ("Education has but one tendency: to give higher hopes and aspirations," a North Carolina newspaper waned. "We want the Negro to remain here, just about as he is - with mighty little change").
42. The Ku Klux Klan was formed in 1871.
43. Lewis, David Levering, *W.E.B. DuBois: Portrait of a Race, 1869-1919* (New York: Henry Holt, 1993) at 260 (discussing the diminished Black vote in the South).
44. Lynching: to execute without due process of law. The American Heritage Dictionary, 4th ed.; lynching could include torture such as burning a person alive, castration, mutilation, amputation of limbs, and/or decapitation.
45. Tolnay, Stewart E. and Beck, E. M., *An Analysis of Southern Lynchings, 1882-1930* (Chicago: University of Illinois Press, 1992) (discussing lynching as a terroristic means of social control) at 19; Odem, at 28-29 (discussing lynching as a mechanism to maintain White supremacy).
46. Fierce, Mildred C., *Slavery Revisited: Blacks and the Southern Convict Lease System, 1865-1933* (Brooklyn, NY: Africana Studies Research Center, 1994) at 6.
47. See *supra* Table 2 and Table 3.
48. Franklin, John Hope, *Race and History: Selected Essays, 1938-1988* (Baton Rouge: Louisiana State University Press, 1989) at 145-146; *Black Survival 1776-1976: The Urban League Perspective* (Philadelphia: Philadelphia Urban League, 1977) at 11.
49. Lewis, David Levering, *W.E.B. DuBois: 1869-1919* (New York: Henry Holt, 1993) at 372 (discussing the Black migration North of the 1800s).
50. W.E.B. DuBois, *The Philadelphia Negro: A Social Study* (Philadelphia: University of Pennsylvania Press, 1899) at 145-146.

51.   Lewis, David Levering, *W.E.B. DuBois: Portrait of a Race, 1869-1919* (New York: Henry Holt, 1993) at 372 (discussing the Black migration North of the 1800s).

52.   *Plessy v. Ferguson*, 163 U.S. 537, 552 (1896).

53.   *Plessy v. Ferguson*, 163 U.S. 537 (1896).

54.   *Plessy v. Ferguson*, 163 U.S. at 552.

55.   *Plessy v. Ferguson*, 163 U.S. at 544.

56.   *Plessy v. Ferguson*, 163 U.S. at 544.

57.   Whites formed abolitionist organizations during slavery, assisted in the Underground Railroad, formed the NAACP, and acted as counsel in numerous civil rights cases.

58.   *Scott v. Sandford*, 60 U.S. 393, 395-396 (1956).

59.   *Plessy v. Ferguson*, 163 U.S. 537 (1896).

60.   *Plessy v. Ferguson*, 163 U.S. at 559.

61.   *Plessy v. Ferguson*, 163 U.S. at 559-560.

62.   The federal government did not have a vested interest in maintaining an accurate number of persons lynched.

63.   Thompson, Mildred, *Ida B. Wells-Barnett: An Exploratory Study of an American Black Woman, 1893-1930* (Brooklyn: Carlson Publishing, 1990) at 198; the exact number of persons lynched in America is difficult to determine.

64.   Wells, Ida B. *Crusade for Justice: The Autobiography of Ida B. Wells* (Chicago: The University of Chicago Press, 1970) ("At the meeting, representatives of every newspaper in New York were present, and they sent reports of my first address throughout the country") at 218.

65.   Wells, Ida B., *Crusade for Justice: The Autobiography of Ida B. Wells*, at 213-15.

66.   David Levering, *W.E.B. DuBois: Portrait of a Race, 1869-1919* (New York: Henry Holt, 1993) at p. 387.

67.   David Levering, *W.E.B. DuBois: Portrait of a Race, 1869-1919* (New York: Henry Holt, 1993) at p. 387.

68.   Carl T. Rowan, *Dream Makers, Dream Breakers: The World of Justice Thurgood Marshall* (Boston: Little, Brown and Company, 1993) at 27.

69.   David Levering, *W.E.B. DuBois: The Fight for Equality and the American Century, 1919-1963* (New York: Henry Holt, 2000) at p.1-3.

70.   Constance Baker Motley, *Equal Justice Under Law* (New York: Farrar, Straus and Giroux, 1998) at pp. 99-101 (Charles Hamilton Houston is known as the architect of the Civil Rights Movement. He graduated from Amherst College, Harvard Law School. Houston was appointed Dean of Howard University School of Law where he developed strategies and fostered a level of intellectual growth needed to create the *Brown* victory. Thurgood Marshall attended Howard University Law School from 1933 to 1936).

71.   Mark V. Tushnet, *Making Civil Rights Law* (New York: Oxford University Press, 1994) at p. 6.

72. See *University of Maryland v. Murray*, 169 Md. 478 (1936); *State of Missouri ex rel Gaines v. Canada*, 305 U.S. 337 (1938).

73. Carl T. Rowan, *Dream Makers, Dream Breakers: The World of Justice Thurgood Marshall* (Boston: Little, Brown and Company, 1993) at 150.

74. Constance Baker Motley, *Equal Justice Under Law* (New York: Farrar, Straus and Giroux, 1998) at pp. 240 - 241.

75. David Levering, *W.E.B. DuBois: The Fight for Equality and the American Century, 1919-1963* (New York: Henry Holt, 2000) at p. 521-523, 532-534 (W.E.B. DuBois drafts An Appeal to the World: A Statement on the Denial of Human Rights to Minorities in the Case of Citizens of Negro Descent in the United States of America and an Appeal to the United Nations for Redress); Constance Baker Motley, *Equal Justice Under Law* (New York: Farrar, Straus and Giroux,1998) at p.70.

76. Constance Baker Motley, *Equal Justice Under Law* (New York: Farrar, Straus and Giroux, 1998) at p.5.

77. Constance Baker Motley, *Equal Justice Under Law* (New York: Farrar, Straus and Giroux, 1998) at p. 191.

78. Mark V. Tushnet, *Making Civil Rights Law* (New York: Oxford University Press, 1994) at p. 204-205.

79. Constance Baker Motley, *Equal Justice Under Law* (New York: Farrar, Straus and Giroux, 1998) at p. 191.

80. Mark V. Tushnet, *Making Civil Rights Law* (New York: Oxford University Press, 1994) at p. 206-207 (discussing the reargument of *Brown* and Congressional questions of intent).

81. Constance Baker Motley, *Equal Justice Under Law* (New York: Farrar, Straus and Giroux, 1998) at p.102.

82. *Brown v. Board of Education*, at 494-495.

83. *Brown v. Board of Education*, at 494.

84. *Brown v. Board of Education*, at 495.

85. See generally *Brown v. Board of Education II*, 349 U.S. 294 (1955).

86. *Brown v. Board of Education II*, 349 U.S. at 301.

87. Constance Baker Motley, *Equal Justice Under Law* (New York: Farrar, Straus and Giroux, 1998) at p.110-111.

88. Mark V. Tushnet, *Making Civil Rights Law* (New York: Oxford University Press, 1994), at p. 206-207 (discussing the reasons which led to local governments control of *Brown*'s implementation).

89. *Brown v. Board of Education II*, 349 U.S. at 300 (the District Court is to consider administration, physical condition of the school plant, school transportation, personnel, attendance areas and admissions). See also the *Green* factors with regard to faculty, staff, transportation, extracurricular activities and facilities were among the most important indicia of a segregated system. *Green v. County School Board*, 391 U.S. 430, 435 (1968).

90. Constance Baker Motley, *Equal Justice Under Law* (New York: Farrar, Straus and Giroux, 1998) at p.110-111.

91. Mark V. Tushnet, *Making Civil Rights Law* (New York: Oxford University Press, 1994) at p. 240 (discussing the "Southern Manifesto").

92. *McDaniel v. Barresi*, 402 U.S. 39 (1971). A "neutral" desegregation plan which does not require integration is reversed as *per se* invalid.

93. *Cooper v. Aaron*, 358 U.S. 1 (1958) (*see generally* the Court decision desegregating Central High School in Little Rock, Arkansas).

94. David J. Garrow, *Bearing the Cross: Martin Luther King, Jr. and the Southern Christian Leadership Conference* (New York: Quill Publishers, 1986) at p. 98.

95. Robert F. Burk, *The Eisenhower Administration and Black Civil Rights* (Knoxville: University of Tennessee Press, 1984).

96. Stephan Lesher, *George Wallace: American Populist* (New York: Addison-Wesley Publishing, 1994) at p.108-109; Robert F. Burk, *The Eisenhower Administration and Black Civil Rights* (Knoxville: University of Tennessee Press, 1984).

97. Stephan Lesher, *George Wallace: American Populist* (New York: Addison-Wesley Publishing, 1994) at p.108; Robert F. Burk, *The Eisenhower Administration and Black Civil Rights* (Knoxville: University of Tennessee Press, 1984).

98. David J. Garrow, *Bearing the Cross: Martin Luther King, Jr. and the Southern Christian Leadership Conference* (New York: Quill Publishers, 1986) at p. 106.

99. *McDaniel v. Barresi*, 402 U.S. 39, 45-46.

100. *McDaniel v. Barresi*, 402 U.S. 39, 45-46.

101. *Green v. County School Board*, 391 U.S. at 435 (the Court sets forth once more the criteria established in *Brown II*).

102. *Swann v. Charlotte-Mecklenburg*, 402 U.S. 1 (1971).

103. *Swann v. Charlotte-Mecklenburg*, 402 U.S. at 15 citing *Green v. County School Board*, 391 U.S. at 439.

104. Mark V. Tushnet, *Making Civil Rights Law* (New York: Oxford University Press, 1994) at p. 240-242 (discussing the litigation and counter-tactics used by school districts to avoid desegregation).

105. See Derek Bell, *Race, Racism, and American Law* (New York: Aspen Law and Business, 2000) at pp.179-180.

106. See Gary Orfield, *Must We Bus? Segregated Schools and National Policy*, 59-62 (1978).

107. *Jenkins v. Missouri*, 515 U.S. 70 (1995).

108. *Jenkins v. Missouri*, 515 U.S. 70 (1995).

109. See Derek Bell, *Race, Racism, and American Law* (New York: Aspen Law and Business, 2000) at pp.179-180.

110. Study by the Joint Center for Political Studies, Washington, D.C.

111. Orfield, Schools More Separate; Janet Ward Schofield. "Review of Research on School Desegregations Impact on Elementary and Secondary School Students," in *Handbook of Research on Multi-cultural*

Education, ed. James Banks and Cherry McGee Banks (New York: Simon & Schuster MacMillan, 1995), at pp. 597-617.

112. Orfield, Schools More Separate; Janet Ward Schofield. "Review of Research on School Desegregations Impact on Elementary and Secondary School Students," in *Handbook of Research on Multi-cultural Education,* ed. James Banks and Cherry McGee Banks (New York: Simon & Schuster MacMillan, 1995), at pp. 600-617.

113. Orfield, Schools More Separate; Janet Ward Schofield. "Review of Research on School Desegregations Impact on Elementary and Secondary School Students," in *Handbook of Research on Multi-cultural Education,* ed. James Banks and Cherry McGee Banks (New York: Simon & Schuster MacMillan, 1995), pp. 597-617; Gary Orfield, Susan Eaton and the Harvard Project on School Desegregation, eds., *Dismantling Desegregation: The Quiet Reversal of Brown v. Board of Education* (New York: New Press, 1996).

114. The stated purpose of the legislation is to close the achievement gap of the disadvantaged. PL 107-110. Specifically, the purpose is "to ensure that all children have a fair, equal and significant opportunity to obtain a high-quality education and reach, at a minimum, proficiency on challenging state academic achievement standards and state academic assessments." Sec. 1001.

115. *Bakke* at 366 nte. 42.

116. *University of California Regents v. Bakke,* 438 U.S. 265 (1978).

117. *University of California Regents v. Bakke,* 438 U.S. at 297.

118. *Bakke* at 297.

119. *Bakke* at 297.

120. *Bakke* at 289.

121. *Bakke* at 297.

122. *Hopwood v. Texas,* 78 F 3d 932, 934-935 (1996).

123. *Hopwood v. Texas,* 78 F 3d 932 (1996).

124. *Hopwood v. Texas,* 78 F 3d at 994.

125. *Hopwood v. Texas,* 78 F 3d at 994.

126. *Hopwood v. Texas,* 78 F 3d at 994.

127. *Cappaccione v. Charlotte-Mecklenburg and Belk v. Charlotte-Mecklenburg School District,* Nos. 99-2389(L);CA-97-482-3-P; CA-65-1974-3-P (September 19, 2001).

128. *Belk v. Charlotte-Mecklenburg School District,* Nos. 99-2389(L);CA-97-482-3-P, CA-65-1974-3-P (September 19, 2001).

129. *Belk v. Charlotte-Mecklenburg School District,* Nos. 99-2389(L);CA-97-482-3-P, CA-65-1974-3-P (September 19, 2001).

130. *Belk v. Charlotte-Mecklenburg School District,* Nos. 99-2389(L);CA-97-482-3-P, CA-65-1974-3-P (September 19, 2001).

131. *Grutter v. Bollinger,* 539 U.S. 306, 322 (2003); See *University of California Regents v. Bakke,* 438 U.S. 265 (1978).

132. *Grutter v. Bollinger*, 539 U.S. 306, 322 (2003); See *University of California Regents v. Bakke*, 438 U.S. 265 (1978).

It is remarkable that Justice Powell's opinion in *Bakke* relies on *Hirabyashi*, 320 U.S. 81, at 100, quoting, "distinctions between citizens solely because of their ancestry are by their very nature odious to a free people whose institutions are founded upon the doctrine of equality," and *Yick Wo*, 118 U.S. 356, at 369, quoting, "are universal in their application to all persons within their territorial jurisdiction without regard to any differences of race, of color, or of nationality; and the equal protection of the laws is a pledge of the protection of equal laws."

Powell's reliance on these two cases distorts the context of the court's holding. In both cases, the United States Government was found to have engaged in overt and invidious discrimination against Americans of Chinese and Japanese ancestry. In *Hirabyashi,* the United States Government forced Japanese-Americans and citizens of Japanese ancestry into concentration camps based on fear, hatred and hostility towards Japan during World War II was upheld. In *Yick Wo,* permits to operate a laundry in the San Francisco area were denied to Chinese aliens (based on the color of their skin) but granted to whites by the city's Board of Supervisors. In both cases, distinctions based on race proffered by the United States Government were intended to oppress and exclude Asians and Asian-Americans as an entire group. Affirmative-action programs, on the other hand, do not oppress and exclude whites or the white American male, as an entire group, from job and educational opportunities.

133. See generally, *Grutter v. Bollinger*, 539 U.S. 306 (2003) (law school admissions policy considers diversity of each applicant); *Gratz v. Bollinger*, 539 U.S. 244 (2003) (undergraduate admissions policy provides 20 points to under-represented minority applicants).

134. See generally, *Grutter v. Bollinger*, 539 U.S. 306, 315 (2003) (Justice O'Connor delivered the opinion of the Court that addressed a "flexible assessment of applicants' talents, experiences and potential").

135. *Grutter v. Bollinger*, U.S. 306, 316 (2003) ("the policy does not define diversity "'solely in terms of racial and ethnic status'").

136. *Gratz v. Bollinger*, 539, U.S. 244 (2003) (Chief Justice Rehnquist delivered the opinion of the Court critical of providing under-represented minorities 20 additional points).

137. *Gratz v. Bollinger*, 539 U.S. at 253-4 (the University policy allows the admissions officers to consider "African-Americans, Hispanics, and Native Americans to be under-represented minorities").

138. See *Grutter v. Bollinger*, 539 U.S. at 244 (2003) (Court's analysis fails to consider past discriminatory policies or history of discrimination in the State of Michigan by governmental entities or arguments of prior discrimination at the university).

139. U.S. Const., Am.14 Sec. 2.
140. *Gratz v. Bollinger*, 539 U.S. at 257; *Grutter v. Bollinger*, 539 U.S. at 336 ("truly individualized consideration demands at race be used in a flexible, nonmechanical way"); See *University of California Regents v. Bakke*, 438 U.S. 265 (1978) (admissions policies must be narrowly tailored and provide for race only as a component of the overall plan.).
141. *Adarand Constructors, Inc. v. Pena*, 515 U.S. 200, 201-202 (1995).
142. *Richmond v. J.A. Croson Co.*, 488 U.S. 469, 493 (1989).
143. *Richmond v. J.A. Croson Co.*, 488 U.S. 469, 493 (1989) (strict scrutiny is applied to 'smoke out' any **illegitimate** use of race *[emphasis added]*; *Grutter v. Bollinger*, 539 U.S. at 331.
144. *Grutter v. Bollinger*, 539 U.S. at 336. Ibid at 334; *Brown v. Board*, 347 U.S. at 493 ("the Court has long recognized that "'education...is the very foundation of good citizenship'").
145. *Grutter v. Bollinger*, 539 U.S. at 342-43 (although the Court cites the educational benefits that flow from a diverse student body, there remains the issue of when such race conscious admissions plans should cease).
146. *Grutter v. Bollinger*, 539 U.S. at 342 (diversity among the student body is th main support for the law school plan ignoring the relevance of prior history of rase relations on the applicants, both white and black).
147. *Grutter v. Bollinger*, 539 U.S. at 330 (the Court's opinion speaks to "preparing students for work and citizenship, ...education is pivotal to sustaining our political and cultural heritage...and fundamental...in maintaining the fabric of society").
148. *Grutter v. Bollinger*, 539 U.S. at 332 (the law school must be inclusive so that "all members of our heterogenous society may participate in the educational institutions that provide the training and education necessary to succeed in America").
149. *Grutter v. Bollinger*, 539 U.S. at 334-5 (although the Court found that the law school plan does not operate as a quota, Chief Justice Rehnquist and Justices Thomas and Scalia dissent stating that the "critical mass" is a "sham to cover a scheme of racially proportionate admissions" at 395).
150. *University of California Regents v. Bakke*, 438 U.S. 265 (1978).
151. *University of California Regents v. Bakke*, 438 U.S. 318, n. 52.
152. *Grutter v. Bollinger*, 539 U.S. at 334 quoting *Richmond v. Croson*, at 469 ("a quota is a program in which a certain fixed number or proportion of opportunities are "'reserved exclusively for certain minority groups,'" The Court fails to provide a word for preference given to members of the majority).
153. *Grutter v. Bollinger*, 539 U.S. at 332 (although the Court does not state the race of these leaders who would hold questionable legitimacy, it is understood that they are all White and their legitimacy depends on having had Black and Latino classmates in law school who then play no other role).

154. *Plessy v. Ferguson*, 163 U.S. at 551, quoting *New York in People v. Gallagher*, 93 N.Y. 438, 448.

Chapter 2

1.   Richard E. Jones. *Brown v. Board of Education: Concluding Unfinished Business*, (2000): 188. Richard E. Jones. *Brown v. Board of Education: Concluding Unfinished Business. Washburn Law Journal* (2000): 39, no. 2: 381-428.
2.   84 F.R.D. 390 (1979) *Brown v. Board of Education of Topeka*
3.   84 F.R.D. 389-391 (1979) *Brown v. Board of Education of Topeka*
4.   84 F.R.D. 405 (1979). *Brown v. Board of Education of Topeka*
5.   84 F.R.D. 405 (1979). *Brown v. Board of Education of Topeka*
6.   Topeka Public Schools Desegregation Case Strategy *http://www.topeka. k12.ks.us/admin/communications/documents/*INFO/FEATURE/DESEG/ *GIdesegHistory3.html*.
7.   671 F. Supp. 1311 (D.Kan. 1987), *Brown III*.
8.   Topeka Public Schools Desegregation Case Strategy *http://www.topeka. k12.ks.us/admin/communications/documents/*INFO/FEATURE/DESEG/ *GIdesegHistory3.html*.
9.   Federal District Court Case No. T-316, Topeka, KS (1999).
10.   Topeka Public Schools Desegregation History http://www.topeka.k12. ks.us/admin/communications/documents/INFO/FEATURE/DESEG/ GIdesegHistory3.html.
11.   Larita Owens, Unpublished Doctoral Dissertation, KSU (2001): 35. Larita Lynette Grant Owens, *Implementation of the Comer School Development Program in Topeka Public Schools,* Unpublished Doctoral Dissertation, Kansas State University (2001).
12.   Topeka Public Schools Desegregation Remedy Plan. June 16, 1994. *http://www.topeka.k12.ks.us/admin/communications/documents/*INFO/ *FEATURE/DESEG/GIdesegRemplan.html*.
13.   McDonald, Hatch, Kirby, Ames, Haynes & Joyner. *School Reform* (1999): Chapter 2. Joseph McDonald, Thomas Hatch, Edward Kirby, Nancy Ames, Norris M. Haynes & Edward T. Joyner. *School Reform Behind the Scenes.* Teachers College Press, New York, NY (1999).
14.   Comer, Haynes, Joyner, Ben-Avie. *Rallying The Whole Village* (1996): Chapter 1. James P. Comer, Norris M. Haynes, Edward T. Joyner & M. Ben-Avie (Eds.)., *Rallying The Whole Village: The Comer Process for Reforming Education.* New York, NY: Teachers College Press (1996).

Chapter 3

1.   James L. Underwood, "African-American Founding Fathers: Making of the South Carolina Constitution of 1868" in James L. Underwood and W. Lewis Burke, Jr.'s, *At Freedom's Door: African-American Founding Fathers and Lawyers in Reconstruction South Carolina* (Columbia: U. of South

Carolina Press, 2000), p. 15; see also Walter Edgar's, *South Carolina: A History* (Columbia: U. of South Carolina Press, 1998), pp. 389-390.

2. George B. Tindall, *South Carolina Negroes, 1877-1900* (Columbia: U. of South Carolina Press, 1952), pp. 215, 222-223.

3. Ibid., 223.

4. Edgar, *South Carolina*, pp. 489-490.

5. Ibid.

6. Ibid., 481.

7. Daniel M. Berman, *It Is So Ordered: The Supreme Court Rules on School Segregation* (New York: W. W. Norton and Company, 1966), p. 18.

8. Idus A. Newby, *Black Carolinians: A History of Blacks in South Carolina From 1895 to 1968* (Columbia: U. of South Carolina Press, 1973), p. 224.

9. Peter Irons, *Jim Crow's Children: The Broken Promise of the Brown Decision* (New York: Viking Press, 2002), p. 333.

10. Newby, *Black Carolinians,* p. 222.

11. Ibid.

12. Ibid., 224.

13. Ibid., 223.

14. James T. Patterson, *Brown v. Board of Education: A Civil Rights Milestone and Its Troubled Legacy* (Oxford: Oxford U. Press, 2001), p. 25.

15. Kahlil G. Chism, A Documentary History of *Brown*: Using Primary Records to Understand *Brown, et al., v. Board of Education of Topeka, Kansas, et al.,* "in James Anderson and Dara N. Byrne, editors, *The Unfinished Agenda of Brown v. Board of Education* (Hoboken, New Jersey, 2004), p. 15.

16. Ibid.

17. Patterson, *Brown v. Board of Education*, p. 15.

18. Edgar, *South Carolina*, pp. 521-522.

19. Patterson, *Brown v. Board of Education*, p. 23.

20. Edgar, *South Carolina*, p. 522; see also Patterson, *Brown v. Board of Education*, p. 23.

21. Patterson, *Brown v. Board of Education*, p. 23.

22. Charles Ogletree, "All Too Deliberate," in Anderson and Byrne, *The Unfinished Agenda of Brown v. Board of Education*, p. 48.

23. Edgar, *South Carolina*, p. 522.

24. Ibid.

25. The official citation for *Briggs v. Elliott* is 132 F. Supp. 776,777; see also Berman, *It Is So Ordered*, p. 134.

26. William D. Smyth, "Segregation in Charleston in the 1950s: A Decade of Transition," *South Carolina Historical Magazine*, 92: 2(April 1991); pp. 104-105; see also Leon Friedman, editor, *Brown v. Board of Education: The Landmark Oral Argument Before the Supreme Court* (New York: The New Press, 2004), pp. 206-207. Section 7, Article 11 of the 1895 South Carolina Constitution called for the separation of blacks and whites in

public schools. The South Carolina Code (1942) Number 5277 reinforced segregation in public schools.

27.   Friedman, *Brown v. Board of Education: The Landmark Oral Argument*, pp. 206-207.

28.   Berman, *It Is So Ordered*, p. 134; Friedman, *Brown v. Board of Education: The Landmark Oral Argument*, pp. 206-207.

29.   Judge Cameron M. Currie, "Before Rosa Parks: The Case of Sarah Mae Flemming," in W. Lewis Burke and Belinda F. Gergel, editors, *Matthew J. Perry: The Man, His Times, and His Legacy* (Columbia: U. of South Carolina Press, 2004), p. 100; Irons, *Jim Crow's Children*, p. 61.

30.   Mark Whitman, *The Irony of Desegregation Law* (Princeton: Markus Wiener Publishers, 1998), p. 18; also Edgar, *South Carolina*, 522.

31.   Richard Kluger, *Simple Justice: The History of Brown v. Board of Education and Black America's Struggle for Equality* (New York: Vintage Books, 1977), p. 335; Smyth, "Desegregation in Charleston," pp. 105-106.

32.   Tindall, *South Carolina Negroes*, p. 307; Smyth, "Desegregation in Charleston," pp. 105-106.

33.   Kluger, *Simple Justice*, p. 334.

34.   Irons, *Jim Crow's Children*, p. 77.

35.   Ibid., 78-79.

36.   Smyth, "Desegregation in Charleston," pp. 105-106.

37.   Clayborne Carson, "Two Cheers for *Brown v. Board of Education*," Journal of American History, 91: 1(June 2004), p. 29.

38.   Ibid. On inferiority and the role of black schoolteachers see Adam Fairclough, "The Costs of *Brown*: Black Teachers and School Integration," *Journal of American History*, 91: 1(June 2004): 43-55. See also Whitman, *Irony of Desegregation*, p. 11.

39.   Newby, *Black Carolinians*, p. 331.

40.   Orville J. Burton, "Dining With Harvey Gantt: Myth and Realities of 'Integration With Dignity,'" in Burke and Gergel, *Matthew Perry*, p. 217, note 20; Charles E. Jenks, "School Desegregation in McCormick, South Carolina," Ph. D. Dissertation, University of Georgia, 1994, p. 54.

41.   Whitman, *Irony of Desegregation*, p. 45.

42.   Patterson, *Brown v. Board of Education*, p. 126; Whitman, *Irony of Desegregation*, p. 45; Burton, "Dining With Harvey Gantt," page 217, note 20.

43.   Irons, *Jim Crow's Children*, pp. 331-332.

44.   Ibid., 333.

45.   Irons, *Jim Crow's Children*, p. 331; Klarman, *From Jim Crow to Civil Rights*, pp. 352-353, 358-359, 362.

46.   Patterson, *Brown v. Board of Education*, pp. 154-155, 185.

47.   Gary Orfield and Carole Ashkinaze, *The Closing Door: Conservative Policy and Black Opportunity* (Chicago: U. of Chicago Press, 1991), p. 209.

48.   Ogletree, "All Too Deliberate," pp. 45, 58.

49.   Orfield and Eaton, *Dismantling Desegregation*, pp. 1-4.

50. Irons, *Jim Crow's Children*, pp. 332, 336-337.
51. Jenks, "School Desegregation in McCormick, South Carolina," p. 54.

Chapter 4

1. National Coalition for Women and Girls in Education (NCWGE). Title IX at 30: Report Card on Gender Equity (2002); Title IX of the Education Amendments of 1972, 20 U.S.C. Sections 1681-1688 (1994).
2. Title VII of the Civil Rights Act of 1964. An act to enforce the constitutional right to vote, to confer jurisdiction upon the district courts of the United States to provide injunctive relief against discrimination in public accommodations, to authorize the attorney general to institute lawsuits to protect constitutional rights in public facilities and public education, to extend the Commission on Civil Rights, to prevent discrimination in federally assisted programs, to establish a Commission on Equal Employment Opportunity, and for other purposes. Be it enacted by the Senate and House of Representatives of the United States of America in Congress assembled that this Act may be cited as the"Civil Rights Act of 1964."
3. NCWGE, 2002.
4. American Council of Education (2002). Minorities in higher education 2001-2002: Nineteenth annual status report. Washington, DC: author; American Council of Education (2003). Minorities in higher education 2002-2003: Twentieth annual status report. Washington, DC: author; American Association of University Professors (AAUP) (1997). Diversity in Higher Education. Retrieved on December 9, 2003 from *http://www. aaup. org/ aafctsht. html.*
5. U. S. Department of Education (1997) Title IX: 25 Years of Progress. Author: Washington, D.C.; AAUP, 1997.
6. Day, J.C. & Newberger, E.C. (2003). *The Big Payoff: Educational Attainment and Estimates of Work-Life Earnings.* Washington, D.C.: U.S. Census Bureau, pp. 4-6.
7. Kim, M. (September 2000). Women paid low wages: Who they are and where they work. *The Monthly Labor Review*, pp. 26-29, see p. 25.
8. Kim, p. 25.

Chapter 5

1. See e.g., *Hopwood v. State of Texas*, 78 F.3d 932, 947 (5th Cir. 1996) (Weiner, Circuit Judge, concurring); *Yellow Springs Exempted Village School District Board of Education v. Ohio High School Athletic Association*, 647 F.2d 651, 667 (6th Cir. 1981) (Jones, Circuit Judge, concurring in part and dissenting in part); *Lee v. Macon Board of Education*, 453 F.2d 1104, 1109, 1110 (5th Cir. 1971); United Packinghouse, Food and Allied Workers International Union, *AFL-CIO v. National Labor Board*, 416 F.2d 1126, 1136 (D.C. Circuit 1968).

2.   See e.g, *Bercovitch v. Baldwin School,* 964 F.Supp. 597, 598 (D. Puerto Rico 1997); *Baldwin v. Ledbetter,* 647 F.Supp. 623, 639 (N.D. Georgia 1986); *Bailey v. Binyon,* 583 F.Supp. 923, 934 (N.D. Illinois 1984); *Hobson v. George Humphreys, Inc.,* 563 F.Supp. 344, 353 (W.D.Tennessee 1982); *Sterling v. Harris,* 478 F.Supp. 1046, 1052 (N.D. Illinois 1979); *St. Augustine High School v. Louisiana High School Athletic Association,* 270 F.Supp. 767, 774 (E.D. Louisiana 1967); *Dawley v. City of Norfolk, Virginia,* 159 F.Supp. 642, 644 (E.D. Virginia 1958).

3.   See e.g., *DeFunis v. Odegaard,* 507 P.2d 1169, 1179 (Washington, en banc 1973); *State of Louisiana v. Brown,* 108 So.2d 233, 234 (Louisiana 1959).

4.   *City of Memphis v. Greene,* 451 U.S. 100, 153 (1981) (Marshall, J., with whom Brennan, J. and Blackmun, J. join, dissenting) (citing *Brown* while observing that closing a street at the edge of a white neighborhood sends a message that damages and stigmatizes the members of the black community who are being blocked from access).

5.   See e.g., *Perez v. State of Florida,* 620 So.2d 1256 (Florida 1993) (Overton, J.) (considering whether to overrule a case interpreting the application of the Florida Constitution to a criminal case); *State of Mississippi ex rel. Moore v. Molpus,* 578 So.2d 624 (Mississippi 1991) (declining to overrule its previous interpretation of the Mississippi Constitution's initiative and referendum provision); *Scott v. News-Herald,* 496 N.E.2d 699 (Ohio 1986) (in a defamation case, interpreting federal and state constitutional provisions relevant to freedom of the press); *State ex rel. Sullivan v. Boos,* 126 N.W.2d 579, 588 (Wisconsin 1964) (Dieterich, J., dissenting) (arguing that the court should depart from precedent and refuse to consider judges to be "officers" within the meaning of the Wisconsin Constitution); *Moskow v. Dunbar,* 309 P.2d 581, 597 (Colorado en banc 1957) (Sutton, J., dissenting) (in examining the constitutionality of a Colorado statute forbidding the Sunday sale of motor vehicles, arguing that the court ought to overrule the existing line of authority permitting such laws).

6.   See e.g., *The People v. King,* 851 P.2d 27, 41 (Supreme Court of California, en banc 1993) (Mosk, J., concurring and dissenting) (dissenting from the majority's decision to overrule a case concerning sentencing enhancement under state sentencing statute); *Gallegos v. Midvale City,* 492 P.2d 1335 (Utah 1972) (declining to overrule existing precedent concerning the proper interpretation of a statute tolling the statute of limitations in personal injury cases against municipalities); *Van Dorpel v. Haven-Busch Company,* 85 N.W.2d 97, 106 (Michigan 1957) (overruling a case interpreting the state's workers' compensation statute).

7.   *Moskow v. Dunbar,* 309 P.2d 581, 597 (Colorado en banc 1957) (Sutton, J., dissenting) (in examining the constitutionality of a Colorado statute forbidding the Sunday sale of motor vehicles, arguing that the court ought to overrule the existing line of authority permitting such laws).

8. See e.g., *Igartua de la Rosa v. United States*, 229 F.3d 80, 88, 89 (1st Cir. 2000) (characterizing *Brown* as involving a situation that "required corrective judicial action even in the face of long-standing legal precedent [such as *Plessy*]"). See also *State ex rel. Sullivan v. Boos*, 126 N.W.2d 579, 590 (Wisconsin 1964) (Dieterich, J., dissenting) (in interpreting the Wisconsin Constitution to determine whether state judges are "officers," citing and describing *Brown* as "the United States Supreme Court's historic school desegregation decision which overturned the age-old 'separate but equal' doctrine first announced by that court in *Plessy* . . .").

9. See e.g., *State ex rel. Sullivan v. Boos*, 126 N.W.2d 579, 590 (Wisconsin 1964) (Dieterich, J., dissenting) (observing that the *Brown* Court based its decision at least in part on an assessment of the changed role of public education in American society circumstances since *Plessy*); *Williams v. City of Detroit*, 111 N.W. 2d 1, 26 (Michigan 1961) (citing *Brown* as an example after stating that "it is the peculiar genius of the common law that no legal rule is mandated by the doctrine of *stare decisis* when that rule was conceived in error or when times or circumstances have so changed as to render it an instrument of injustice."); *Van Dorpel v. Haven-Busch Company*, 85 N.W.2d 97, 106 (Michigan 1957) (asserting that changed conditions permitted it to overrule an earlier interpretation of a workers' compensation statute even though the relevant statutory language had not changed, the court cited *Brown* as an example of a court overruling a case where "[b]etween th[e] two decisions the Constitution had not changed. Nothing had changed but the hearts and minds of men.").

Chapter 6

1. *Alabama State Teachers Association v. Alabama Public Schools and College Authority*, 289 F. Supp. 784 (Mid. D. Ala. 1968), *aff'd*, 393 U.S. 400 (1969), p. 789.

2. *ASTA v. APSACA*, 1969.

3. *Sanders v. Ellington*, 288 F. Supp. 937 (M. D. Tenn. 1968).

4. *Sanders v. Ellington*, 1968.

5. *Geier v. Dunn*, 337 F. Supp. 573 (M. D. Tenn. 1972).

6. *Geier v. Dunn*, 1972.

7. *Norris v. State Council of Higher Education*, 327 F. Supp. 1368 (E. D. Va. 1971).

8. The development, outcome and impact of the *Bakke* decision have received much attention (Ball, H. (2000). *The Bakke case: Race, Education & Affirmative Action*. Lawrence, KS: University Press of Kansas; Edley, C., Jr. (1996). *Not all black and white: Affirmative action and American values*. New York: Hill and Wang; Moses, M. S. (2002). *Embracing Race: Why we need race-conscious education policy*. New York: Teachers College Press; Orfield, G. & Miller, E. (Eds.). (1998). *Chilling admissions: The affirmative-action crisis and the search for alternatives*. Cambridge, MA: Harvard Educa-

tional Publishing Group, Civil Rights Project; Skrentny, J. D. (1996). *The ironies of affirmative action: Politics, culture and justice in America.* Chicago: The University of Chicago Press; Spann, G. A. (2000). *The law of affirmative action: Twenty-five years of Supreme Court decisions on race and remedies.* New York: New York University Press; Stefkovich, J. A. & Leas, T. (1994, Summer). A legal history of desegregation in higher education. *The Journal of Negro Education,* 63(3), 406-420. However, similar to the *Hocutt* and *Murray* cases, *DeFunis v. Odegaard* planted the seed that made *Bakke* possible.

9.   *DeFunis v. Odegaard,* 416 U.S. 312 (1974), *rev'd,* 82 Wn.2d 11 (1973).
10. *DeFunis v. Odegaard,* 416 U.S. 312 (1974), *rev'd,* 82 Wn.2d 11 (1973).
11. *Regents of the University of California v. Bakke,* 438 U.S. 265 (1978).
12. *Wygant v. Jackson Board of Education,* 476 U.S. 267 (1986).
13. *City of Richmond v. J. A. Croson Co.,* 488 U.S. 469 (1989).
14. *Regents of the University of California v. Bakke,* (1978).
15. *Hopwood v. Texas,* 78 F.3d 932 (5ᵗʰ Cir. 1996), *rev'd & rem'd,* 861 F. Supp. 551 (W. D. Tex. 1994).
16. *Hopwood v. Texas,* 236 F.3d 256 (5ᵗʰ Cir. 2000). [*Hopwood III*]
17. California Constitution, Article I §31 (2004); Revised Code of Washington, § 49.60.400 (2004).
18. *Johnson v. Board of Regents of the University of Georgia,* 263 F. 3d 1234 (11ᵗʰ Cir. 2001); State of Florida (2002). *One Florida: Equity in Education* [Online]. Retrieved July 24, 2004, from http://www. oneflorida.org/ myflorida/government/governorinitiatives/one_florida/equity_educa tion.html.
19. Green, D. (2004). *Gratz v. Bollinger,* 123 S. Ct. 2411, 2003 U.S.LEXIS 4801 (2003), and *Grutter v. Bollinger,*123 S. Ct. 2325, 2003 U.S.LEXIS 4800 (2003). In J. Beckman (Ed.), *Affirmative action: An encyclopedia* (Vol. 1, A-I, pp. 455-462). Westport, CT: Greenwood Press.
20. *Gratz v. Bollinger,* 123 S. Ct. 2411, 2003 U.S.LEXIS 4801, (2003), *aff'd & rev'd,* 135 F. Supp. 2d 790 (E. D. Mich. 2001).
21. Green, D. (in press). Fighting the battle for racial diversity: A case study of Michigan's institutional responses to *Gratz* and *Grutter. Educational Policy.*
22. *Geier v. University of Tennessee,* 297 F.2d 1056 (6 Cir. 1979).
23. *Geier v. Blanton,* 427 F. Supp. 644 (M. D. Tenn. 1977).
24. *Geier v. University of Tennessee,* 1979.
25. *Geier v. University of Tennessee,* 1979, p. 1068.
26. Tennessee system fails diversity test (1997, May 29). *Black Issues in Higher Education,* 14, 7.
27. Geier v. Alexander, 801 F. 2d 799 (6ᵗʰ Cir. 1986), *aff'd,* 593 F. Supp. 1263 (M. D. Tenn., 1984); "Tennessee System Fails Diversity Test," 1997.
28. "Tennessee System Fails Diversity Test," 1997.

29. National Center for Education Statistics (n. d.). IPEDS: College Opportunities Online, Fall 2002 Enrollment [Online]. Retrieved July 26, 2004 from http://nces.ed.gov/ipeds/cool/.

30. Owensby, D. D. (2002, Spring). Affirmative action and desegregating Tennessee's higher education system: The *Geier* case in perspective. *Tennessee Law Review Association, Inc.,* 69, 701-745.

31. *Ayers v. Allain,* 674 F. Supp. 1523 (N. D. Miss.1987).

32. *Ayers v. Allain,* 1987; *Ayers v. Fordice,* 879 F.Supp. 1419 (N. D. Miss. 1995); Brown, M. C. (1999). *The quest to define collegiate desegregation: Black colleges, Title VI compliance, and post-Adams litigation.* Westport, CT: Bergin & Garvey.

33. Roach, R. (1998, February 19). Mississippi appeal refused. *Black Issues in Higher Education,* 14, 34-35; *United States v. Fordice,* 505 U.S. 717 (1992).

34. *Ayers v. Fordice,* 1995.

35. *Ayers v. Thompson,* No. 02-60493, 2004 U.S. App. LEXIS 1149, at *1 (5th Cir. January 27, 2004).

36. *Ayers v. Thompson,* No. 02-60493, 2004 U.S. App.LEXIS 1149, at *1 (5th Cir. January 27, 2004), at *40.

37. *Hunter, R. C. & Donahoo, S. (2004). The implementation of Brown in achieving unitary status.* Education and Urban Society, 36(3), 342-354.

38. Young, I. M. (1995). Polity and group difference: A critique of the ideal of universal citizenship. In R. Beiner (Ed.), *Theorizing citizenship* (pp. 175-207). New York: State University of New York Press.

Chapter 7

1. Ayers, Jake. "Notes." Qtd. in Humphries, Frederick S. (1991). The Impact of the Mississippi Desegregation Case on Historically Black Colleges and Universities. *Racial Crisis in American Higher Education.* Phillip G. Allback and Kofi Lomotey, eds. Albany: State University of New York Press, p. 207.

2. Ayers, Lillie. Interviewed by author. 5 June 2004. Telephone interview.

3. Ibid.

4. Mary Ann Connell, 1993, p. 287. The Road to United States v. Fordice: What is the Duty of Public Colleges and Universities in Former *De Jure* States to Segregate. *Mississippi Law Journal,* 62, 285-357.

5. Humphries, Frederick S. (1991). The Impact of the Mississippi Desegregation Case on Historically Black Colleges and Universities. *Racial Crisis in American Higher Education* (pp.), Phillip G. Allback and Kofi Lomotey, eds. Albany: State University of New York Press.

6. *Meredith v. Fair,* 674 F. Supp. 1523.

7. *Meredith v. Fair,* 674 F. Supp. 1523, pp. 1526-1527.

8. *Meredith v. Fair,* 674 F. Supp. 1523.

9. Connell, p. 287.

10. Ibid.

11. Appeal Rejected in College Desegregation Case (28 January 2004). The Associated Press. http://www.cnn.com/2004/EDUCATION /01/28/ college.desegregation.ap.

12. Ibid.

13. P. 33. Tate, William F., Gloria Ladson-Billings, and Carl A. Grant (1996). The *Brown* Decision Revisited: Mathematizing a Social Problem. *Beyond Segregation: The Politics of Quality in African-American Schooling* (pp. 29-50). Mwalimu J. Shujaa (Ed.). Thousand Oaks: Corwin Press, Inc., Sage Publication.

14. Tate, Ladson-Billings, and Grant, 1996, p. 35.

15. Phillips, Ivory. Interviewed by author. 28 June 2004. Telephone interview.

16. Blake, Wilton E. (1991, p. 398). Ayers Threatens the Survival of State-Supported Historically Black Universities. *Howard Law Journal*, 34, 397-409.

17. Jones, Darryll (1993, Fall). An Education of Their Own: The Precarious Position of Publicly Supported Black Colleges after *United States v. Fordice*. *Journal of Law and Education*, 22, no.4, 485-524.

18. Frederick Humphries, 1991, p. 202

19. Ibid.

20. West, Cornel (1993). *Race Matters*. Boston: Beacon Press; Bowen, William G. and Derek Bok (1998). *The Shape of the River*. Princeton: Princeton University Press; Patterson. James T. (2001). *Brown v. Board of Education: A Civil Rights Milestone and Its Troubled Legacy*. Oxford University Press; *Grutter v. Bollinger* (2004). The Supreme Court Collection. *Legal Information Institute* (Cornel Law School). www.supct.law.cornell.edu/supct/html/ 02-241.ZS.html; Orfield, Gary and Chungmei Lee (2004). *Brown* at 50: King's Dream or *Plessy's* Nightmare? *The Civil Rights Project at Harvard University*. www.civilrightsproject. harvard.edu.

21. James T. Patterson, 2001, xiii…xiv.

22. P. 22. United States Commission on Civil Rights (1997, March 6-8). Race and the Public Education System in Mississippi: *U.S. v. Fordice. The Mississippi Delta Report,* accessed 16 Feb. 2004; available at http:www. usccr.gov/pubs/msdelta/pref.html.

23. P. 148. Jones, Elaine R. (1998). Race and the Supreme Courts 1994-1995 Term. In *Affirmative-Action Debate*, 5th Reprint (pp. 146-156). George E. Curry (Ed.). Reading, MA: Perseus Books.

Chapter 8

1. Martin Luther King, Jr. "Advice for Living." *Ebony* 12, no. 12 (October 1957): 53.

2. Martin Luther King, Jr. *Stride Toward Freedom: The Montgomery Story*. New York: Harper & Row, 1958, pp. 18-19.

3. W.E.B. DuBois. The Souls of Black Folk,. 1903. Reprint, Greenwich: Fawcett, 1961.

4. Booker T. Washington. *Up From Slavery*. New York: Dell Publishing Co., 1965.

5. Henry Louis Gates, Jr. and Cornel West. *The Future of the Race*. New York: Random House, Inc., 1996, pp.133-177. Gates and West provide an excellent debate and critique of DuBois' concept of the Talented Tenth. Copies of DuBois' essay on the concept in 1903 and his rethinking of the concept in 1948 are presented in the appendix.

6. W.E.B. DuBois. *Black Reconstruction in America: 1860-1880*. New York: Atheneum, 1973.

7. Amiri Yasin Al-Hadid, "Africana Studies at Tennessee State University: Diversity and Traditions," pp. 93-114, and Alan Colon, "Black Studies and Historically Black Colleges and Universities: Towards a New Synthesis," pp. 287-314 in Delores P. Aldridge and Carlene Young. *Out of the Revolution: The Development of Africana Studies*. Lanham: Lexington Books, 2000.

8. Komandduri S. Murty and Julian B. Roebuck, "The Case for Historically Black Colleges and Universities," *Journal of Social and Behavioral Sciences* 36, no. 4 (1990-1991), 171.

9. James E. Blackwell. *The Black Community: Diversity and Unity, Third Edition*. New York: Harper Collins, 1991, p. 249.

10. Martin Luther King, Jr. "Letter from Birmingham Jail." In James M. Washington (editor) *A Testament of Hope: The Essential Writings of Martin Luther King, Jr*. New York: Harper & Row, 1986, p.293.

11. Kendra Hamilton. "A Shared Responsibility: Bluefield State's new president makes college's success a community agenda," *Black Issues in Higher Education*, December 5, 2002.

12. Earl J. McGrath. *The Predominantly Negro Colleges and Universities in Transition*. New York: Columbia University, 1965, p. 176.

13. George Cox, Thomas Gentry and Dolphus L. Spence, "Case Study of A Black College in Transition," unpublished paper, March 13, 1970.

14. *West Virginia State College Catalog 1996-97*.

15. *West Virginia State College Catalog 1996-97*, p.11.

16. Earl J. McGrath. *The Predominantly Negro Colleges and Universities in Transition*, p. 176.

17. *Tennessee State University Undergraduate Catalog 2003-2005*, p. 5.

18. *Tennessee State University Fact Book, Fall 2002*, published by Institutional Effectiveness and Research at Tennessee State University.

19. Earl J. McGrath. *The Predominantly Negro Colleges and Universities in Transition*, p. 176.

20. Amiri Al-Hadid. "Africana Studies at Tennessee State University: Traditions and Diversity" in Delores P. Aldridge and Carlene Young

(editors). *Out of the Revolution: The Development of Africana Studies.* New York: Lexington Books, 2002, pp. 99-100.

21. Amiri Yasin Al-Hadid, "Africana Studies at Tennessee State University," pp. 100-101.

22. Jeffrey Lehman. *The African-American Almanac, 9th Edition.* Detroit: Thompson Learning, Inc., 2003, p. 706.

23. Jeffrey Lehman. *The African-American Almanac, 9th Edition,* p. 705.

24. Langston Hughes. *Selected Poems of Langston Hughes.* New York: Vintage Books, 1974, p. 268.

25. Charles J. Ogletree, Jr. *All Deliberate Speed: Reflections on the First Half Century of Brown v. Board of Education.* New York: W.W. Norton & Company, 2004, pp. 309-310.

Chapter 9

1. Roebuck, J. B. and K. S. Murty, 1993. *Historically black colleges and universities: Their place in American higher education.* Westport, CT: Praeger, p. 40.

2. The University of North Carolina is the proper name for the system of sixteen public universities in North Carolina as legally reconfigured in 1972.

3. Consent Decree, *North Carolina, et al., v. Department of Education. et al.,* No. 79-217-CIV-5, (E.D.N.C., filed Apr. 24, 1980).

4. William C. Friday, interview by author in Chapel Hill, N. C., July 8, 2004.

5. Raymond H. Dawson, interview by author in Chapel Hill, N. C., July 8, 2004.

6. Charles Lyons, telephone interview by author, July 22, 2004.

7. Albert N. Whiting, telephone interview by author, July 23, 2004.

8. Cleon F. Thompson, Jr., telephone interview by author, July 28, 2004.

9. Garlene Penn, *Enrollment Management for the 21st Century,* 26: 7, 1.

10. Ibid., iii.

11. Ibid.

12. U. S. Bureau of the Census, Population Division, "2003 State Population Estimates: 3.25 Year Population Growth."

13. Initially titled *University v. Murray.* The name changed to *Pearson v. Murray* in 2001.

14. The University of Florida posthumously awarded Virgil D. Hawkins a Doctors of Law degree in 2001. See Doody, 2001.

Chapter 10

1. Thomas Jefferson quoted in Michael Kammen, *A Machine That Would Go of Itself: The Constitution in American Culture* (New York: St. Martin's Press, 1994), 3.

2. All quotes from Thurgood Marshall's Bicentennial Speech at the Annual Seminar of the San Francisco Patent and Trademark Law Association,

    May 6, 1987. Printed as "The Constitution's Bicentennial: Commemorating the Wrong Document?" *Vanderbilt Law Review* 40 (1987) 1337-1342.

3.   The *Black* and *Alston* cases are covered in several locations. I found the following works most helpful: Earl Lewis, *In Their Own Interests: Race, Class and Power in Twentieth Century Norfolk, Virginia* (Berkeley: University of California Press, 1991), 155-166; J. Douglas Smith, *Managing White Supremacy: Race, Politics and Citizenship in Jim Crow Virginia* (Chapel Hill, North Carolina: University of North Carolina Press, 2002), 256-272; and Bruce Beezer, "Black Teachers' Salaries and the Federal Courts Before *Brown v. Board of Education*: One Beginning for Equity," *The Journal of Negro Education* 55 (Spring 1986): 200-213.

4.   Norfolk's school integration crisis is discussed in numerous books and articles. I found the following most helpful: Forrest R. White, *Pride and Prejudice: School Desegregation and Urban Renewal in Norfolk, 1950–1959* (Westport, Connecticut: Praeger, 1992); Alexander Leidholdt, *Standing Before the Shouting Mob: Lenoir Chambers and Virginia's Massive Resistance to Public School Integration* (Tuscaloosa: University of Alabama Press, 1997); Antonio T. Bly, "The Thunder During the Storm–School Desegregation in Norfolk, Virginia, 1957-1959: A Local History." *Journal of Negro Education* 67 (1998): 106-114.

5.   The *Riddick* case is covered in Susan E. Eaton and Christina Meldrum, "Broken Promises: Resegregation in Norfolk, Virginia," in *Dismantling Desegregation*, ed. Gary Orfield and Susan Eaton (New York: The New Press, 1996); and Deborah Moira Jewell-Jackson, "Ending Mandatory Busing for Desegregation in Norfolk, Virginia: A Case Study Explaining the Decision-Making Process in a Formerly *De Jure* Southern School District" (Ph.D. diss., Harvard Graduate School of Education, 1995).

6.   For general coverage of Norfolk see Thomas C. Parramore, Peter C. Stewart and Tommy L. Bogger, *Norfolk: The First Four Centuries* (Charlottesville, Virginia: University Press of Virginia, 1994).

7.   Henry S. Rorer, *History of Norfolk Public Schools: 1681-1968* (Norfolk, Virginia: Henry S. Rorer, 1968), 11-15. See also Gary Ruegsegger, *The History of Norfolk Public Schools: 1681-2000* (Norfolk, Virginia: Norfolk Public Schools, 2000), 7-8.

8.   Tommy Bogger, *Free Blacks in Norfolk, Virginia, 1790-1860: The Darker Side of Freedom* (Charlottesville, Virginia: University Press of Virginia, 1997), 140-143.

9.   Rorer, *History of Norfolk Public Schools*, 25-31. See also Ruegsegger, *The History of Norfolk Public Schools*, 9-18. In 1867, the *Norfolk Journal* proposed that the city begin educating its African-American children. The paper was not bold enough to suggest that white and black children attend the same schools, but instead argued that separate schools should be established for the African-American students in the community. "If we fail to move, others will take the initiative, and we shall reap a plentiful

crop of tears," the paper said. Establishing African-American schools was "a wise measure," the *Journal* argued, because "educating the Negro … [would] improve his condition …[and] make him a better member of society." This statement reveals much about the racist underpinnings of late nineteenth century Virginian society, and it goes a long way in explaining why even moderate whites in Norfolk could not get the city to establish black public schools during Reconstruction. Although Norfolk's white leaders failed to establish any public schools for black children in the years immediately following the Civil War, the American Missionary Society stepped in and filled the void. Four private church-related schools were established in 1867 for Norfolk's black community. These schools operated independently of the city's public system until 1871. See Rorer, *History of Norfolk Public Schools,* 25-31.

10. For information on Norfolk during these years see Parramore, *Norfolk: The First Four Centuries,* chapters 17-23.

11. Rorer, *History of Norfolk Public Schools,* 26.

12. Richard A. Dobie's Superintendent's Report, 1896. Quoted in Rorer, *History of Norfolk Public Schools,* 27.

13. Lewis, *In Their Own Interests,* 24. See also: Rorer, *History of Norfolk Public Schools,* for student enrollment in 1886: 1180 whites and 875 blacks.

14. Rorer, *History of Norfolk Public Schools,* 31. See also Ruegsegger, *The History of Norfolk Public Schools,* 30.

15. Smith, *Managing White Supremacy,* 135.

16. Lewis, *In Their Own Interests,* 157-158.

17. Ibid., 160.

18. "Court Denies Salary Claim Of Teacher," Norfolk's *Virginian Pilot,* June 1, 1939. Lewis, *In Their Own Interests,* 159.

19. "No Contract for Teacher Who Filed Pay Suit," *Norfolk Journal and Guide,* June 24, 1939. Lewis, *In Their Own Interests,* 160.

20. "School Board is Urged to Reappoint Fired Teacher," *Norfolk Journal and Guide,* July 1, 1939.

21. "Equal Salary Case in U.S. Court Monday," *Norfolk Journal and Guide,* February 10, 1940. Lewis, *In Their Own Interests,* 161.

22. For Alston's case see: *Alston et al., v. School Board of City of Norfolk et al.,* 112 F.2d 992. In addition see: "Here's How the Alston Case Stands," *Norfolk Journal and Guide,* June 29, 1940 and "Supreme Court Refuses Review of Equal Teacher's Salary Decision," *Norfolk Journal and Guide,* November 2, 1940.

23. Mark Tushnet, The NAACP's Legal Strategy against Segregated Education, 1925-1950 (Chapel Hill: The University of North Carolina Press, 1987), chapters 6 and 7. In addition see Wilkerson, Doxey A. "The Negro School Movement in Virginia: From 'Equalization' to 'Integration,'" *The Journal of Negro Education* 29 (Winter 1960): 17-29.

24. White, *Pride and Prejudice,* chapter 1.

25. Rorer, *History of Norfolk Public Schools,* 85.

26. "Cost of Negro Schooling Hits 217.55 Per Pupil," *Norfolk Ledger-Dispatch,* August 21, 1953, and "New Districts are Formed," *Norfolk Ledger-Dispatch,* December 12, 1951 quoted in White, *Pride and Prejudice,* 65.

27. Brewbaker and Schweitzer quoted in White, *Pride and Prejudice,* 71.

28. See Leidholdt, *Standing Before the Shouting Mob,* chapters 11-12. On Harry F. Byrd see Matthew Lassiter and Andrew B. Lewis' "Massive Resistance Revisited: Virginia's White Moderates and the Byrd Organization" in *The Moderates' Dilemma: Massive Resistance to School Desegregation in Virginia* (Charlottesville, Virginia: University Press of Virginia, 1998). Also valuable are: James W. Ely, Jr., *The Crisis of Conservative Virginia: The Byrd Organization and the Politics of Massive Resistance* (Knoxville: University of Tennessee Press, 1976), and Robbins L. Gates, *The Making of Massive Resistance: Virginia's Politics of Public School Desegregation, 1954–1956* (Chapel Hill: University of North Carolina Press, 1964).

29. *Leola Pearl Beckett et al., v. The School Board of the City of Norfolk, Virginia,* 148 F. Supp. 430.

30. Jim Henderson, "Norfolk Schools Ordered to Integrate in Fall," *Norfolk Virginian-Pilot,* February 13, 1957; "13 Schools Affected by Integration," *Norfolk Virginian-Pilot,* February 13, 1957. In addition see Leidholdt, *Standing Before the Shouting Mob,* chapter 11.

31. P. Bernard Young, Jr., "Key Participants in Norfolk School Integration Suit, *Norfolk Journal and Guide,* August 30, 1958; John I. Brooks, "Six Norfolk Schools Facing Closings Threat as Board Agrees to Admit 17 Negro Students," *Norfolk Virginian-Pilot,* August 30, 1958. See also Leidholdt, *Standing Before the Shouting Mob,* chapter 11.

32. Prieur quoted in Leidholdt, *Standing Before the Shouting Mob,* 86.

33. Interview, Delores Johnson Brown, March 2004, in the possession of the author.

34. Bly, "Thunder During the Storm," 109-111. See also Leidholdt, *Standing Before the Shouting Mob,* chapters 11 and 12.

35. James Baker, "Integration in Virginia Schools," *Virginia Journal of Education* 56 (1962):18.

36. "Norfolk City Schools Special Report on Enrollment as of October 1, 1968." Norfolk Public Schools, Office of the Chief Operating Officer, File Cabinet for Busing, Transportation Folder.

37. See Deborah Moira Jewell-Jackson, "Ending Mandatory Busing for Desegregation in Norfolk, Virginia: A Case Study Explaining the Decision-Making Process in a Formerly *De Jure* Southern School District" (Ph.D. diss., Harvard Graduate School of Education, 1995). In addition see Susan E. Eaton and Christina Meldrum, "Broken Promises: Resegregation in Norfolk, Virginia," in *Dismantling Desegregation,* eds. Gary Orfield and Susan Eaton (New York: The New Press, 1996).

38. Judge MacKenzie quoted in *Riddick v. School Board of the City of Norfolk,* 627 F. Supp, 814, 819 (U.S. Dist. 1984). See also Eaton, "Broken Promises," 117.

39. *Riddick v. School Board of the City of Norfolk,* 627 F. Supp, 814, 817 (U.S. Dist. 1984).

40. Ibid.

41. *Riddick v. School Board of the City of Norfolk,* 784 F.2d 521, 527 (4th Cir. 1986).

42. Ibid., 526.

43. Ibid.

44. See Deborah Moira Jewell-Jackson, "Ending Mandatory Busing for Desegregation in Norfolk, Virginia: A Case Study Explaining the Decision-Making Process in a Formerly *De Jure* Southern School District," Dissertation, Harvard Graduate School of Education, 1995.

45. *Riddick v. School Board of the City of Norfolk,* 627 F. Supp, 814, 816 (U.S. Dist. 1984).

46. Ibid., 821.

47. Ibid.

48. *Riddick v. School Board of the City of Norfolk,* 784 F.2d 521, 543 (4th Cir. 1986).

49. See Eaton, "Broken Promises," 118.

50. 1959 figures, Leidholdt, *Standing Before the Shouting Mob,* 1. 2003 figures, "2002-2003 Division Performance Report: Executive Summary, Norfolk Public Schools," 23.

51. "2002-2003 Division Performance Report: Executive Summary, Norfolk Public Schools," 23.

Chapter 11

1. Muhammad, D., Davis, A., Lui, M. and Leondar-Wright, B. *The State of the Dream 2004: Enduring Disparities in Black and White.* Boston: United for a Fair Economy, 2004.

2. *In* Brown, Susan, Kysilka, Marcella. *What Every Teacher Should Know About Multicultural And Global Education,* Boston: Allyn and Bacon, 2003.

3. Brown, Linda M. *Black Issues in Higher Education,* "Going global; traditionally, the percentage of African-American students who studied abroad has been low; however many university officials are looking into ways to increase numbers" (Special report: International Education). May 9, 2002: http://findarticles.com.

4. "Educating for Global Competence: the Report of the Advisory Council for International Education Exchange," *Black Students and Overseas Programs: Broadening the Base of Participation,* New York: Council on International Educational Exchange, 1991.

5. Response to *"A National Mandate for Education Abroad: Getting on With the Task"* in Council on International Educational Exchange, *Black Students*

and Overseas Programs: Broadening the Base of Participation, New York: Council on International Educational Exchange, 1991.

6. Chin, Hey-Kyung Koh.,ed. *Open Doors: Report on International Educational Exchange*. New York: Institute of International Education, 2003.

7. Council on International Educational Exchange, *Black Students and Overseas Programs: Broadening the Base of Participation*, New York: Council on International Educational Exchange, 1991.

8. "International Comparative Approaches to the problem of Under represented Groups" in Council on International Educational Exchange, *Black Students and Overseas Programs: Broadening the Base of Participation*, New York: Council on International Educational Exchange, 1991.

9. Burris, "Introducing International Studies and International Civil Society Research at Historically Black Colleges and Universities" in Onwudiwe, Ebere, ed. <u>Globalization, Civil Society and the HBCUs</u>. New York: Global Humanities Press, 2002.

10. Johnnetta Cole (1990), "Opening Address of the 43rd International Conference on Educational Exchange," in Council on International Educational Exchange, *Black Students and Overseas Programs: Broadening the Base of Participation*, New York: Council on International Educational Exchange, 1991.

11. Holly Carter (1990), "Minority Access to International Education" in Council on International Educational Exchange, *Black Students and Overseas Programs: Broadening the Base of Participation* , New York: Council on International Educational Exchange, 1991.

12. Chin, Hey-Kyung Koh.,ed. *Open Doors: Report on International Educational Exchange*. New York: Institute of International Education, 2003

13. Carter, 1990.

14. Cole, 1900.

15. Oyelaran in Brown, Linda M. <u>Black Issues in Higher Education</u>, "Going global; traditionally, the percentage of African-American students who studied abroad has been low; however, many university officials are looking into ways to increase numbers" (Special report: International Education). May 9, 2002.

16. Brown, Linda M. <u>Black Issues in Higher Education</u>, "Going global; traditionally, the percentage of African-American students who studied abroad has been low; however many university officials are looking into ways to increase numbers" (Special report: International Education). May 9, 2002.

17. Onwudiwe, Ebere, ed. *Globalization, Civil Society and the HBCUs*. New York: Global Humanities Press, 2002, p.27.

18. Craig, Starlette. *The Black Collegian Online*. "Global leadership for African-American Collegians: A 21st Century Imperative."

19. Brown, Susan, Kysilka, Marcella. *What Every Teacher Should Know About Multicultural And Global Education,* Boston: Allyn and Bacon, 2003, p. 10.

20.   Brown, Susan, Kysilka, Marcella. *What Every Teacher Should Know About Multicultural And Global Education,* Boston: Allyn and Bacon, 2003, p.35 B &K.

21.   L.M. Brown, 2002.

22.   Ibid.

23.   Council on International Educational Exchange, *Black Students and Overseas Programs: Broadening the Base of Participation,* New York: Council on International Educational Exchange, 1991.

24.   Craig, Starlette. *The Black Collegian Online.* "Global leadership for African-American Collegians: A 21st Century Imperative."

Chapter 12

Portions of this chapter are taken from conference papers prepared for "*Brown Plus 50: A Renewed Agenda for Social Justice,*" sponsored by the New York University Metro Center, New York, NY, USA, May 19, 2004 and for "Lessons from the Past, Vision for the Future: Celebrating 50 Years of *Brown v. Board of Education,*" sponsored by the Africana Studies Program at Central Missouri State University, Warrensburg, MO, USA, April 2, 2004.

1.   For example, for a detailed discussion on competing views of the capacity of courts to bring about social change, see Gerald Rosenberg, *The Hollow Hope: Can Courts Bring about Social Change?* (Chicago and London: The University of Chicago Press, 1991).

2.   Joseph Wronka, "Human Rights and Social Policy in the United States: An Educational Agenda for the 21st Century," *Journal of Moral Education,* 23, no. 2 (1994): pp. 261-272.

3.   Unless indicated, names of all persons and institutions are pseudonyms.

4.   For a theoretical discussion on the racial dimension of the moral character of education, see Garrett Albert Duncan, "Black Youth, Identity and Ethics," *Educational Theory* (in press).

5.   See for example, James Anderson, *The Education of Blacks in the South, 1860-1935* (Chapel Hill: The University of North Carolina Press, 1988); Martin Carnoy, *Education as Cultural Imperialism* (New York: David McKay Company, Inc., 1974); W.E.B. DuBois, "Does the Negro Need Separate Schools?," *Journal of Negro Education,* 4 (1935): pp. 328-335; W. E. B. DuBois, "Negro Education," in David Levering Lewis (Ed.), *W. E. B. DuBois, Reader* (New York: Henry Holt and Company, 1995: pp. 261-269); George Noblit & Van Dempsey, *The Social Construction of Virtue: The Moral Life of Schools* (Albany, NY: State University of New York Press, 1996); and William H. Watkins, *The Architects of Black Education: Ideology and Power in America, 1865-1954* (New York: Teachers College Press, 2001).

6.   Douglas Massey & Nancy Denton, *American Apartheid: Segregation and the Making of the Underclass* (Cambridge: Harvard University Press, 1993) and

Melvin Oliver & Thomas Shapiro, *Black Wealth/White Wealth: A New Perspective on Racial Inequality* (New York: Routledge, 1995).

7. William Tate, Gloria Ladson-Billings & Carl Grant, "The *Brown* Decision Revisited: Mathematizing a Social Problem," in Mwalimu Shujaa (Ed.), *Beyond Desegregation: The Politics of Quality in African-American Schooling* (Thousand Oaks, CA: Corwin Press, 1996).

8. Derek Bell, "Serving Two Masters: Integration Ideals and Client Interests in School Desegregation Litigation," in Richard Delgado (Ed.), *Critical Race Theory: The Cutting Edge* (Philadelphia, PA: Temple University Press, 1995: p. 231).

9. Bell, "Serving Two Masters," p. 232.

10. Pauline Lipman, *Race, Class and Power in School Structuring* (New York: State University of New York, 1998) and Iris Marion Young, *Justice and the Politics of Difference* (Princeton, NJ: Princeton University Press, 1990).

11. Garrett Albert Duncan, "Critical Race Ethnography in Education: Narrative, Inequality and the Problem of Epistemology," *Race Ethnicity and Education*, 8, no. 1 (in press).

12. Derek Bell, *Silent Covenants: Brown v. Board of Education and the Unfulfilled Hopes for Racial Reform*, (New York: Oxford University Press, 2004); for a discussion of how such politics informed busing patterns, see Amy Stuart Wells & Robert L. Crain, *Stepping over the Color Line: African-American Students in White Suburban Schools* (New Haven, CT: Yale University Press, 1997) and Joe Williams, "'White Benefit' was Driving Force of Busing: 20 Years Later, Architects of MPS Plan Admit They Didn't Want to Disrupt City's White Residents," *Journal Sentinel* Online (1999)<http://www.jsonline.com/news/metro/oct99/newbus101999a.asp> (Accessed February 29, 2004).

13. Paulo Freire, *Pedagogy of the Oppressed* (New York: Continuum, 1996).

14. Derek Bell, "Waiting on the promise of *Brown*," in B. Levin & W. Hawley (Eds.), *The Courts, Social Science and School Desegregation* (New Brunswick, NJ: Transaction Books, 1977); Derek Bell, *And We are Not Saved: The Elusive Quest for Racial Justice* (New York: Basic Books, 1987); Bell, "Serving Two Masters"; Devon Carbado, "Afterword: (E)racing Education," *Equity and Excellence in Education*, 35, no. 2 (2002): pp. 181-194; Kimberlé Crenshaw, Neil Gotanda, Gary Peller & Kendall Thomas, K. (Eds.), *Critical Race Theory: The Key Writings that Formed the Movement.* (New York: Routledge, 1995); Richard Delgado, *The Rodrigo Chronicles: Conversations about America and Race.* New York: New York University Press, 1995); and Tate et al., "The *Brown* Decision Revisited."

15. J. Harvie Wilkinson, From *Brown* to *Bakke: The Supreme Court and School Integration: 1954-1978.* (Oxford: Oxford University Press, 1979: p. 46).

16. Vivian Gunn Morris & Curtis L. Morris, *The Price They Paid: Desegregation in an African-American Community* (New York: Teachers College Press, 2002).

17. See, for example, Signithia Fordham, *Blacked Out: Dilemmas of Race, Identity and Success at Capital High* (Chicago and London: The University of Chicago Press, 1996); John Ogbu, *Black American Students in an Affluent Suburb: A Study of Academic Disengagement* (Mahwah, NJ: Lawrence Erlbaum Associates, Publishers, 2003); and Claude Steele, "A Threat in the Air: How Stereotypes Shape Intellectual Identity and Performance," *American Psychologist*, 52: pp. 613-629.

18. Michelé Foster, *Savage Inequalities: Where Have We Come From? Where are We Going?*, *Educational Theory*, 43, no. 1 (1993): pp. 23-32.

19. Kenneth Meier, Joseph Stewart & Robert England, *Race, Class, and Education: The Politics of Second-Generation Discrimination* (Madison, WI: The University of Wisconsin Press, 1989).

20. Gloria Ladson-Billings and William F. Tate IV, "Toward a Critical Race Theory of Education," *Teachers College Record*, 97, no. 1: pp. 47-68.

21. Applied Research Center, *Education and Race* (Oakland, CA: The Authors, 1998).

22. Jeffrey R. Henig, Richard C. Hula, Marion Orr, Desiree S. Pedescleaux, *The Color of School Reform : Race, Politics, and the Challenge of Urban Education* (Princeton, NJ: Princeton University Press, 2001).

23. *Methodological Notes:* In December 1998, I introduced myself to the principal of CHS and was invited to conduct research to identify the factors that contributed to both the attrition and the retention of black male students at her school. From January 1999 through June 2001, with the assistance of a team of university student research assistants, I conducted individual and focus-group interviews and participant observations at the school. We also obtained data related to CHS demography, standardized testing, attendance and graduation rates, and documents related to the historical, ideological and programmatic features of the school. We devoted most of the spring and fall of 2000 to interviewing black male students. These interviews elicited their insights about the culture of and their experiences at CHS and informed the theoretical framework to guide our ethnographic examination of the broader institution. In addition, we recorded formal and informal dimensions of the school that captured the day-to-day culture of CHS in a number of settings, including classrooms, hallways during passing periods, the main office, lunchroom, extracurricular activities and faculty and staff professional development workshops. Data were also recorded in entries made in a reflective journal over the course of the study that recorded my subjective responses to the project.

My analytic framework draws on critical theories of ethnography and discourse. I use hermeneutic inference to adopt the multiple positions, or points of view, of individuals within a particular situation to describe possible meaning fields. Meaning reconstructions allow me to clarify what I sensed was going on in a particular interaction. I also constitute pragmatic horizons to make explicit intersubjective symbol systems that make it possible for us to share understandings of objective events. Finally, I subject the meanings that I reconstruct and the symbol systems that I render to triangulation, with an eye for disconfirming evidence; to periodic member checks to share my ongoing work with the CHS principal teachers, and students; and to peer reviews to assess the "trustworthiness" of my findings and conclusions. For further discussion on methodological and analytic strategies related to the current study, see Phil Francis Carspecken, *Critical Ethnography in Educational Research* (New York and London: Routledge, 1996); Lilie Chouliaraki & Norman Fairclough, *Discourse in Late Modernity: Rethinking Discourse Analysis* (Edinburgh: University of Edinburgh Press, 1999); and Duncan, "Critical Race Ethnography in Education."

24.   Sarah Lawrence Lightfoot, *The Good High School: Portraits of Character and Culture* (New York: Basic Books, 1983, p. 309).

25.   See, for example, Maud Blair, *Why Pick on Me? School Exclusion and Black Youth* (Stoke on Trent, UK: Trentham Books, 2000); M. Christopher Brown & James Earl Davis (Eds.), *Black Sons to Mothers: Compliments, Critiques and Challenges for Cultural Workers* (New York: Peter Lang, 2000); Larry Davis (Ed.), *Working with African-American Males: A Guide to Practice* (Thousand Oaks, CA: Sage Publications, 1999); George Dei, Josephine Mazzuca, Elizabeth McIsaac & Jasmin Zine, *Reconstructing "Dropout": A Critical Ethnography of the Dynamics of Black Students' Disengagement from School* (Toronto: University of Toronto Press, 1997); Ann Arnett Ferguson, *Bad Boys: Public Schools in the Making of Black Masculinity* (Ann Arbor: The University of Michigan Press, 2000); Fordham, *Blacked Out*; Ronnie Hopkins, *Educating Black Males: Critical Lessons in Schooling, Community and Power* (State University of New York Press, 1997); Máirtín Mac an Ghaill, *The Making of Men: Masculinities, Sexualities and Schooling* (Buckingham: Open University Press, 1994); Pedro Noguera, "Preventing and Producing Violence: A Critical Analysis of Responses to School Violence," *Harvard Educational Review*, 65, no. 2 (1995): pp. 189-212; Ogbu, *Black American Students in an Affluent Suburb*; Vernon Polite & James Earl Davis (Eds.), *African-American Males in School and Society: Practices and Policies for Effective Education* (New York: Teachers College Press, 1999); Jeremy Price, *Against the Odds: The Meaning of School and Relationships in the Lives of Six Young African-American Men* (Stamford, CT: Ablex Publishing Corporation, 2000); and Tony Sewell, *Black Masculinities and Schooling. How Black Boys Survive Modern Schooling* (Stoke-on-Trent, Staffordshire: Trentham Books Limited, 1997).

26.   Garrett Albert Duncan, "Beyond Love: A Critical Race Ethnography of the Schooling of Adolescent Black Males," *Equity and Excellence in Education*, 35, no. 2 (2002): pp. 131-143; Garrett Albert Duncan and Ryonnel Jackson, "The Language We Cry In: Black Language Practice at

a Post-desegregated Urban High School," *GSE Perspectives on Urban Education*, (in press).

27. Richard Delgado, *The Coming Race War? And Other Apocalyptic Tales of America after Affirmative Action and Welfare* (New York: New York University Press, 1996).

28. See, for example, Bram Hamovitch, "More Failure for the Disadvantaged: Contradictory African-American Student Reactions to Compensatory Education and Urban Schooling," *The Urban Review*, 31, no. 1: pp. 55-77 and Noguera, "Preventing School Violence."

29. W. E. B. DuBois, *The Souls of Black Folk* (New York: Bantam Books, 1903: p. 3).

30. Duncan, "Beyond Love."

31. Duncan and Jackson, "The Language We Cry In."

32. Victor Anderson, *Beyond Ontological Blackness: An Essay on African-American Religious and Cultural Criticism* (New York: Continuum, 1995: p. 13).

33. Crenshaw et al., *Critical Race Theory*.

34. W. E. B. DuBois, *The Souls of Black Folk*; Garrett Albert Duncan, "Race and Human Rights Violations in the United States: Considerations for Human Rights and Moral Educators," *Journal of Moral Education*, 29, no. 2 (2000): 183-201; Wronka, "Human Rights and Social Policy in the United States."

35. Erik H. Erikson, "A Memorandum on Identity and Negro Youth," *Journal of Social Issues,* 24, no. 10 (1964): 29-42.

36. Maya Angelou, *Current Biographies*, 1974.

Chapter 13

1. Blanchett, W. J., Mumford, V. & Beachum, F. (in press). *Urban School Failure & Disproportionality in a Post-Brown Era: Benign Neglect of Students of Color's Constitutional Rights.*

2. Losen, D.J. & Orfield, G. (2002). *Racial inequity in special education.* Cambridge, MA: Harvard Education Press.

3. Ibid.

4. Ibid.

5. Smith, D. D. (2004). *Introduction to special education: Teaching in an age of opportunity* (5th ed). Needham Heights, MA: Allyn & Bacon.

6. Ibid.

7. Ibid.

8. Ibid.

9. Losen & Orfield, 2002.

10. Blanchett, W. J., Mumford, V. & Beachum, F. (in press). *Urban School Failure & Disproportionality in a Post-Brown Era: Benign Neglect of Students of Color's Constitutional Rights.*

11. Blackorby, J. & Wagner, M. (1996). Longitudinal post-school outcomes of youth with disabilities: Findings from the national longitudinal transition study. *Exceptional Children,* v62, (5), 399-413.

12. Ibid.

13. President's Commission on Excellence in Special Education Report: A New Era: Revitalizing Special Education for Children and Their Families. Washington, DC: Author.

14. The Civil Rights Project, 2001.

15. Harry, B., & Anderson, M.G. (1995). The disproportionate placement of African-American males in special education programs: A critique of the process. *Journal of Negro Education,* 63(4), 602-616.

16. U.S. Department of Education (2002). *Twenty-fourth annual report to Congress on the implementation of the Individuals with Disabilities Education Act.* Washington, DC: Author.

17. Dunn, L.M. (1968). Special education for the mentally retarded–Is much of it justifiable? *Exceptional Children,* 35, 5-22.

18. Ibid.

19. Artiles, A.J., Trent, S.C., Hoffman-Kipp, P. & Lopez-Torres, L. (2000). From individual acquisition to cultural-historical practices in multicultural teacher education. *Remedial and Special Education,* 21, 79-89, 120; Voltz, D. L. (1998). Cultural diversity and special education teacher preparation: Critical issues confronting the field. *Teacher Education and Special Education.* 21, 63-70.

20. King, S. H. (1993). The limited presence of African-American teachers. *Review of Educational Research,* 63 (2), 115-149l; Townsend, B. L., Thomas, D. D., Witty, J. P. & Lee, R. S. (1996). Diversity and School Restructuring: Creating partnerships in a world of difference. *Teacher Education and Special Education,* 19, 102-118; Voltz, 1998; Voltz, D. L., Dooley, E. & Jeffries, P. (1999). Preparing special educators for cultural diversity: How far have we come?: *Teacher Education and Special Education,* 22, 66-77.

21. Brownell, M.T., Sindelar, P.T., Bishop, A.G., Langley, L.K. & Seo, S. (2002). *Special education teacher supply and teacher quality: The problems, the solutions.* Focus on Exceptional Children, 35(2), 1-16.

22. U.S. Department of Education (2003). Individuals with disabilities Education Act (IDEA) data. Available at www.ideadata.org.

23. Darling-Hammond, L. & Sclan, E. (1996). Who teaches and why. In J. Sikula, T.J. Buttery, E. Guyton (Eds.). *Handbook on research on teacher education* (2nd ed., p. 67-101). New York: Macmillan; Ingersoll, R. (2001). *Teacher turnover, teacher shortages, and the organization of schools.* Seattle: University of Washington, Center for the Study of Teaching and Policy.

24. Crutchfield, M. (1997). Who's teaching our children with disabilities? *News Digest,* 27, 1-23.

25. Newby, D.E., Swift, K.L. & Newby, R.G. (2000). Encouraging and recruiting students of color to teach. *Multicultural Education,* 8, 8-14.

26.   Skiba, R. J., Peterson, R. L., Williams, T. (1997). Office referrals and suspension: Disciplinary intervention in middle schools. *Education and Treatment of Children,* 20(3), 1-21.

27.   Harry, B. & Anderson, M.G. (1995). The disproportionate placement of African-American males in special education programs: A critique of the process. *Journal of Negro Education,* 63(4), 602-616; Patton, J.M. (1998). The disproportionate representation of African-Americans in special education: Looking behind the curtain for understanding and solutions. *Journal of Special Education,* 32(1), 25-31.

28.   U.S. Department of Education (2001). *Twenty-third annual report to Congress on the implementation of the Individuals with Disabilities Education Act.* Washington, DC: Author.U.S. Department of Education (2000). *Twenty-second annual report to Congress on the implementation of the Individuals with Disabilities Education Act.* Washington, DC: Author.

29.   Kozleski, E., Mainzer, R.W., Deshler, D., Coleman, M.R. & Rodriguez-Walling, M. (2000). *Bright futures for exceptional learners: An agenda to achieve quality conditions for teaching and learning.* Arlington, VA: Council for Exceptional Children.

30.   Olson, L. (2000). Finding and keeping quality teachers. Quality Counts: Who should teach? *Education Week Special Issue XIX,* 12-17.

31.   Individuals with Disabilities Education Act Amendments of 1995: Reauthorization of the Individuals with Disabilities Education Act (IDEA). Publication: Washington, D.C., U.S. Dept. of Education.

32.   24th Annual Report to Congress, 2004.

33.   Hosp, J.L. & Reschly, D.J. (2002). Predictors of restrictiveness of placement for African-Americans and Caucasian students. *Exceptional Children,* 68(2), 225-238.

34.   Ladner, M. & Hammonds, C. (2001). Special but unequal: Race and special education. In C.E. Finn, A.J. Rotherham & C.R. Hokanson (Eds.), *Rethinking special education for a new century.* Washington, DC: Thomas B. Fordham Foundation and Progressive Policy Institute.

35.   National Research Council (2002). *Minority Students in Special and Gifted Education.* Committee on Minority Representation in Special Education, M.Suzanne Donovan and Christopher T. Cross, editors. Division of Behavioral and Social Sciences and Education. Washington, DC: National Academy Press.

36.   Lerner, J.W. (1989). Educational interventions in learning disabilities. *Journal of American Academy of Child and Adolescent Psychiatry,* 28, 326-331.

37.   Lyon, G.R., Fletcher, J.M., Shaywitz, S.E., Shaywitz, B.A., Torgesen, J.K., Wood, F.B., Schulte, A. & Olson, R. (2001). Rethinking learning disabilities. In C.E. Finn Jr., A.J. Rotherham & C.R. Hokanson, Jr. (Eds.), *Rethinking special education for a new century* (pp. 259-288). Washington, DC: Thomas B. Fordham Foundation.

38. Rosenshine, B. (1979). Content, time and direct instruction. In P.L. Peterson and H. Walberg (Eds.), *Research on teaching: Concepts, findings and implications.* Berkeley: McCutchan.

39. Au, K. H. (2002). Multicultural Factors and the Effective Instruction of Students of Diverse Backgrounds. In A.E. Farstrup and S. J. Samuels, *What Research Has to Say About Reading Instruction* (pp. 835-852). Newark, Delaware: International Reading Association; Delpit, L. (1995). *Other people's children: Cultural conflict in the classroom.* New York: The New Press; Pressley, M., Rankin, J. & Yokoi, L. (1996). A survey of instructional practices of primary teachers nominated as effective in promoting literacy. *Elementary School Journal,* 96(4), 363-382.

40. Olson, J.R. & Singer, M. (1994). Examining teacher beliefs, reflective change, and the teaching of reading. *Reading Research and Instruction,* 34(2), 97-110.

41. Artiles, A. & Zamora-Duran, G. (1997). *Reducing disproportionate representation of culturally diverse students in special and gifted education.* Reston, VA: The Council for Exceptional Children.

42. Ibid.

43. Diamond, B.J. & Moore, M.A. (1995). *Multicultural literacy: Mirroring the reality of the classroom.* New York: Longman; Nichols, W. D., Rupley, W.H., Webb-Johnson, G. (2000). Teachers role in providing culturally responsive literacy instruction. *Reading Horizons,* 41(1), 1-18.

44. Tate, W.F. (1995). Returning to the root: A culturally relevant approach to mathematics pedagogy. *Theory into Practice,* 34(3), 166-173, see p. 168.

45. Siddle-Walker, E. (1993). Caswell County Training School, 1933-1969: Relationships between community and school. *Harvard Educational Review,* 62(2), 161-182.

46. Tate, 1995.

47. Gay, G. (2000). Culturally responsive teaching. New York: Teachers College Press; Ladson-Billings, G. (1994). *The dreamkeepers.* San Francisco: Jossey-Bass.

48. Delpit, 1995.

49. Michael-Bandele, M. (1993). *Who's missing from the classroom? The need for minority teachers.* Washington, DC: American Association of Colleges for Teacher Education.

50. Mitchell, A. (1998). African-American teachers: Unique roles and universal lessons. *Education and Urban Society,* 31(1), 104-122.

51. Foster, M. (1994). Effective Black teachers: A literature review. In E.R. Hollins, J.E. King & W.C. Hayman (Eds.), *Teaching diverse populations: Formulating a knowledge base* (pp. 225-242). Albany, NY: State University of New York Press.

52. Howard, T. (2003). Culturally relevant pedagogy: Ingredients for critical teacher reflection. *Theory into Practice,* 42(3), 195-202.

Chapter 14

This study was made possible through a University of Minnesota Grant in Aid of Research, Artistry and Scholarship Program. An earlier draft of this chapter was presented at the 2004 American Educational Research Association Annual Conference in San Diego, CA. The author wishes to thank Brandon Rowland for his assistance with the AP research.

1. Clifford Adelman, *Answers in the Toolbox: Academic intensity, attendance patterns, and bachelor's degree attainment* (Washington, D.C.: U.S. Department of Education, 1999), http://www.ed.gov/pubs/Toolbox/ Exec.html; Susan P. Choy, *Access & persistence: Findings from 10 years of longitudinal research on students* (Item No. 309375) (Washington, DC: American Council on Education, 2002); College Board, *Access to Excellence: A Report of the Commission on the Future of the Advanced Placement Program*, 2001, http://ap central. collegeboard.com/repository/ ap01. pdf. ac_7907.pdf; U.S. Department of Education, *Bridging the gap: Academic preparation and post-secondary success of first-generation college students* (Item No. NCES-2001-153) (Washington, DC: National Center for Educational Statistics, 2001).

2. Adelman, *Answers in the Toolbox.*

3. College Board, *AP Facts*, retrieved March 1, 2004, from http://www. collegeboard.com.

4. Office of Civil Rights, U.S. Department of Education, *Achieving Diversity: Race-Neutral Alternatives in American Education* (Washington, DC: U.S. Department of Education, 2004), http://www.ed.gov/about offices/ list/ocr/edlite-raceneutralreport2.html.

5. The six states are: California, Florida and Washington (race-based admission policies made illegal); Georgia, Michigan, and Texas (race-based admission policies challenged in the courts).

6. Michael W. McCann, Rights At Work: Pay-Equity Reform and the Politics of Legal Mobilization (Chicago: Chicago University, 1994); M. Paris, "Legal Mobilization and the Politics of Reform: Lessons from School Finance Litigation in Kentucky, 1984-1995," *Law and Social Inquiry,* 26 (2001): 631-684.

7. College Board, *AP Facts.* Participation is calculated by looking at which high schools have at least one student take an AP examination.

8. The fee for each examination is $82, although fee reductions are available for low-income students.

9. The College Board plans to release the full study in 2005. Analysis of course performance is available at http://www.apcentral. collegeboard. com. The study replicates an earlier study on AP and college grades. See College Board, *AP Students in College: An Investigation of Course Grades at 21 Colleges* (Washington, DC: College Board,1998).

10. Susan P. Santoli, "Is there an Advanced Placement advantage?" *American Secondary Education,* 30, no. 3 (2002): 23-35. According to College Board research, a majority of AP students graduate from college in at least 4

years with a GPA of over 3.0. College Board, *AP Students in College: An Investigation of Their Course-Taking Patterns and College Majors* (Washington, DC: College Board, 2000).

11. Walter R. Allen, Marguerite Bonous-Hammarth and Robert Teranishi, *Stony the Road We Trod: The Black Struggle for Higher Education in California* (Los Angeles, CA: CHOICES, 2002); Douglas S. Massey, Camille Z. Charles, Garvey F. Lundy and Mary J. Fischer, *The source of the river: The social origins of freshmen at America's selective colleges and universities* (Princeton, NJ: Princeton University, 2003); Daniel G. Solorzano and Armida Ornelas, "A Critical Race Analysis of Advanced Placement Classes: A Case of Educational Inequality," *Journal of Latinos and Education* 1, no. 4 (2002): 215-229.

12. U.S. Department of Education, *Bridging the Gap*, 9.

13. Ibid.

14. See Adelman, *Answers in the Toolbox*; Institute for Higher Education Policy, *Getting through college: Voices of low-income and minority students in New England* (Washington, DC: Institute for Higher Education Policy, 2001); Santoli, *Is there an AP Advantage*, 29-31.

15. See Choy, *Access & persistence*; Andrea Venezia, Michael W. Kirst and Anthony L. Antonio, *Betraying the College Dream: How Disconnected K-12 and Post-secondary Education Systems Undermine Student Aspirations* (Stanford, CA: The Stanford Institute for Higher Education Research, 2003), 40-41, http://bridgeproject. stanford.edu.

16. Adelman, *Answers in the Toolbox*, viii.

17. Venezia, *Betraying the College Dream*, 40.

18. Santoli, *Is there an AP Advantage?* 25.

19. Ibid. See also College Board, *AP Facts.*

20. Susan Johnsen, "One-Inch Wide and a Mile Deep," *Gifted Child Today*, 25, no. 4 (2002): 5.

21. Eric Neutuch, "Advanced Placement in United States History: A Student's Perspective," *The History Teacher* 32, no. 2 (1999): 245-248.

22. See Santoli, *Is There an AP Advantage?* 31. For example, three select public institutions, the University of Michigan, the University of Texas at Austin, and the University of Virginia only accept AP Examination scores of 4 or 5 as passing. A score of three may allow a student to avoid a prerequisite, but will not count for college credit at these institutions.

23. Jeannie Oakes, *Keeping track: How schools structure inequality* (New Haven, CT: Yale University Press, 1995); Kevin Welner and Jeannie Oakes, "Ability Grouping: The New Susceptibility of School Tracking Systems to Legal Challenges," *Harvard Educational Review* 66, no. 3 (1996): 451-470.

24. Karin Chenoweth, "The College Board Decries Participation Gap," *Black Issues in Higher Education*, Sept. 17, 1998, 24. It should be underscored that ability grouping based on improper use of standardized tests violates civil

rights laws, according to the Office of Civil Rights (OCR), as does tracking based on race.

25. See College Board, *Access to Excellence*; Education Trust, *Education Watch: Key Education Facts and Figures* (Washington, DC: The Education Trust, 2004); Solorzano, *A Critical Race Analysis of AP.*

26. National Research Council, *Learning and understanding: Improving advanced study of mathematics and science in U.S. high schools* (Washington, DC: National Academy Press, 2002).

27. University of Georgia Web Page, http://www1.admissions.uga. edu/freshman_adm/crit.html.

28. University of Michigan Admissions Process Web Page, http://www. admissions.umich.edu/process/review/intro/.

29. See Jonathan Kozol, *Savage Inequalities: Children in America's Schools* (New York: Crown, 1991); Karen Miksch, "Education Law and Student Access: Why isn't Education a Fundamental Right?" In *Developmental education: Policy and practice*, eds. Jeanne Higbee, Dana Lundell and Irene Duranczyk (Auburn, CA: National Association of Developmental Education, 2002), 65-76.

30. Welner and Oakes, *Ability Grouping.*

31. Claude Steele, "A threat in the air: How stereotypes shape intellectual identity and performance," *American Psychologist* 52, no. 5 (1997): 613-629.

32. See Patricia McDonough, *Choosing colleges: How social class and schools structure opportunity* (Albany, NY: SUNY Press, 1997).

33. Joseph B. Berger, Suzanne M. Smith and Stephen P. Coelen, *Race and the Metropolitan Origins of Post-secondary Access to Four-Year Colleges: The Case of Greater Boston* (Cambridge, MA: Harvard University, The Civil Rights Project, 2004).

34. Donald Heller and Patricia Marin, eds., *Who should we help? The negative social consequences of merit scholarships* (Cambridge, MA: Harvard University, The Civil Rights Project, 2002).

35. *Daniel v. State of California*, No. RDVSOC174397 (Super. Ct. filed July 27, 1999).

36. Jeannie Oakes, John Rogers, Patricia McDonough, Daniel Solorzano, Hugh Mehan and Pedro Noguera. *Remedying Unequal Opportunities for Successful Participation in Advanced Placement Courses in California High Schools: A Proposed Action Plan.* An expert report submitted on behalf of the plaintiffs and the American Civil Liberties Union in the case *Daniel v. California* (2001).

37. Miksch, *Why isn't Education a Fundamental Right?*

38. *Castaneda v. The Regents of the University of California*, No. C 99-0525 SI (N.D. Cal. *Consent decree* approved June 9, 2003), http://www. naacpldf. org/ whatsnew / pdfs/ Castaneda_ Consent_ Decree. pdf.

39. The *Castaneda* complaint also alleged a disparate impact cause of action pursuant to Title VI of the Civil Rights Act of 1964. For a discussion of

the difficulties of bringing a disparate impact claim under VI after the U.S. Supreme Court ruling in *Sandoval v. Alexander*, 532 U.S. 275 (2001), see Sam Spital, "Affirmative Action Under Attack: Restoring *Brown*'s Promise of Equality After *Alexander v. Sandoval*: Why We Can't Wait," *Harvard Blackletter Journal* 19 (2003): 93.

40.   The *Castaneda* research reports have generated a number of published reports and articles, for example, "Knocking at Freedom's Door: Race, Equity and Affirmative Action in U.S. Higher Education," an edition of *The Journal of Negro Education* guest edited by Grace Carroll and Walter R. Allen has several articles by members of the research team disseminating the results of the *Castaneda* research. See, for example, Mitchell Chang, "The Relationship of High School Characteristics to the Selection of Undergraduate Students for Admission to the University of California-Berkeley," *The Journal of Negro Education* 69, no. 1/2 (2000): 49-59; Daniel Solorzano, Miguel Ceja and Tara Yosso, "Critical Race Theory, Racial Microaggressions and Campus Racial Climate: The Experiences of African-American College Students," *The Journal of Negro Education* 69, no. 1/2 (2000): 60-73.

41.   Steele, *Stereotype Threat*.

42.   Kozol, *Savage Inequalities*.

43.   Oakes, *Keeping Track*; Welner, *Ability Grouping*.

44.   Michelle Locke, "Black Admissions Drop 30 Percent at Berkeley," *Los Angeles Times*, May 29, 2004, Sec. B.

45.   Ibid.

46.   Because all of the interviews were conducted with researchers, attorneys and plaintiffs who reside in California–where race-based admissions are no longer allowed under Proposition 209–I told the informants that they could choose to imagine that they are instead working in a state where educational institutions are legally allowed to use race-based affirmative action. Otherwise, the starting conditions of the simulation would be too limited to accurately capture the informants' perspectives.

47.   Allen, *Stony the Road We Trod: The Black Struggle for Higher Education in California*; Oakes, *Remedying Unequal Opportunities for Successful Participation in Advanced Placement Courses*.

48.   *Gratz v. Bollinger*, 539 U.S. 244 (2003); *Grutter v. Bollinger*, 539 U.S. 306 (2003).

Chapter 15

1.   Jackson, J. F. L., Snowden, M. T & Eckes, S. E. (2002). *Fordice* as a window of opportunity: The case for maintaining Historically Black Colleges and Universities (HBCUs) as predominantly black institutions. *West's Educational Law Reporter,* 161, 1-19.

2.   Teddlie, C. & Freeman, J. A. (2002). Twentieth-century desegregation in U.S. higher education: A review of five distinct historical eras. In W. A.

Smith, P. G. Altbach & K. Lomotey (Eds.) (Revised), *The racial crisis in American higher education* (pp. 77 - 99). Albany: State University of New York Press.

3.   *Adams* cases, brought by the NAACP to ensure Title VI compliance, included a series of separate court decisions beginning with *Adams v. Richardson*, 356 F.Supp. 92 (D.C.C. 1973) through *Adams v. Bell*, Civil Action No. 70-3095 (D.C.C. 1982). These cases challenged the dual system of higher education.

4.   *The University of California Regents v. Bakke* case (438 US 265 [1978]) challenged the Medical School's race-based admissions policy. The term 'reverse discrimination' was introduced as a result of the court's favor for *Bakke*.

5.   Teddlie & Freeman, 2002.

6.   Almanac (2003). Chronicle of Higher Education [Special Issue].

7.   Allen, W. R., Epps, E. G. & Haniff, N. Z. (Eds.) (1991). College in Black and White: African-American students in predominantly white and in historically black public universities. Albany: State University of New York Press.

8.   Antonio, A. L. (2002). Diversity and the influence of friendship groups in college. In C. S. Turner, A. L. Antonio, M. Garcia, B. V. Laden, A. Nora, C. L. Presley (Eds.) (2nd Ed.). *ASHE reader series: Race and Ethnicity in Higher Education* (pp. 359-375). Boston: Pearson Custom Publishing.

9.   Astin, A. W. 1993. *What matters in college? Four critical years revisited.* San Francisco: Jossey-Bass Publishers.

10. Pascarella, E., Edison, M., Nora, A., Hagedom, L. S. & Braxton, J. (1996). Effects of teacher organization/preparation and teacher skill/clarity on general cognitive skills in college. Journal of College Student Development, 37 *(1), 7-19.*

11. *Astin, 1993; Milem, J. F. & Hakuta, K. (2000). The benefits of racial and ethnic diversity in higher education. In D. Wilds, Minorities in higher education: Seventeenth annual status report (pp. 39-67). Washington, DC: American Council on Education; Pascarella, Edison, Nora, Hagedorn & Terenzini, 1996.*

12. *Cole (2003, November). The impact of interracial interactions on student-faculty contact and intellectual development. Paper presented at the meeting of the Association for the Study of Higher Education, Portland, Oregon.*

13. *Antonio, 2002; Chang, M. J. (1996). Racial diversity in higher education: Does a racially mixed student population affect educational outcomes? Unpublished doctoral dissertation, University of California at Los Angeles.*

14. *Please see Tinto, V. (1975). "Dropout from Higher Education: A Theoretical Synthesis of Recent Research", Review of Educational Research, 65 (Winter): 89-125; Tinto, V. (1987). Leaving college: Rethinking the causes and cures of student attrition. Chicago: University of Chicago Press; Tinto, V. (1993). Leaving college: Rethinking the causes and cures of student attrition (2nd ed.). Chicago: University of Chicago Press.*

15. *For example: Cole, D. G. (1999). Faculty-student Interactions of African-American and White College Students at Predominantly White Institutions. Unpublished doctoral dissertation, Indiana University, Bloomington; Endo, J. & Harpel, R. (1982). The effect of student-faculty interaction on students' educational outcomes. Research in Higher Education 16(2), 115-138; Pascarella, E., Duby, P., Terenzini, P. & Iverson, B. (1983). Student-faculty relationship and freshman-year intellectual and personal growth in a nonresidential setting. Journal of College Student Personnel, 24(5), 394-402; Pascarella, E. & Terenzini, P. (1978). Student-faculty informal relationships and freshman year educational outcomes. Journal of Educational Research, 71, 183-189; Wilson, R., Wood, L. & Gaff, J. (1974). Social-psychological accessibility and faculty-student interaction beyond the classroom. Sociology of Education, 47, 74-92.*

16. *Astin, 1993; Pascarella, E. T. & Terenzini, P. T. (1991). How college affects students. San Francisco: Jossey-Bass.*

17. *Tinto, V. (1993). Leaving college: Rethinking the causes and cures of student attrition (2nd ed.). Chicago: University of Chicago Press.*

18. *Hurtado, S. T. & Carter, D. (1997). Effects of college transition and perceptions of the campus racial climate on Latino college students' sense of belonging. Sociology of Education, 70, 324-345; Nora, A. (2002). A theoretical and practical view of student adjustment and academic achievement. In W. G. Tierney & L. S. Hagedorn (Eds)., Increasing Access to College: Extending Possibilities for All Students. Albany: State University of New York Press.*

19. *Hurtado & Carter, 1997.*

20. *Hurtado & Carter, 1997; Tinto, 1993.*

21. *E.g., Nora, 2002.*

22. *E.g., Tierney, W. G. (1999). Models of minority college-going and retention: Cultural integrity versus cultural suicide. Journal of Negro Education, 68(1), 80-92.*

23. *Hurtado, S., Milem, J.F., Clayton-Pedersen, A.R. & Allen, W. R. (1998). Enhancing campus climates for racial/ethnic diversity: Educational policy and practice. Review of Higher Education, 21(3), 279-302.*

24. *Allport, G. W. (1954, 1978). The nature of prejudice. Cambridge, MA: Addison-Wesley.*

25. *Gurin, P., Nagda, R., & Lopez, G. (2004). The Benefits of Diversity in Education for Democratic Citizenship. Journal of Social Issues, 60 (1), 17-34, (pp. 17-18)*

26. *Allport, 1954, 1978*

27. *See also Aitken, N. D. (1982). College student performance, satisfaction and retention. Journal of Higher Education, 53 (1), 32-50; Bean, J.P. & Bradley, R.K. (1986). Untangling of satisfaction-performance relationships for college students. Journal of Higher Education, 57(4), 393-412; Volkwein, J. F. & Carbone, D. A. (1994). The impact of departmental research and teaching climates on undergraduate growth and satisfaction. Journal of Higher Education, 65(2), 147-167.*

28. Harvey, W. B. (2003). *Minorities in higher education 2002-2003: Twentieth annual status report.* Washington, DC: American Council on Education.
29. Astin, 1993; Pascarella & Terenzini, 1991.
30. Jones, L., Castellanos, J. & Cole, D. (2002). Examining the Ethnic/Minority Student Experience at Predominantly White Institutions: A Case Study. *Journal of Hispanic Higher Education, 1*(1), 19-39.
31. Anaya, G. & Cole, D. (2001). Latina/o student achievement: Exploring the influence of student-faculty interaction on college grades. *Journal of College Student Development, 42*(1), 3-14.

Chapter 16

1. A. Leon Higginbotham was born February 25, 1928 in Trenton, New Jersey. He graduated from Antioch College in 1949 and Yale Law School in 1952. He was Chief Judge Emeritus of the United States Court of Appeals for the Third Circuit where he served for sixteen years and was among the youngest individuals appointed to a federal bench. He was assigned to the U.S. District Court for the Eastern District of Pennsylvania for thirteen years. In 1968, President Johnson appointed him vice chairman of the National Commission on the Causes and Prevention of Violence, known as the Kerner Commission, which investigated riots of the 1960s. In 1969, he was named Yale's first black trustee. He also served as a district court judge in the U.S. Virgin Islands. He retired from the bench March 5, 1993. He received the Presidential Medal of Freedom in 1995. He died December 14, 1998.
2. An open letter to Justice Clarence Thomas from a federal judicial colleague. A. Leon Higginbotham, Jr. University of Pennsylvania Law Review, Jan. 1992 v. 140(3) pp. 1005-1028.
3. Ibid., p.2.
4. Ibid.
5. Colleen L. Adams, Rubin M. Sinins & Linda Y. Yueh (2000). A Life well-lived: Remembrances of Judge A. Leon Higginbotham, Jr.–His days, his jurisprudence, and his legacy. *Loyola of Los Angeles Law Review*, Vol. 33:987.
6. Higginbotham, A. Leon (1994, August). Justice Clarence Thomas in retrospect. 45 *Hastings Law Journal*, 1405.
7. Higginbotham, 1991, p.2.
8. Adams, Sinins and Yueh, 2000.
9. Palmer, Barbara (2002, April). Ten years later, Anita Hill revisits the Clarence Thomas controversy. Retrieved July 8, 2004 from http://newsservice. standford.edu/news/2002/april3/anitahill-43.html.
10. Comiskey, M. (2003, April). The Senate confirmation process and the "quality" of the U.S. Supreme Court Justices in the twentieth century. Paper presented at the Annual Meeting of the Midwestern Political Science Association, April 3-6, 2003, Chicago, Illinois, p.6.

11. Comiskey, p. 7.
12. Rankin, Anna Beth (1998, July). America's abandonment of the founding of the absence of natural law. Retrieved July 3, 2004 from http://www. ashbrook.org/tools/printerpage.asp.
13. Clarence Thomas. Retrieved June 19, 2004 from http://encyclopedia. thefree dictionary.com/Clarence%20Thomas; Clarence Thomas. Retrieved June 23, 2004 from http://www.supremecourthistory.org/ myweb/ justice/ thomas. html.
14. Efron, Edith (1992, February). Native Son: Why a black Supreme Court Justice has no rights a white man need respect. Retrieved July 6, 2004 from http://reason.com/9202/fe.ee.natives.html, p.10.
15. Higginbotham, 1991, p.4.
16. Wermiel, S. J. (2002, March). Clarence Thomas after ten years: Some reflections. *Journal of Gender, Social Policy and Law*, 10(2), 315-325.
17. Higginbotham, A. Leon (1996). Shades of freedom: Racial politics and presumptions of the American Legal Process, pp. 195-96. The ten precepts outlined by Higginbotham (1996) deserve revisiting to refresh your memory. They are: 1. *Inferiority*: Presume, preserve, protect and defend the ideal of the superiority of whites and the inferiority of blacks. 2. *Property*: Define the slave as the master's property, maximize the master's economic interest, disregard the humanity of the slave except when it serves the master's interest, and deny slaves the fruits of their labor. 3. *Powerlessness*: Keep blacks—whether slave or free—as powerless as possible so that they will be submissive and dependent in every respect, not only to the master but to whites in general. Limit blacks' accessibility to the courts and subject blacks to an inferior system of justice with lesser rights and protections and greater punishments. Utilize violence and the powers of government to assure the submissiveness of blacks. 4. *Racial "Purity"*: Always preserve white male sexual dominance. Draw an arbitrary racial line and preserve white racial purity as thus defined. Tolerate sexual relations between white men and black women; punish severely relations between white women and nonwhite men. As to children who are products of interracial sexual relations, the freedom or enslavement of the black child is determined by the status of the mother. 5. *Manumission and Free Blacks*: Limit and discourage manumission; minimize the number of free blacks in the state. Confine free blacks to a status as close to slavery as possible. 6. *Family*: Recognize no rights of the black family, destroy the unity of the black family, deny slaves the right of marriage; demean and degrade black women, black men, black parents and black children; and then condemn them for their conduct and state of mind. 7. *Education and Culture*: Deny blacks any education, deny them knowledge of their culture, and make it a crime to teach those who are slaves how to read or to write. 8. *Religion*: Recognize no rights of slaves to define and practice their own religion, to choose their own

religious leaders, or to worship with other blacks. Encourage them to adopt the religion of the white master, teach them that God, who is white, will reward the slave who obeys the commands of his master here on earth. Use religion to justify the slave's status on earth. 9. *Liberty–Resistance*: Limit blacks' opportunity to resist, bear arms, rebel or flee; curtail their freedom of movement, freedom of association and freedom of expression. Deny blacks the right to vote and to participate in government. 10. *By Any Means Possible*: Support all measures, including the use of violence, that maximize the profitability of slavery and that legitimizes racism. Oppose, by the use of violence if necessary, all measures that advocate the abolition of slavery or the diminution of white supremacy.

18.   Bell, Genniver C., Jones, Enid B. and Johnson, Joseph F. (2002, May). School reform: Equal expectations on an uneven playing field. *Journal of School Leadership*, Vol. 12, p.318.

19.   *Adarand Constructor, Inc. v. Pena*, 515 U.S. 200 (1995) (USSC+).

20.   *Grutter v. Bollinger*, 123 S. Ct. 2325 (2003).

21.   *Missouri v. Jenkins*, 515 U.S. 70, 132 L. Ed. 2d 63, 115 S. Ct. 2038 (1995).

22.   Higginbotham, 1992.

23.   Gerzon, Mark (1996). A house divided: Six belief systems struggling for America's soul. Putnam Books: New York, New York.

24.   Thomas, Clarence (1998, July 29). *I am a Man, a Black Man, an American.* Speech delivered at the annual meeting of the National Bar Association.

25.   Guinier, Lani (1998). Lift Every Voice: Turning a civil rights setback into a new vision of social justice. Simon and Schuster: New York.

26.   Ibid.

27.   Higginbotham, 1994.

28.   Cheshire, Susan M. (2004, March). A Letter to Justice Clarence Thomas. Unpublished paper, Fayetteville State University.

29.   Dickerson, Debra (2004). *The end of blackness: Pantheon Books.*

30.   Dickerson as quoted in Merida, Kevin and Fletcher, Michael A. (2002, August). Supreme Discomfort: More   than a decade after his bitter confirmation battle, African-Americans are still judging Clarence Thomas guilty. Is that justice? Retrieved August 1, 2004 from http://www.washingtonpost.com/ac2/wp-dyn/A23641-2002Jul30?language=printer.

31.   Higginbotham, 1991, p. 10.

CONTRIBUTORS

Amiri Yasin Al-Hadid
Amiri Yasin Al-Hadid is Chair and Professor of Africana Studies at Tennessee State University. He is the principal organizer of the department's Annual Africana Studies Conference. Dr. Al-Hadid is Founder and Emir of the Great Debate Honor Society, which is based on the philosophies of El-Hajj Malik El-Shabazz and Dr. Martin Luther King, Jr. He earned his B.A. degree in Sociology and Psychology from Alabama State University and his Ph.D. in Sociology from the University of California-Santa Barbara. Dr. Al-Hadid's research focuses on Africa, the African Diaspora, Education, the Great Debate, Inter-faith Dialogue, Islam and Pan-Africanism.

Dwayne Ashley
Dwayne Ashley is Chief Executive Officer and President of the Thurgood Marshall Scholarship Fund (TMSF). He leads the overall strategic direction to raise funds for merit scholarships, programmatic and capacity-building support to the 47 public Historically Black Colleges and Universities (HBCUs). Ashley holds a master's degree in Governmental Administration from the University of Pennsylvania Fels School of Government and graduated *Cum Laude* from Wiley College (the oldest black college in Texas) with a Bachelor of Science degree. He is the third generation in his family to attend a historically black college. He was also awarded an Honorary Doctorate of Law from the University of the District of Columbia, a Thurgood Marshall Scholarship Fund member school, in May 2001.

Wanda J. Blanchett
Wanda J. Blanchett is Associate Professor, Urban Special Education in the Department of Exceptional Education, University of Wisconsin-Milwaukee. Dr. Blanchett's research interests include transition planning for students with disabilities from secondary settings to all facets of adult life; comprehensive health education programming including sex education and HIV/AIDS education for students with special needs; urban teacher preparation, urban education, mentoring; and severe disabilities. Professor Blanchett holds an M.S.E. in special education from the University of Central Arkansas and a Ph.D. in special education from Penn State University where she was a Holmes Scholar. She is now a mentor for current Holmes Scholars and a member of the executive board of TASH (an international disability advocacy organization).

Jackie R. Booker

Jackie R. Booker is Chair and Associate Professor of the Department of History and Sociology at Claflin University in Orangeburg, South Carolina. Dr. Booker holds a Ph. D. in History from the University of California-Irvine. She is also the author of *Veracruz Merchants, 1770-1829: A Mercantile Elite in Late Bourbon and Early Independent Mexico* (Boulder: Westview Press, 1993).

Gloria J. Browne-Marshall

Gloria J. Browne-Marshall is an Assistant Professor of Constitutional Law at John Jay College of Criminal Justice in New York City and the founder of The Law Policy Group, Inc. Professor Browne-Marshall a civil rights litigator, has written extensively in the area of Racial Justice, Constitutional Law, Criminal Justice and International Human Rights. She is a graduate of St. Louis University School of Law, University of Pennsylvania Fels Institute of Government, and the University of Missouri-Columbia.

Mickey L. Burnim

Mickey L. Burnim is the Chancellor of Elizabeth City State University in Elizabeth City, North Carolina. Dr. Burnim is an economist having earned three degrees in economics–a B.A. and M.A. from the University of North Texas, and a Ph.D. from the University of Wisconsin at Madison. His fields of specialization were public finance and labor economics, and he has written papers and published scholarly articles in these areas. Prior to joining Elizabeth City State University, Dr. Burnim served as Provost and Vice- Chancellor for Academic Affairs at North Carolina Central University. Earlier in his career, he worked as Assistant Vice President for Academic Affairs in the general administration of the University of North Carolina; as a staff economist at the U.S. Department of Housing and Urban Development and as a faculty member and researcher at Florida State University.

Dara N. Byrne

Dara N. Byrne is an Assistant Professor at John Jay College of Criminal Justice of the City University of New York in the Department of Speech, Theater, and Media Studies. Dr. Byrne holds a Ph.D. in Rhetoric and Intercultural Communication from Howard University in Washington, D.C. She earned a B.A. Honors degree in English and Sociology as well as an M.A. in English from Carleton University in Ottawa, Canada.

Dr. Byrne is a specialist in critical language studies, intercultural communication and African Diaspora Studies. In 2003, Dr. Byrne served as the Project Editor for the *Black Issues in Higher Education* contributed volume, *The Unfinished Agenda of Brown v. Board of Education* (2004, Wiley).

She is also the Editor for the *The Unfinished Agenda of the Selma-Montgomery Voting Rights March* (2005, Wiley).

Darnell G. Cole

Darnell G. Cole is Associate Professor at the University of Hawaii - Mânoa. He earned his Ph.D. in Higher Education Administration & Education Psychology, Indiana University-Bloomington. Dr. Cole's recent publications include: "Increasing Access to College: Extending Possibilities for All Students" in the *Journal of General Education*; "Teacher education in a collaborative multicultural classroom: Implications for critical-mass-minority and all-minority classes at a predominantly white university" in the *Journal of Classroom Interaction*; and "Perceptions and experiences of Muslim women who veil on college campuses" in the *Journal of College Student Development*.

Elizabeth K. Davenport

Elizabeth K. Davenport is an Associate Professor and Coordinator of the Ph.D. program in Educational Leadership at Florida A&M University. Dr. Davenport is a graduate of Michigan State University's College of Education, receiving a Doctorate in Teacher Education, Curriculum and Social Analysis. Dr. Davenport holds a Bachelor of Arts degree in Education and a Juris Doctorate from the University of Michigan as well as a LL.M from New York University School of Law. She also has a Master's degree in Telecommunications and Adult and Lifelong Learning from Michigan State University.

Saran Donahoo

Saran Donahoo is an Assistant Professor in the Department of Educational Administration and Higher Education at Southern Illinois University. She earned her Doctorate in Higher Education Administration at the University of Illinois at Urbana-Champaign. She earned her B. A. in Secondary Education at the University of Arizona and her M. A. in History at the University of Illinois. Her research interests include history of higher education, legal issues affecting post-secondary institutions, higher education policy, and women and minorities in higher education.

Garrett Albert Duncan

Garrett Albert Duncan is Associate Professor of Education of African and Afro-American Studies, and of American Culture Studies at Washington University in St. Louis. His research focuses broadly on the relationships of race, culture and education as they shape the post-civil rights schooling of students of color in public schools. His work has been published in journals such as the *Journal of Moral Education, Teachers College Record*, and the *Journal of Negro Education*. In addition to teaching classes that align with his research, writing and methodological interests, Garrett also teaches social and philosophical foundations of education courses. His work experience also includes eight years teaching science in public secondary schools and a brief stint teaching incarcerated teenage males in the Fred C. Nelles School for Boys, California Youth Authority. He earned his Ph.D. from the Claremont Graduate School.

Gloria A. Dye

Gloria A. Dye is an Associate Professor in Secondary Special Education at Washburn University, Topeka, KS. She teaches undergraduate and graduate courses in special education, and earned her Doctorate in Special Education at the University of New Mexico.

Denise O'Neil Green

Denise O'Neil Green is an Assistant Professor in the Department of Educational Organization and Leadership at the University of Illinois at Urbana-Champaign. She earned her Ph.D. in Higher Education from the University of Michigan-Ann Arbor. She received her M.P.A. from the Woodrow Wilson School at Princeton University and a B.A. from the University of Chicago. Her research focuses on affirmative action, organizational behavior and conflict.

Blythe Hinitz

Blythe Hinitz is Professor and Assistant Chair of Elementary and Early Childhood Education at The College of New Jersey. Dr. Hinitz's research interests include: early childhood teacher education, the history of education, creative arts, social studies (history, geography, economics), early childhood curriculum and administration and supervision of early education programs.

Jerlando F. L. Jackson

Jerlando F. L. Jackson is an Assistant Professor of Higher and Post-secondary Education in the Department of Educational Administration and Faculty Associate for the Wisconsin Center for the Advancement of Post-secondary Education at the University of Wisconsin-Madison. He serves as a Research Associate for the Center for the Study of Academic Leadership. Dr. Jackson's recent research includes studies of factors associated with the retention and advancement for administrators of color and the nature of administrative work in higher and post-secondary education.

Joseph F. Johnson

Joseph F. Johnson is Dean of the School of Education and Professor of Educational Leadership at Fayetteville State University, a constituent institution of the University of North Carolina. He teaches graduate courses in school law, school finance and organizational development at the master's and doctoral levels of study for aspiring principals and school superintendents. He received his B.S. degree in Biology from Fayetteville State University and his M. Ed. degree in Science Education from Virginia State University. He earned a Certificate of Advanced Graduate Studies in Educational Administration (C.A.G.S.) and a Doctorate in Educational Administration (Ed. D.) from Virginia Polytechnic Institute and State University.

Andrew Ann Dinkins Lee

Andrew Ann Dinkins Lee is the Interim Assistant Dean of Fort Valley State University's College of Arts, Sciences and Education. Dr. Lee is also an Associate Professor in the Charter Teacher Education Program. She has held positions as an assistant and associate professor at Albany State University, as a teaching fellow and teaching assistant at the University of Pittsburgh and as a consumer counselor and crisis intervention aide for the VISTA Program, Family Service Association in Jackson, MS. Dr. Lee is a member of the National Communication Association, the National Council of Teachers of English, the Consortium for Africana Film Education, and the NCA/ Carnegie Academy Scholarship on Teaching and Learning. Dr. Lee holds a Ph.D. and M.A. in Rhetoric and Communication from the University of Pittsburgh and a B.S., Special Education, Jackson State University.

Jeffrey Lynn Littlejohn

Jeffrey Lynn Littlejohn is Assistant Professor in the History Department at Norfolk State University. His areas of specialization include Colonial and Revolutionary America; The U.S. Constitution and Civil Rights. In 2004, Dr. Littlejohn served as director for the e-learning project, "The *Brown* Decision in Norfolk: Local Leaders, National Politics and Cold War Significance," which was funded by the National Endowment for the Humanities. Dr. Littlejohn holds an M.A. and Ph.D. from the University of Arkansas-Fayetteville and a B.A. from Belmont University in Nashville.

Judith Lynne McConnell

Judith Lynne McConnell is Professor of Early Childhood Education at Washburn University in Topeka, Kansas. She has published numerous articles and book chapters and spoken at national and international conferences, including conferences in Spain, China and the United Kingdom. She has co-ordinated the Early Childhood Oxford Round

Table at Oxford University in the United Kingdom each spring since 2003. She holds Doctorate and Master's degrees in Education from Teachers College at Columbia University as well as a Master's degree from the University of Virginia.

Karen Miksch

Karen Miksch is an Assistant Professor at the University of Minnesota, General College. She teaches social science courses focusing on social justice, including "Law in Society." Her research in higher education access policy and multi-cultural education for a more-inclusive developmental education classroom complements her teaching mission. She received her Juris Doctorate (J.D.) from the University of California, Hastings College of the Law. Prior to teaching at the undergraduate level, she was a civil rights attorney for six years and lectured nationally about access policy.

N. Joyce Payne

N. Joyce Payne is the Founder of the Thurgood Marshall Scholarship Fund, which she considers her greatest achievement, and serves as Chair of its nominating committee. To date, the fund has awarded over $42 million in scholarship assistance and capacity-building support. Dr. Payne is also Director of the Human Resources and Minority Programs for the National Association of State Universities and Land-Grant Colleges, where she serves as senior staff member for presidents and chancellors of historically black public colleges/universities. She is responsible for congressional and federal relations and for developing and coordinating initiatives that contribute to the advancement of these universities. Among her numerous honors, Dr. Payne received an Honorary Doctorate degree from Lincoln University in Missouri, a Presidential Leadership Award from Delaware State University, and a fellowship from the Ford Foundation. Dr. Payne earned her Master's of Arts and a Doctorate in Education from Atlanta University.

Monika Williams Shealey

Monika Williams Shealey teaches in the Department of Exceptional Education and the Collaborative Teacher Preparation Program specializing in primary/middle learners. Her research interests include urban school renewal, culturally appropriate research methodologies, and culturally responsive literacy instruction for students with and without disabilities. Dr. Shealey is an active member of professional organizations in the area of education research, reading and special education. She received her B.S. and M.A. degrees from the University of South Florida, an Ed.S. from the University of Miami, and a Ph.D. from the University of Central Florida. Dr. Shealey is also a Holmes Scholar alumna.

Kevin H. Smith

Kevin H. Smith is Professor of Law, Cecil C. Humphreys School of Law, the University of Memphis. Professor Smith has published on topics such as disability law, Supreme Court certiorari decision-making, secured transactions, law school pedagogy and legal reasoning in the *Akron Law Review*, the *Albany Law Review*, the *Denver Law Review*, the *Hofstra Law Review*, the *Law Review of Michigan State University*–Detroit College of Law, the *Loyola University Chicago Law Journal*, the *Oklahoma Law Review*, the *Seton Hall Law Review*, the *University of Kansas Law Review*, the *University of Memphis Law Review*, and the *Wayne Law Review*. He received his B.A. from Drake University, his M.A., JD and Ph.D. from the University of Iowa.

Roberta J. Wilburn

Roberta J. Wilburn is Associate Professor of Education at LeMoyne-Owen College in Memphis. Dr. Wilburn's research focuses on early childhood education, special education and international studies and cultural awareness. As such she serves as director of Early Childhood Education & International Studies. In addition to receiving numerous research grants, Dr. Wilburn frequently conducts workshops and professional presentations on education, children and families, diversity and cultural awareness. Her most recent publication is *Primer to Developing a Successful Preservice Teacher Portfolio* (University Press of America, 2004). Dr. Wilburn holds an Ed.D. and M.A. from George Washington University and a B.A. from Mount Holyoke College.

Juan Williams

Juan Williams has been a political analyst and National Correspondent for the past twenty-one years for *The Washington Post*. Currently, a senior correspondent for National Public Radio News, Williams is the author of the best-selling documentary (which accompanied the PBS television series of the same title) *Eyes on the Prize: America's Civil Rights Years, 1954-1965* (Penguin USA, 1988), which won him critical acclaim and an Emmy Award. He also penned the biography *Thurgood Marshall: American Revolutionary* (Times Books, 2000).